Opheliamachine

Magda Romanska

Opheliamachine

methuen | drama

LONDON · NEW YORK · OXFORD · NEW DELHI · SYDNEY

METHUEN DRAMA
Bloomsbury Publishing Plc
50 Bedford Square, London, WC1B 3DP, UK
1385 Broadway, New York, NY 10018, USA
29 Earlsfort Terrace, Dublin 2, Ireland

BLOOMSBURY, METHUEN DRAMA and the Methuen Drama logo are trademarks
of Bloomsbury Publishing Plc

First published in Great Britain 2024

A catalogue record for this book is available from the British Library.

Library of Congress Cataloging-in-Publication Data
Names: Romanska, Magda, author. | Shakespeare, William, 1564–1616. Hamlet. |
Romanska, Magda. Opheliamachine. | Romanska, Magda. Opheliamachine. German. |
Romanska, Magda. Opheliamachine. French. | Romańska, Magda. Opheliamachine. Italian. |
Romanska, Magda. Opheliamachine. Spanish. | Romanska, Magda. Opheliamachine. Japanese. |
Romanska, Magda. Opheliamachine. Korean. | Romanska, Magda. Opheliamachine. Romanian. |
Romanska, Magda. Opheliamachine. Polish.
Title: Opheliamachine / Magda Romanska.
Description: London ; New York : Methuen Drama, 2024. | Series: Methuen drama play collections |
Identifiers: LCCN 2023024073 | ISBN 9781350398818 (paperback) |
ISBN 9781350398825 (epub) | ISBN 9781350398832 (pdf)
Subjects: LCSH: Ophelia (Fictitious character)–Drama. |
Hamlet (Legendary character)–Drama. | LCGFT: Drama.
Classification: LCC PS3618.O5956 O64 2024 | DDC 812/.6—dc23/eng/20230920
LC record available at https://lccn.loc.gov/2023024073

ISBN: PB: 978-1-3503-9881-8
        ePDF: 978-1-3503-9883-2
        eBook: 978-1-3503-9882-5

Series: Methuen Drama Play Collections

Typeset by RefineCatch Limited, Bungay, Suffolk
Printed and bound in Great Britain

To find out more about our authors and books visit www.bloomsbury.com
and sign up for our newsletters.

Contents

How to Lose a Guy in Ten Wars:
Introduction to *Opheliamachine*

Ilinca Todorut

In the twenty-first century, Ophelia won't throw herself into a river because the guy she likes killed her entire family and, on top of it all, treats her like trash. That's melodrama, that's Romanticism, that's the female sacrifice required from all past pure and great heroines. Now Ophelia refuses that role. At some point she realized that when everything is trash, having self-esteem is unladylike, but that's no reason to die. Life goes on. And on. And on. And on (Beckett). 'BLAH BLAH BLAH, behind me the ruins of Europe' (Heiner Müller).[1] 'The length of your penis is proportional to the anguish I'll feel', Ophelia says to Hamlet, while writing and delivering her own monologues (Romanska).[2]

Opheliamachine (2002–12) agrees with *Hamletmachine* (1977), the Müller play that Romanska retorts to, that the setting is destruction. Even the urtext, Shakespeare's *Hamlet* (which Müller aimed to 'destroy' with masculine confidence),[3] half a millennium earlier is set in a disintegrating European state about to collapse under Fortinbras' invasion, a place where 'something is rotten' (Act I, Sc. 4) for centuries. In *Opheliamachine*, the landscape is a cemetery of things, a trash heap of *objets d'art*, rotting corpses, broken devices, and assorted detritus of Western civilization. Now Ophelia is an immigrant to the US, whose 'grandmother's father perished mysteriously somewhere between Prague and Vienna'. She spends a lot of time moving about in buses, planes, airports, like all physically and psychologically displaced cosmopolitan people born

---

[1] Heiner Müller, 'The Hamletmachine', in *Theatermachine*, translated and edited by Marc von Henning (London and Boston: Faber and Faber, 1995), 87.

[2] This and all subsequent quotations from *Opheliamachine* are from a Word manuscript created in 2012 that Magda Romanska graciously shared with me.

[3] Heiner Müller, in a short introductory note on page 86 of the printed text of *Hamletmachine*, translated by von Henning: '*Hamlet was for me an obsession, so I wrote a short text*, Hamletmachine, *with which I tried to destroy Hamlet.*'

in territories smooshed in between empires. She is an adult making ends meet. She is the centre of her story.

Ophelia hardly ever spoke before. What was *her* opinion on the brotherly crimes, the neighbourly invasions, the Christian genocides? No one asked. When she did speak, it was because she was crazy. When she did speak, Müller made 'her heart [into] a clock', the poor object that she is.[4] Ophelia was Europe, her body to be conquered. Ophelia was the body, 'alone with [. . .] breasts [. . .] thighs [. . .] womb',[5] Ophelia was the victim, 'the woman dangling from the rope', the item traded, bled, gassed.[6] *Opheliamachine* gives subaltern Ophelia the chance to speak. It turns out she has an actual heart, one that 'bleeds', even though 'her veins are made of wire'. Rebecoming a person is a tough journey; she will never fit the standards of the universal human. She misses the mark. She is cyborgian. She talks about irrelevant things. But she does have a mouth on top of breasts, and that mouth is not just another hole. She has thoughts she articulates into words. She is an intellectual. She is still mad, but this time angry-mad. She talks too much about other women, babies and marriage, sex and love, good-for-nothing, couch-potato Hamlet vacillating between TV channels, but what can you do, she thinks, *ego sum femina*. So are the other two characters besides Hamlet. Horatio appears feminized, 'wearing a tux, fishnet stockings, and red heels. Her hair is pulled back'. Horatio is now Ophelia's best friend, not Hamlet's. Gertrude, looking like a Jersey immigrant matriarch in robe and hair rollers, plays the mother of the bride. How the tables have turned. There have never been so many good female roles in a Shakespearean play.

So Ophelia begins the text dressed as a soldier, taking seriously her new world-historical role to play. She is typing ferociously words on a (Soviet or German, I presume) typewriter, guzzling red wine and sucking on cigarettes. She is half Carrie Bradshaw, modern woman of the 2000s quipping about sex and the city (read: the global village, the omnipresent hamlet), half continental European intellectual, a Walter Benjamin ragpicking through the trash heap of

---

[4] Müller, 'The Hamletmachine', 89.
[5] Ibid.
[6] Ibid.

history, a Hannah Arendt who fled the Nazi camps to find a new home in America and write about totalitarianism. With his cowboy hat, Hamlet is here American, the young prince heir to European civilization. Really, a New Yorker, conflating in his being a mishmash of American emblems. America welcomed Arendt with open arms, but Hamlet's 'tired arms' do not open for Ophelia, and it might be because she's Eastern European, in which case the empires employ another meaning for 'open arms'.

Opheliamachine is a love story because Ophelia is a woman, because the author is a woman, and love stories are what women write. Love stories are war stories. The plot of *Opheliamachine* follows the courtship between Ophelia and Hamlet, their wedding day, their marriage settled into the routine of her-talking-while-working to a him-devouring-TV-on-a-couch. Along this narrative, bodies float, army boots clobber to death, babies are merchandise, mothers eat children's brains, gun shots splatter brains, flesh is set on fire. The usual. Intermittently, in the background, the National Geographic channel blasts information on the grim mating rituals in the animal kingdom where love equals consumption. It is obviously a comedy. It is low class (read: crass) humour, it is 'Making Do' humour (de Certeau). It is as camp as it can get. It is a camp performance as it would be played in a refugee camp, in a forced labour camp, in an extermination camp.

* * *

Rich influences pump through *Opheliamachine*. There's twentieth-century European theatre, marked by grief, war, genocides and botched revolutions, that comes out on the pages of Ionesco, Genet, Beckett, Sartre, Camus, Peter Weiss or Dürrenmatt. These dramatists torture plays out of neat dramaturgical structures, muse sardonically on the grotesque, absurd human condition, despair over the burden of mass trauma.

There's the cultured and professional Western and Central European source, the one running through centuries from Shakespeare through Goethe to Brecht and Heiner Müller, the one that often aligned itself with the low, but not always successfully. The one tortured by its shared ancestry with fascism, the ghost of the Father-Führer knocking from under the stage boards. The sophisticated, theory-fluent artistic tradition that enabled Müller's postmodern/postdramatic theatre to experiment with form, play with language, meaning and narrative rules, or employ striking images. Romanska tests with gusto the postdramatic's aptitude for intertextuality and self-referentiality, for language games and plastic use of story-telling clichés. Unexpected imagery explodes into the visual field freely and aggressively. Lines mix as in a salad bowl chopped references to feminist, postcolonial, media and political theory. Make of it what you will.

But the play is unmistakably feminist, channelling those remarkable women playwrights trained in and revolting against the patriarchal theatre tradition: Adrienne Kennedy, Lorraine Hansberry, María Irene Fornés, Sarah Kane, Elfriede Jelinek, just to name a few. Kennedy and Jelinek share with Romanska an interest in media culture and its impact on the female psyche, which leads to formal experimentations. Fornés zoomed in courageously on relationships between women, laying it all out, the good with the bad. Kane's goriness echoes through *Opheliamachine*, while the long monologues that punctuate the action channel Jelinek, weaponizing pornography against itself, meaning*full* but not always logical. *Opheliamachine* allows for theoretical and aesthetic flights of fancy, but it's an American influence, such as Hansberry's, that doesn't allow them to soar too high, grounding them in discernible, domestic, concrete sociopolitical situations. Gertrude's appearance and demeanour in *Opheliamachine* might be outlandish, her manner of speaking hardly naturalistic, but she does refer to (at length, repeatedly, and with crystal clear clarity) the exploitative and privileged practice of adopting babies from impoverished parts of the world with the entitled attitude of ordering yet another commodity. The European and American heritages combine in Romanska's writing, reflecting her formation on one continent and development on the other.

*   *   *

Before moving to the US to study, and then to teach and work herself, Magda Romanska was born and raised in the former Polish People's Republic. *Opheliamachine*'s conversation with Polish theatre might be less obvious to English-speaking readers. The play has a wedding at its core. This is not merely a feminine, domestic theme. It is a central trope of Polish drama, epitomized by the canonized masterpiece *The Wedding* (1901) by Stanisław Wyspiański, a modernist, nationalist poet and playwright who combined the preexisting folk-derived, Romantic, naturalist metaphysics of weddings with a dense historical metanarrative. *The Wedding* turns the figure of the national bard, the poet hero, the *wieszcz*, into a character. Poland's three real-life nineteenth-century prophetic bards, the three *wieszcz* – Mickiewicz, Słowacki and Krasiński – wrote at a time when Poland was wiped off the map, dismembered and partitioned among Russia, Austria and Prussia. The Romantic authors elegiacally but hopefully created and sustained the idea of a Polish identity and a Polish State of consciousness. Wyspiański's play ruminates philosophically and complicates notions of national identity and national destiny, anticipating a dark and murderous twentieth century filled with violence, wars, and renewed internal, ethnic divisions and external territorial divisions (as the 1939 Molotov–Ribbentrop Pact that planned to split Poland between the Third Reich and the Soviet Union).

The Wedding portrays the marriage feast between a peasant girl and a Poet, a symbolic union of the populace and the leading intelligentsia who, with the addition of fantastical apparitions from Polish folklore and history, invoke a national consciousness to bridge social divisions in the attempt to conjure into existence the Polish national state. Yet this nationalistic rhetoric, delivered in the verse epic poetic style of the Romantics and using the same mythical setting, is subtly undermined by Wyspiański: the Golden Horn delivered by the legendary bard and prophet Vernyhora to sound the unification of Poland is lost due to sheer incompetence. The wedding feast ends in quiet despair with the couples dancing in a somnambulist trance, incapable of action and taking on a historically passive and questionable role. Polish dramatists used farce to convey a bleak vision of history and to overturn and re-appropriate their literary tradition. *The Wedding* 'is considered the most accurate portrayal of the "Polish soul" and at the same time the sharpest attack upon it'.[7]

---

[7]Maciej Karpinski, *The Theater of Andrzej Wajda*, translated by Christina Paul (Cambridge: Cambridge University Press, 1989), 24.

Twentieth-century Polish playwrights continued to use the wedding trope as a way of discussing the state of the nation and its historical role, further developing an inter-textual allegorical mode of tragic farces that can escape the censors. Plays such as Witold Gombrowicz's *The Marriage* and *Princess Ivona* (written in 1946 and 1938 respectively, but only first performed in the 1960s), Slawomir Mrożek's *Tango* (1965), and *White Wedding* (1975) by Tadeusz Różewicz conflate the *wieszcz* Poet groom, the once brave liberator of the nation, with the figure of Hamlet as an anti-hero of indecision. Hamlet as a heroic figure was lost at war. The *wieszcz* in the plays above – Philip, Henry, Arthur and Benjamin (all English names) – grow ambivalent, portrayed as both victims and torturers. The Central European Hamlet doesn't first and suddenly appear in Müller's *Hamletmachine*. In Polish drama, he is meditating since the Second World War in the graveyard of civilization as a ludicrous parody of a European prince and a much more dangerous figure whose passivity and cowardice gleefully condones violence and repression. The 'grotesque is more cruel than tragedy' explained Polish critic Jan Kott in his bestseller on modern uses of Shakespeare.[8] In these 'marriage' plays, sex is always violent. The passive female body subjected to sexual abuse alludes to the passive territory of Poland ripped apart by imperialism. Bianca, the bride in *White Wedding*, equates sex with death: 'I can't be married. He'll thrust though me and kill me.'[9] In parodies of great Romantic dramas, Polish playwrights excelled at formal travesties, at mixing elevated literary register with the ruthless, crass and scatological.

Continuing in the Polish vein of detourned literary traditions, bleak comedies and brutal romances with befouled, engorged language, *Opheliamachine* gives a retort to *Hamletmachine*, but also to a national theatre culture by trying out a shifting of agency away from an incompetent or vicious-turning Hamlet/male heroic figure (since we've had enough of those) to the previously deemed passive bride that stood for the land, the mass of people, an

[8] Jan Kott, *Shakespeare, Our Contemporary*, translated by Boleslaw Taborski (New York; London: W.W. Norton, 1974), 83.
[9] Tadeusz Różewicz, *Mariage Blanc; and, The Hunger Artist Departs*, translated by Adam Czerniawski (London; New York: Marion Boyars, 1983), 60.

amorphous body at the mercy of historical forces. If the Hero-Groom that was supposed to lead the passive 'female' masses turned out to be the most passive of all, rolling over into violence, succumbing to mass-media induced catatonia, can the active element in this duo be instead the Bride? Romanska's Ophelia takes on the crumbled, charred mantle of the *wieszcz* and begins writing at the typewriter: she is the Poet-Seer. Can she do it any better? This question is at the heart of *Opheliamachine*, stirring up hope and empowerment together with doubt, anxiety and imposter syndrome. Ophelia enacts a subaltern reversal. After individual male heroes drove communist and democratic experiments into mass repressions, the play connects the challenge to patriarchy on the family level with the anti-hierarchical impulse of collective leadership from below.

* * *

In a conversation reported by Maria Pia Pagani, Romanska shares that *Opheliamachine* 'was inspired by Witold Gombrowicz's concept of *"filistria*: the realm of displaced persons of uncertain gender and sexuality living in a postcolonial – and now postideological – world"'.[10] Like the Romantics writing in exile during Poland's erasure from the map for more than a century, Gombrowicz lived and wrote in Argentina for twenty-four years, starting in 1939, when Germany invaded Poland. Romanska's work continues a national literature with a personal and intimate knowledge of displacement from geographical boundaries and national cultures. Yet Gombrowicz's openness to influences and his corruptions of far-right identities regressively conceived of as 'pure' – be they national, ethic or sexual – enriched his work, just as it did Romanska's. Their hybridity of identities and aesthetics

---

[10] Maria Pia Pagani sources the quote as '*Writing Opheliamachine*, private conversation with Magda Romanska' in her introduction to *Opheliamachine*'s Italian translation, 'From Elsinore to American Techno-Solitude', translated by Margaret Rose. *Mimesis Journal* 3, no. 1 (July 2014): 4–13, at 7. Quote comes from Allen Kuharski, 'Witold, Witold, Witold', *Gombrowicz' Grimaces: Modernisn, Gender, Nationality*, edited by Allen Kuharski (New York: State University Of New York Press), 285.

models a way of being and a post-nationalist art-making needed in a global world of mass migrations and refugee crises increasingly inter-mixed and inter-connected.

Gombrowicz's statelessness and queerness enabled him to see that what are upheld as fixed, essential, natural forms (from organizational models to individual and collective identities to artistic rules) are artificial constructions subject to change. His *filistria* is an 'anti-form', a call to fluidity in all aspects of life and work.[11] Romanska's immigration status, disability and female perspective arm her with the standpoint from which naturalized acts of violence are fully exposed. Her literary work communicates the pain and anger of experiencing injustice, but also envisions alternatives. The characters in *Opheliamachine* are casually gender-fluid and of mixed and indeterminate national and ethnic origin. Whereas Müller's 'feminized' Hamlet, with '*hand covering his face*' in shame declares 'I want to be a woman', which means little more than wearing revealing clothes and a '*whore's mask*', gender-fluid Horatio is not debased by feminine attributes.[12] The final image in *Hamletmachine* is of Ophelia '*in a wheelchair*' speaking as 'TWO MEN' wrap her in muslin and silence her: an image of the Victim.[13] When Ophelia appears in a wheelchair in Romanska's play, she is not silenced or stopped or victimized by it. She 'rolls out [in the wheelchair] laughing hysterically'. The tone of *Hamletmachine*, its postideological stance, reads as bleak, where values and certainties collapse into the absurdity of world wars and repressive crackdowns spreading disillusionment. *Opheliamachine*, however, rummages through the debris to reaffirm the sense of possibility and freedom within a postideological fluidity. The play ends with the image of Ophelia lighting up a match as dusk falls. She may use it to torch Hamlet doused in gasoline, symbolic of the old world with its heroes, cultures and ideas that failed us; she may use it to guide us and Hamlet through the night.

---

[11] Silvia G. Dapía, '"Living in Another Language": Witold Gombrowicz's Experience', *Polish American Studies* 71, no. 2 (2014): 79–89, at 89. https://doi.org/10.5406/poliamerstud.71.2.0079.

[12] Müller, 'The Hamletmachine', 89–90.

[13] Ibid., 94.

From Elsinore to American Techno-Solitude

Maria Pia Pagani

Translated from Italian by Margaret Rose

The earlier version of this introduction was published in *Mimesis*. July 2014

Magda Romanska explains as follows the long creative process of *Opheliamachine*, which opened to acclaim at the City Garage Theatre, Santa Monica, 14 June 2013,[1] later received reading at Brooklyn's Brick Theatre, New York, in 2014, and had its European premiere at Berliner Ensemble in Germany on 30 September 2022:

> I wrote *Opheliamachine* about ten years ago, at the heyday of my fascination with Heiner Muller. It was meant to be a response and a polemic with Mueller's *Die Hamletmaschine*. In *Hamletmachine*, Muller tries to deconstruct the impossible position of an Eastern European intellectual at the peak of the Cold War as well as the seemingly disappearing agency of the author. The gender, sex and violence are part of the equation, particularly in Germany which has been struggling to come to terms with its own historical glorification of raw power and masculinity. As Muller tried to capture the particular historical moment, in *Opheliamachine* I tried to capture our historical moment with all its entrapments: the

---

[1] For the acclaimed debut of the play, see Ben Miles, 'Opheliamachine', *Showmag. com*, 12 June 2013; Jessica Rizzo, '*Opheliamachine* Takes on Influential 20th-Century Theatre Work', *Cultural Weekly*, 13 June 2013; Philip Brandes, '*Opheliamachine*: An Uncompromising Vision at City Garage', *Los Angeles Times*, 20 June 2013; Sarah A. Spitz, 'The New Age of Ophelia', *Santa Monica Daily Press*, 20 June 2013; Anthony Byrnes, 'Opening the Curtain', Radio programme, 25 June 2013.

dissolution of our national and gender identities, the loss of
agency and terrifying solipsism of our lives in an increasingly
fragmented – if connected – world, the brutal, animal-like
quality of our relationships, the collapse of a social order and
its distinction, the chaos and violence that follows.[2]

Born in Poland, Magda Romanska emigrated to the USA in the
1990s. A graduate from Stanford, she also studied at Yale Drama
School, and received her doctorate at the Cornell University's
Theatre and Film Department where she wrote her PhD thesis on the
representation of death and femininity. She is an award-winning
academic, with many outstanding publications such as: *The Post-
Traumatic Theatre of Grotowski and Kantor: History and Holocaust
in 'Akropolis' and 'Dead Class'* (London: 2012),[3] *Boguslaw
Schaeffer: An Anthology* (London: Oberon Books, 2012), *The
Routledge Companion to Dramaturgy* (New York: 2014), *Comedy:
An Anthology of Theory and Criticism* (New York: 2014).

Furthermore, she is making her way as a dramatist in contemporary
American theatre. In her plays she often explores a largely uncharted
area, namely 'migration theatre' linked to the diaspora of many
Eastern European artists and intellectuals. Indeed, the figure of the
migrant frequently recurs in her creative work, ranging from the
autobiographical short story, *How I Survived Socialism*,[4] to her
postmodern, *Opheliamachine*, whose first Italian translation we are
presenting here.

I think that my status as an immigrant – someone living on
the borderline of two cultures – was important for creating
this play. Immigrants have diasporic psyches. We're
detached from our origins and often not really attached to our

---

[2] *About Ophelia*, a private conversation with Magda Romanska.
[3] See Maria P. Pagani, *A Gift of Freedom from Grotowski and Kantor*, in *Jerzy
Grotowski: L'eredità vivente*, edited by Antonio Attisani, 44–5 (Turin: Accademia
University Press, Mimesis Journal Books, 2012).
[4] Magda Romanska, 'How I Survived Socialism: A Self-Help Guide for Worried
Americans', *Cosmopolitan Review: A Transatlantic Review of Things Polish, in
English* 4, no. 1, Spring 2012, http://cosmopolitanreview.com/how-i-survived-
socialism/.

new places. In some way, what used to be an immigrant condition is now a global condition. We are constantly bombarded by so many contradictory messages, it becomes impossible to create a stable coherent self-image. I think that as a humanity we are experiencing a fundamental shift – akin to what happened during the Age of Enlightenment – in the way we understand ourselves, our relationship to each other and to our world.[5]

Like many migrants, who have graduated and engaged in postgraduate studies in their adopted country, Magda Romanska wrote *Opheliamachine* directly in English. Still, she sometimes thinks in Polish in some everyday situations, such as when she is out walking.[6] Her Ophelia play reflects the real and metaphorical steps of her diaspora journey which grows steadily more real.

Written in the tradition of such experimental texts as Picasso's *Four Little Girls*, Artaud's *Jet of Blood*, or Jarry's *Ubu Roi*, *Opheliamachine* is a collage, pastiche, conglomeration of images that rule over our modern, global, virtual sexuality. The play doesn't have a plot as such. It is a postmodern tale of love and sex in a fragmented world of questionable values. Hamlet and Ophelia are represented by multiple characters, each in conflict with him- or herself and the other. *Opheliamachine* captures the dissolution of the national (local, sexual, etc.) identities leading to the kind of physical and psychological displacement that used to be the traditional immigrant, diasporic condition and which now has become the new normalized global mode of being, a new human condition. The play was inspired by Witold Gombrowicz' concept of 'filistria: the realm of displaced persons of uncertain gender and sexuality living in a postcolonial – and now postideological – world.'[7]

---

[5] *Bit about Opheliamachine's background*, private conversation with Magda Romanska.
[6] *Translation from . . .*, private conversation with Magda Romanska.
[7] *Writing Opheliamachine*, private conversation with Magda Romanska.

In her own way, Magda Romanska's Ophelia is *borderline*: she lives on the edge of everything. She is ready to leave, but doesn't really know where she can go. She is unable to dispel the ghosts from her past. She's afraid of the future. She is unable to contain her mad bursts of emotion. Above all, she feels Hamlet isn't hers and is too 'American'. Separating the two, the Atlantic Ocean. Sitting at a floating desk on a scaffolding, she looks out at the New World from 'her' Elsinore and finds herself unable to hold back fits of anger and ironic darts mingled with tenderness, waves of doubt and pessimism.

In a series of kaleidoscopic episodes, during which a discussion with Müller unfolds[8] – a closer look shows Shakespeare's long shadow – *Opheliamachine* reveals the complex experiences and feelings of a contemporary woman. Cruelly entrapped in a machine created by her own conscience, Ophelia exploits this to unravel her contradictions and those of our age. Showing no shame and making no compromises, Ophelia wants to be an authentic woman, but feels the continual danger of losing herself among the women milling at New York's Port Authority Bus Station. Unlike Chekhov's three sisters: 'To Moscow! To Moscow! To Moscow!',[9] she is so mixed up she can't even make up her mind where she is going. Just like them, Ophelia feels uncertain: even if she is in a relationship, she feels lonely and unable to manage her maternal instinct. She struggles to make her voice heard. And filled with doubt, she doesn't find definitive answers. She weeps but finds no consolation for her tears.

And, again from 'her' Elsinore, Ophelia tells Hamlet about one of her ancestors who died in an unnamed place between Prague and Vienna (conjured up in contrapunto as in Grotowski's *Akropolis*),[10] thereby foreseeing that the two of them will share the same fate. But also Hamlet comes from the Old World . . . And does Ophelia feel worried, because she feels he is too 'Americanized'.

*   *   *

[8] See Magda Romanska, 'Gender, Ethics and Representation in Heiner Müller's *Hamletmachine*', in *The Cultural Politics of Heiner Müller*, edited by Dan Friedman, 61–86 (Newcastle, UK: Cambridge Scholars Publishing, 2008).

[9] See Magda Romanska, 'Between History and Memory: Auschwitz in *Akropolis*, *Akropolis* in Auschwitz', *Theatre Survey* 50, no. 2 (2009): 223–50.

[10] *Polish and American*, private conversation with Magda Romanska.

Her words address a man who is always absent-minded, who wears jeans and cowboy boots, with a sixteenth-century jacket. In the present he lives in America, but it seems he wants to ignore the fact that you can't forget your origins. Instead, Magda Romanska's theatre aims to show that we've got roots and they'll always make themselves felt:

> Being located in Central Europe, Poland has always been a center of Europe's contradictory impulses, a place where forces from the West and East, North and South, would battle their tensions. Growing up in Poland, a country which had been the stage for some of the most important events of the twentieth century, had a formatting effect on how I construe my own worldview: dialectically and with the type of laissez faire awareness of how relative my own judgments are. Czeslaw Milosz captured that sense of self-awareness that all Eastern and Central Europeans have: 'the man of the East cannot take Americans seriously because they have never undergone the experiences that teach men how relative their judgments and thinking habits are' (this comes from *The Captive Mind*) Milan Kundera has a similar quote: 'It takes so little, so infinitely little, for a person to cross the border beyond which everything loses meaning: love, convictions, faith, history. Human life – and herein lies its secret – takes place in the immediate proximity of that border, even in direct contact with it; it is not miles away, but a fraction of an inch' (from *The Book of Laughter and Forgetting*). These two quotes, from Milosz and Kundera, should probably be placed at the top of *Opheliamachine* . . . It's a play that takes place on the borders – between countries, cultures, nationalities, genders, relationships . . .[11]

---

[11] See Magda Romanska, 'Hamlet, Masculinity and the Nineteenth Century Nationalism', in *Ghosts, Stories, Histories: Ghost Stories and Alternative Histories*, edited by Sladja Bladan, 114–41 (Newcastle, UK: Cambridge Scholars Publishing, 2007).

In his own way, Magda Romanska's Hamlet is an exile crushed by a tragedy of incomprehension.[12] He neither understands, nor is he understood, with no way out. He wants to understand the world, but the only thing he knows how to do is watch through the lens of virtual reality. He refuses some shrimps, telling his friend, the genderfluid Horatio, he is on a diet. However, he knows perfectly well that his daily diet is 'whatever appears on the screen'; he binges on videogames, computers and television. He knows that he is anorexic in real life, but has bulimia in Second Life. Still, he does nothing to try and change.

Federique Michel's hyper-technological 2013 production is therefore very powerful. According to Rose Desena, writing in *The Los Angeles Post*, it reveals, 'Stunning piece of performance art'.[13] Myron Meisel, writing in *The Hollywood Reporter*, remarks that the production couldn't have been done in any other way, 'This funny yet brutal play needs the inventive mis-en-scène to support its fecundity of ideas amidst the tumult of its conflicting impulses. And don't be afraid: It is OK, even purgative, to laugh.'[14]

The hard-hitting humour pervading Magda Romanska's postmodern play is underscored by critic Steven Leigh Morris in *LA Weekly*: 'This is theater that's not easily accessible and is devilishly bleak at times, but it's not without shards of humor, and is relentlessly provocative and challenging.'[15]

Troubled by the terrible voice of the mother-mistress, Gertrude is busy shopping online for foreign 'dolls', when Hamlet throws a shoe at her but misses. In the hope that one of these creatures will be right for her son, Gertrude insists on buying the best one in the catalogue. Hamlet's failure to hit the target seems to suggest the dark despair of the potshot in *Uncle Vanya*. Today Doctor Chekhov might say that this Hamlet in exile is suffering from:

---

[12] Rose Desena, 'This Week in Theatre: *Opheliamachine*', *The Los Angeles Post*, 25 June 2013.

[13] Ibid.

[14] Myron Meisel, '*Opheliamachine*: Theatre Review', *The Hollywood Reporter*, 17 June 2013.

[15] Steven Leigh Morris, '*Opheliamachine*: Theatre to See This Week in LA', *LA Weekly*, 20 June 2013.

'techno-loneliness'or 'techno-solitude', a global disease steadily taking more victims, particularly in America.

Hamlet never mentions his father. His dignity as a modern-day heir to the throne transpires from the way he handles the remote control, or the great care he shows regarding his late father's sceptre. (Italian audiences will probably recall Renzo Arbore's song, 'Life is a quiz' and the line when a father tells his son: 'Listen / to this advice / here's what I say / in your life / keep control / as long as you are holding your remote control.')

Who knows if Hamlet saw his father's ghost on the screen, thereby increasing his technological addiction? And could it have been his father who, during their silent virtual dialogue, suggested he watch the animal documentaries on the National Geographical Channel to understand better how a couple functions?

In our contemporary society, characterized by a confused progression of life and death, beauty and terror, innocence and violence, is there still room for poets? Who understands them? Can they still love? Do they make us love them? Hamlet doesn't speak much, and when he does, he delivers cryptic verses that make communication with Ophelia increasingly difficult. The psychoanalyst, moreover, that Magda Romanska brilliantly models on the Commedia dell'Arte Doctor figure, declares that Hamlet's stubborn behaviour points to a serious illness.

In fact, Ophelia is fed up with Hamlet's silence and poetic flights; his behaviour turns their life together into a battlefield, where they need to wear army uniform and sometimes wield detonators.[16] (For Italian audiences Gianna Nannini's song, 'Fotoromanza', will probably spring to mind. It goes: 'This love is a gas chamber / it's a building on fire in the city, / this love is a thin knife blade / it's a scene in slow motion / This love is a bomb in a hotel, / this love is a ring / and a flame, bursting in the sky, *this love is a poisoned ice cream*'.)

Still is Ophelia a victim or a threat for Hamlet?

---

[16] See Magda Romanska, 'Playing with the Void: Dance Macabre of Object and Subject in the Bio-Object of Kantor's Theater of Death', *Analecta Husserliana* 81 (2004): 269–87.

Their best moments together see them plunged into a soap, but even then their feelings towards each other are different and there's never a moment when they really come together. As a director, we see Hamlet's creativity as he directs Ophelia's murder; he suggests four different hypotheses to her, all feasible in everyday life and which deftly join the metatheatrical dimension to the crime news everywhere in the media.

Between a cigarette and a drop of blood red wine, Ophelia is forever busy writing her memoirs. Her Dostoyevskian, visionary exploration of herself inevitably leads her to consider her double face, represented by a woman in army uniform to the mad bride, the puppet of Kantorian inspiration who moves round the stage in a wheelchair.[17]

In this contemporary wasteland, whose terrible landscape looms on the screen, there seems no room for human happiness A videogame mechanically plays, 'Dream a Little Dream of Me'. But will Hamlet and Ophelia manage to accept this invitation? Have they still enough strength and will to dream? And to do this together?

Hamlet's techno-solitude and his subsequent behaviour obviously make Ophelia wonder if she has the right man by her side. Horatio comforts her with words worthy of Oscar Wilde's best society comedies. Unfortunately, his reply only increases Ophelia's distress. 'Of course you're not, darling. You could never actually be with the right person. What makes him right is the fact that you're not with him. What makes him wrong is the fact that you're with him.'

Still, simultaneously Ophelia is obsessed with the idea of belonging to another man (only one?) and being judged for this. From her 'Elsinore', clinging to an old-fashioned typewriter, she tries to casually engage in the destruction of a traditional marriage, represented by the bride wearing a wedding dress and veil, welcomed by a peal of joyous bells and the preparation of a lavish banquet.

Her madness stems from this and is represented by Horatio – the groom's best friend, who is also in charge of the catering. Horatio shows everybody a severed head on a silver tray, mirroring what Salome did with John the Baptist's skull.

---

[17] See Magda Romanska, 'Ontology and Eroticism: Two Bodies of Ophelia', *Women's Studies: An Interdisciplinary Journal* 34, no. 6 (2005): 485–503.

Ophelia's wild meditation inevitably leads to suicidal thoughts. Instead of drowning, however, she decides to have her double, dressed in army uniform, put a pistol to her temple and fire. This solution tallies perfectly with the unprincipled (ab)use of arms in America and the wicked shootings to which the media lavish disproportionate attention (Maksudov, dramatist of Bulgakov's *Theatrical Novel,* supports the spectacular aspect of death with a gunshot, but director Ivan Vasil'evic – alias Stanislavski – scraps the idea to avoid problems with the censure. Deeply disillusioned with his life in the theatre, E. Maksudov ends his days by throwing himself off a bridge and drowning like Shakespeare's heroine).

But despite everything, can Hamlet live without Ophelia?

Life has taught Ophelia that 'pleasure' and 'pain' are two sides of the same coin. She thought she could find happiness with Hamlet, but instead she found the emptiness of techno-solitude. However, techno-solitude has also made Hamlet feel suicidal. So the two are now united –for the first time   in the murder-suicide of the play's ending. We watch as Hamlet pours petrol over the stage and Ophelia lights a match. If it's true, as the *Cantico dei cantici* says, that love is as strong as death, then Magda Romanska's contemporary exiles (in their own pathological fashion) love each other.

Photo 1 *Opheliamachine*, City Garage Theatre in Los Angeles (2013). Directed by Frédérique Michel. Produced and designed by Charles A. Duncombe. Left to right: Joss Glennie-Smith, R. J. Jones. Photo credit Paul Rubenstein.

Photo 2 *Opheliamachine*, City Garage Theatre in Los Angeles (2013). Directed by Frédérique Michel. Produced and designed by Charles A. Duncombe. Left to right: Saffron Mazzia, Joss Glennie-Smith. Photo credit Paul Rubenstein.

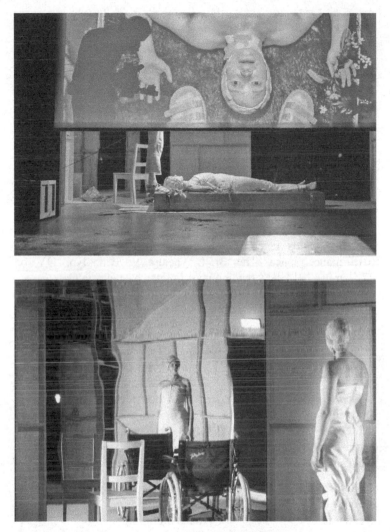

Photo 3 *Opheliamaschine*. Berliner Ensemble, Berlin, Germany (2022). Directed by Uršulė Barto. Designed by by Katja Pech. Nina Bruns as Ophelia. Photo credit Moritz Haase.

Production History

Opheliamachine premiered at City Garage Theatre in Los Angeles 14 June – 28 July 2013. It was directed by Frédérique Michel and produced and designed by Charles A. Duncombe.

Hamlet	Joss Glennie Smith
Therapist/Talk Show Host	Leah Harf
Ophelia/Writer	Kat Johnston
Ophelia/Fighter	Megan Kim
Ophelia/Traveler	Saffron Mazzia
Gertrude	Jeanine Serralles
Horatio	RJ Jones

Opheliamachine received a staged reading at the experimental performance space, The Brick Theatre in Brooklyn, NY on 27 October 2014. The reading was directed by Jackson Gay.

Hamlet	Patch Darragh
Ophelia/Writer	Danielle Slavick
Ophelia/Fighter	Ceci Fernandez
Ophelia/Traveler	Sarah Sokolovic
Gertrude	Jeanine Serralles

Opheliamachine was produced by the Berliner Ensemble in Germany on 30 September 2022. It was translated by Theresa Schlesinger and directed by Uršulė Barto. The assistant director was Kathinka Schroeder and the dramaturg was Jan-Stephan Schmieding. Stage and costume design by Katja Pech.

Ophelia	Nina Bruns
Hamlet	Max Diehle
Gertrude	Hilke Altefrohne

Opheliamachine

A car shop, a storage room or kid's playroom, full of objects gathered there by a lost traveler: armless Michelangelo's David wearing a motorcycle helmet, a pile of broken African masks, the skeleton of a dead poet laughing hysterically at his own shadow, a baby doll with missing limbs sucking on a pink lollipop, Magritte's broken umbrella, Andy Warhol's old telephone to God, a dirty white wedding veil hanging somewhere with other clothes, piles of old shoes and wigs.

It is a modern wasteland, with broken console games, TV screens, and computer screens showing random mute scenes of our virtual lives: war scenes, mass murders, genocides, Auschwitz bodies, porn, political ads, Wall Street women, fat women, anorexic women, Japanese schoolgirls, women clad in burkas, wild safaris, comic book explosions. **Hamlet** *and* **Ophelia** *drink this daily soup of news and images: a mishmash of the human contrast between beauty and horror, innocence and violence.*

Everything is covered by radioactive ash.

Hamlet, *dressed in jeans, sixteenth-century jacket, and cowboy hat, sits on the couch facing the audience. He watches TV, mindlessly flipping channels with his remote control. On the backdrop of the stage, a projection of the mishmash.* **Hamlet** *wants to understand the world, but all he can do is stare at it.*

Stage left, behind him, **Ophelia**, *dressed in green army camouflage, sits behind a floating desk typing something on an old-fashioned typewriter. A glass of blood red wine sits on the side. She smokes a cigarette and is focused intently on typing.*

Hamlet *and* **Ophelia** *are at the two ends of the world. Between them, the Atlantic Ocean full of rotting corpses, dead birds and urine.*

Ophelia (*typing*)   Hamlet, my darling, I do not wish to identify with you or with her; your toy soldiers invaded my side of the bed. The oceans and continents exchange easily for political nostalgia and endurance. Let the dead bury the dead, the plague of our fathers. (*She pauses and takes a sip of her wine.*)

Hamlet (*absentmindedly, recalling better times*)   In the unblessed dice

– six beds by seven nights –
newly hatched larvae docked themselves
on the shores of their own sawdust.

Ophelia (*continuing, undisturbed*)   . . . writing is a form of intellectual masturbation. I spill my poor, pathetic self over the white eye of my computer, proud to master this difficult art of self-indulgence, and hence to enter the new era of solipsistic pleasures. My self-sufficiency astonishes me. Oh, those erotogenic points on my brain, examined thoughtfully in megalomaniac fits of self-adoration. Yes, yes, right now, I'll save herself automatically for later. (*She pauses and takes a drag of her cigarette.*)

TV (*National Geographic Channel*)   During its mating ritual, the female white eagle locks her talons with the male, demanding his total submission as the two of them plunge inertly to the ground. If he tries to free himself before she's ready, she'll never let him mount her. If she waits just a few seconds too long, they'll both crash to their deaths onto the ground.

The sound of a passing train riding at full speed, whistling as if trying to warn someone standing on the train tracks. The train passes. Midnight at the Port Authority. Ding dong, the sound of the announcer, mumbling something. **Hamlet** *continuously watches TV.*

Ophelia (*as a matter of fact*)   Most girls at the Port Authority are either from the Bronx or Harlem. They are dressed in fake Chanel scarves on their heads and fake Louis Vuitton bags under their shoulders. They try to look fashionable and taken care of, like they have a man for whom they are worth the couple hundred dollars of the seemingly useless luxuries. Some of them have small babies or toddlers with them, holding them with quiet desperation. I am never sure who needs whom more: they their babies, or their babies them. They sit on the ground or on their suitcases, waiting patiently for their buses. Sometimes, they have a man with them, and then their eyes shine through with gentle satisfaction. They seem both fragile and tough, like they could start crying or cursing any minute.

Ophelia *goes back to typing. Phone rings. The sound of the passing tram. Child cries in the neighboring apartment.* **Gertrude** *enters. She crosses the stage, wearing a robe and fiery rollers on her head. She picks her teeth and talks on the phone. Her eyes are aglow.*

Gertrude   Oh my goodness, no! She had freckles?! Well, hallo, you KNOW what I THINK about that. I mean . . . look all I'm saying is as simple as this. You look at a regular china doll, does she have freckles? Huh? No, she doesn't. Does the one they send you have freckles? So, . . . send it back!. . . . . No, you shouldn't have to do that! You should NOT have to pay for the return postage. You put it right back in that box and you send it back. Oh, no! You paid for that! . . . You saw the picture in the catalog, you put it on your credit card and now you should get what you paid for! . . . Were there pictures of a girl with freckles? No! ok. My point . . . have I made my point?! . . . NO, because this is called MISREPRESENTATION!   . . They can get sent to jail for that, you know?. . . . Yeah, you can get lots of nice girls from China . . .

She disappears behind the stage door. Her robe gets stuck in the door and she pulls it angrily. **Hamlet** *turns around and throws a shoe behind her, but misses. He grows bat wings and goes back to watching TV.*

Ophelia (*continues typing as if nothing has happened*)   The dread, darling, the dread; I want you to fill it up or take it upon yourself. It's your choice: prosperity awaits impatiently our sorry genes to be passed over, and immortalized in twelve pounds of carbon and intellect. Yes, yes, darling, I am sure procreation can be a source of unending joy for the masses, but we're so much more refined. You must understand, the voices in my head cannot be deafened by a child's cry; you must know, even the screams I produce with such grace when you mercifully exercise your right to post-coital numbness . . . numbness . . . (*Pause. As she types,* **Hamlet** *watches soft porn.*) the dread, darling, the dread I was talking about, not numbness. I am sure if you try just a little harder, you'll reach it. Your penis was measured carefully and its existential qualities were assessed with full responsibility for my own failure to cure your wounded self and define the convention of our charming encounter which I hope will leave us equally unfulfilled. The length of your penis is proportional to the anguish I'll feel smoking a cigarette in your tired arms, and contemplating the statistical probability of lung cancer or a heart attack brought on by sexual insatiability, and dreads not taken care of properly. Hamlet, darling, don't talk about politics, your desires, the world, death and the blood you shed crying over the starving children.

Ophelia, *wearing a wedding gown, crosses over, accompanied by* **Horatio** *and* **Gertrude**. **Gertrude** *is driving a rockabye horse, waving a sword behind her head.* **Horatio** *is wearing a tux, fishnet stockings, and red heels. Her hair is pulled back. She holds a platter of shrimp and a notebook.*

Ophelia (*walking up and down the stairs in wedding dress*)   Blessed are You . . .

Horatio   That shrimp looked a little peavy. Maybe I should call the catering company. You don't want anyone to get sick. They really should start selling wedding insurance for things like that. What do you think?

Ophelia   Do you ever wonder if you're with the right person?

Horatio (*looking up from her notebook*)   Of course you're not, darling. You could never actually *be* with the right person. What makes him right is the fact that you're not with him. What makes him wrong is the fact that you're with him. (*Going back to the notebook.*) Where did the shrimp came from? La Bella Tosca, or Christie's?

Ophelia   Christie's. You should make sure that he's the one. The one.

Gertrude   Oh, the one. . .

Ophelia (*crying her heart out*)   I want the one and forever, together, until death . . .

Gertrude   Life, death, love or lust, the universe is infinite and expanding. Where you came from? Where you're going? *Quo vadis. Panta rei.* Great questions, darling, but, despite what your father says, they will not pay your rent. You should write them down now, put them away in your secret hiding place, and take them out when you're retired. They'll come really handy then, between golf lessons, Pilates, and hot flashes. You really should stop squinting like this. Your makeup gets all smudgy.

Hamlet (*entering, in tux*)   You're not really going to marry *him,* are you?

Horatio (*rolling her eyes*)   He's the one. He isn't the one.

Gertrude   The one to do what?

Ophelia   To heal your soul . . .

Gertrude *and* **Horatio** *look at each other and start laughing hysterically.*

Gertrude   Like the other one?

Horatio   Or the other one.

Gertrude (*philosophically*)   Or another one.

Church bells start ringing and **Gertrude** *and* **Horatio** *turn into avatars; they leave, their synthesized voices dissolving into absurd repetitions: 'the one, or another one, which one, someone, anyone, no one, the one we've been waiting for, or the other one, the one they've been waiting for, you've been waiting for? Who's been waiting for? Which one?'.*

Hamlet (*speaking from the screen as the bells toll*)   Sedate yourself with cries of the wolf's children

nothing's real but
hair stiff from vomit
tonight –
you'll sleep not dreaming.
Tomorrow –

unzip your skin and let us in
Dr Tulp's anatomy lesson can begin

Ding dong – *the sound of the bus station. The announcer's voice is mumbling, unintelligible.*

Ophelia *is carrying a suitcase and a pillow sham full of mannequin heads. She enters carefully, looking up the bus schedule and trying to figure out what time the bus leaves. She is stopped by* **Hamlet**. *He wears a heavy gold chain around his neck.*

Hamlet   Hey, where are you going.

Ophelia   To visit a friend.

Hamlet (*checking her out*)   Where're you from?

Ophelia   Huston, Maine.

Hamlet   Where is it?

Ophelia   It's a small town; nobody knows where it is.

Hamlet   It's a college town? You're in college?

Ophelia   No.

Hamlet   What are you doing there? (*She's silent, smiling faintly, clearly uncomfortable.*) Hehe, I know, it's a guy thing. He got you all cooked up over there. Hehe. He's got you all cooked up over there. You should come here to New York.

Ophelia   Hmm.

Hamlet   What do you have in there?

Ophelia   This?

Hamlet   Uh-huh.

Ophelia   Those are mannequin heads. I am training to be a hairdresser.

(*Ding dong.* Port Authority announcer: 'The 2:30 am bus to Cleveland is leaving Gate 5. Please, don't forget your bags.')

Ophelia   That's my bus.

He waits for her to say something, but she is silent, so he leaves. She struggles with the pillow sham and slowly drags it behind her, disappearing backstage. He spits over his shoulder and follows her.

'Dream a Little Dream of Me' starts playing. **Ophelia**, *sitting behind her desk, takes a sip of wine.* **Hamlet** *abandons his remote control and starts playing a video game. Dry autumn leaves start falling on them. The music stops abruptly as the door opens.*

Gertrude *enters, talking on the phone. She is wearing the same robe, but half of her head is out of the rollers. Her hair, like Medusa's, flows in all four directions of the world. She walks across the stage, talking on the phone and browsing through the catalog.*

Gertrude   . . . which one do you think I should get? The one from Russia, Romania, or from China? The ones from Russia look good, all nice and blonde, but they say they're damaged. All that Russian vodka their mothers drank . . . I am not so sure about the ones from Romania; they look pale, blonde but too pale. They might be malnourished. Same with the African ones. But they are so exotic. I would look good with one on my shoulder next to my Chanel bag. Or better yet, Hermès. . . . What's the warranty on them?. . . . Two years? Can you buy an extended warranty? . . . What if it dies?. . . . Do they send you a new one to replace it? Do they cover the funeral costs? . . . What about the shipping? I am not going to pay for shipping again. Twenty-five thousand for all the paperwork – that's it. . . . Yes, you're right my dear, the ones from South America look so nice, not too dark, not too pale. . . . Uh-huh. . . .

She leaves, quite content with her idea.

TV *(from the screen, it's hard to tell if it's a soap opera or a classic novel)*   This duality of her nature scared him. Each time he was sure he possessed her, her eyes became those of a stranger. In an instance she was so familiar he could hear her voice inside him, and so distant that the sudden loneliness that entered every cell of his body hurt physically and suffocated him like the awareness of his death.

Hamlet *sits on the couch playing a video game. His face slowly morphs into* **Ophelia**'s *face. She is wearing an army helmet, which she covers in a black headscarf.*

Ophelia (*from the screen, as if she was saying a kid's nursery rhyme*)   one day
my flesh walked out on us
leaving me and my skin in a stupor of surprise
we looked at each other amused
we had nothing else to lose

Horatio (*reading from some legal documents*)   For months now they have been preparing for this baby. They were buying everything together, the crib, the stroller, the clothes. Everything was the best, the most expensive, from the most exclusive catalogs. He bought her a brand-new car so she could get to the University and back without waiting on the bus. When they learned it would be a girl, he was disappointed. He really wanted to have a boy to carry on what he started. He fantasized about the things he would teach him. Ashamed of his own feelings, he hid his disappointment, got used to the idea of a girl and cheered her on during the pregnancy, handling patiently her fits of bad humor and random melancholy. She was carrying his baby. For the first time, she was officially permitted to torture him and she slowly discovered that there was no limit to what she could do. The resentment she felt towards him for all the times that she had to humor his fragile ego, only exasperated her imagination. She crushed him time after time with increasingly refined cruelty and he bore it all with a mixed sense of duty, awe and wonder.

The sound of a plane or helicopter flying overhead and the shadow of wings on the set. **Ophelia** *spreads her black arms and starts floating above. She turns into a raven. Sounds of the big city: an ambulance, a shooting spree, laughing girls, someone screaming and a dog barking in the street.* **Ophelia** *watches from above. Her body breaks into a million little pieces which she tries to gather into a shopping basket. The supermarket cleaning lady kicks* **Ophelia** *out, and* **Ophelia** *rips her eyes out.*

Hamlet   Light drops by
caressing the shadows on white sheets
smelling of blood, Lysol and
yesterday's urine.

In which drawer have you put all your insomnias
and mosaics composed of the mould stains on the ceiling
where your horizon ends?

Ophelia *in a wheelchair enters, pushed by an army nurse.*

Ophelia   As a girl in a wheelchair, I was suddenly torn: to whom
I should pledge my alliances? If someone was a woman, the
answer was simple. If someone was a cripple, the answer was
simple. If someone was a woman and a cripple, the answer was
simple. But, there was an intrinsic existential impossibility there in
the figure of the crippled man: was he an enemy or a martyred
brother? Bound to his sex or to his wheelchair? Since I couldn't
decide my politics around crippled men, I decided preemptively to
avoid them altogether. Fundamentally screwed in their wounded
masculinity, crippled men were something that I, with my wounded
femininity, was naturally prone to avoid. Unable to deal with my
own contradictions – between wanting to be desired and wanting to
be respected – I needed an emotionally low-maintenance man, one
infinitely generous, whose own ego and mind were strong and
sturdy like his never-faltering cock, with which he would convince
me over and over again of my boundless sex-appeal, even if for
acquired tastes, and ever-fascinating personality that captured him
totally and without reserve.

The wheelchair spins around and the **Ophelia** *mannequin
evaporates. The nurse dusts off the pillow and begins running in
circles: she knows she can't have an empty wheelchair so she stuffs
it with anything she can.*

TV: *Talk show or prime-time series. Marriage counselling.*
Ophelia *and* **Hamlet** *sit on the couch.*

Therapist   Hello, thank you for coming. It is so nice of you to
have a problem to share.

Hamlet   No problem.

Therapist (*disappointed*)   No problem?

Hamlet   Oh, no, there is problem. No problem we came to share the problem with you.

Therapist   Oh right, how wonderful. So what is the problem?

Hamlet   It is horrible, I can't believe what she did. She ruined our lives.

Ophelia   Oh, honey, what did I do, what did I do, if you just told me . . . oh honey (*crying*). If you could just tell me what it is I am sure we'll be all right. Don't endanger our love and marriage with your silence.

Therapist   Yes, it is all about communication. If you could tell us, we will know. If you could share your feelings with your wife, your feelings will be shared.

Hamlet   What she did? What she did? I can't even talk about it. Look, I am still shaking just thinking about it. I can't believe she did this. I can't believe she did this to me. . . .

Ophelia & Therapist   What did she (*I*) do?

Hamlet   You want to know? You want to know? All right, I will tell you. Yesterday morning, at breakfast . . . (*He whispers in Therapist's ear.*)

Therapist   Oh, my gooooood!

Hamlet   Yes, that is what she did.

Therapist   It is definitively a difficult situation, but I am sure that if we solve it, it will be solved. Divorces are the number one reason for divorces. But, everything else is good?

Ophelia   Oh, yes, everything is good. We have a great marriage.

Hamlet   Oh, yes, work is good, money are good, children are dead.

Therapist   Only then can you say you've reached a state of true wisdom, when you don't let your emotions interfere with your impartial objective intellectual judgment. The conclusion you draw must be always given a priori or deducted from the empirical experience which you've accumulated. You must never rest at making statements that are devoid of profound intellectual impartiality. Only then, can you say something truly profoundly impartial, truly impartially profound. (*He is surprised at himself for being so clever; he smiles and shakes his head, pondering what he has just said, but quickly forgets, starting to pick his nose.*)

Ophelia (*behind her desk, typing*)   How singular is the thing called pleasure and how curiously related to pain, which might be thought to be the opposite of it; for they never come to a man together, and yet he who pursues either of them is generally compelled to take the other.[1]

TV (*lecture*)   The woman whose sexual pleasure is originarily self-representative in a way different from man's might just as well not have a clitoris; the hymen that remains forever (in)violate, upon which the seed is forever spilled afield in dissemination, has no use for the hysteron. Is this the scene of violence that is called love in transformation contained within our only perfect triad? If women have always been used as the instrument of male self-deconstruction, is this philosophy's newest twist?[2]

Ophelia (*a therapist*)   I like to believe that you know what you're doing and you're not just trapped in the predicaments of self-defeating American masculinity, that will eventually leave you emotionally drained, intellectually famished and sexually incompetent.

Hamlet (*while playing a video game, casually*)   Do you want me to kill you in a dramatic act of jealously so overpowering I would lose my senses? Do you want me to kill you while you're coming

---

[1] Plato, *Phaedo* (59c–69e), in *The Dialogues of Plato*, translated by Benjamin Jowett. 3rd edition. Five volumes (London: Oxford: University Press, 1892) 23.
[2] Gayatri Spivak. 'Displacement and Discourse of a Woman.' In *Displacement: Derrida and After*, edited by Mark Krupnick (Bloomington: Indiana University Press, 1983).

so that you can melt with the universe in the eternal climax, so you could think you'll live forever captured in this moment? Do you want me to kill you while I whisper in your ears sweet nothings about my own despair? Do you want me to kill you and myself to follow you in the drama of death so carefully directed?

Ophelia *floats in space. She tries to grasp at straws, but the world disappears on the horizon.* **Ophelia** *tries to walk but there is no surface to walk on. She finds the remote control and presses it desperately a few times. Human and animal carcasses float down the Ganges River.* **Ophelia** *washes her hair and steps on the desert sand. Her heart bleeds. Her veins are made of wires.* **Ophelia** *carries her own corpse across the desert border.*

Hamlet   Though I walk through the valley of the shadow of death, I will fear no evil: For thou art with me;
Thy rod and thy staff, they comfort me.
Thou preparest a table before me in the presence of mine enemies.[3]

Ophelia (*sitting behind her desk in army green. Calm and stoic, continuing to type, as if nothing has happened*)   Please, darling, self-deprecation is not a necessary agent of one's market value; our purity is purely formal as are our perversions so cherished by your mother and advertised in every soap commercial. Darling, you must know she saved herself automatically for the wedding night with candles and desires carefully sculptured by TV, hence new to our generation. The dread, darling, the dread. I truly believe in God and human dignity, except when it lies in the trenches with its head blown away by someone else's virtue and commitment to passion for life, as I believe you're the one to reach deep inside with profundity closed to my weakening limbs. Yes, yes, darling, you can write me a poem, or just fuck me hard enough; I am sure either way, we'll remain faithful to our long-held conviction of immortality accomplished by goodness of the heart, and union of the souls ridden of their mutual hatred and love towards one

---

[3] *King James Bible*, Psalm 23.4-5.

another, passing their days in the harmony of hygienic rituals, post-modern discourse of various intellectual levels and labor that will make us free of materialistic abundance or shortages depending on whether the procreation reached its statistical average or expressed itself in the egotistical individualism of self-adoration. I am sure my conviction will leave me confident in myself as it would any other, for which you'll thank me when I pour you a glass of wine and massage your shoulders. The tip of your penis has an ontological potential, so I stick your sword into your urethra to examine whether the space is sufficiently specious to absorb my dread and all the others left accidentally by the future fathers of America and five other continents considering the globalization of our sexual habits. My grandmother's father perished mysteriously somewhere between Prague and Vienna, exactly the way we will.

Horatio *enters with a silver platter of shrimp.*

Horatio *(to* **Hamlet***, who still sits on the couch)*   Shrimp?

Hamlet   Thanks, I am on a diet.

Horatio *suddenly remembers something and raises his fist, screaming: 'Freedom!' He is run over by the tank and his body disappears into the black asphalt. A group of smiling children runs over the pavement, laughing and holding hands. The black ravens pick at* **Horatio***'s flesh. The sound of the bus station. Ding dong.*

The Announcer   The bus from Paris to New York, through London and Tokyo, leaving from Gate 5. The bus from Paris to New York, through London and Tokyo, leaving from Gate 5.

The announcement repeats a few times as if the mechanism has gotten stuck. As the announcement starts, enter **Ophelia** *wearing a blood-stained wedding dress and head scarf. She is trying to find the right gate. She is followed by* **Horatio***, who carries a silver platter with a human male head on it, surrounded by shrimp.*

Ophelia *enters.*

Ophelia *(madly)*   The one, the one. I am the one. I am the one I've been waiting for. I am the one. One, only one, which one. The one, the Holy One, the inherently **one, the blessed one.**

Horatio (*not paying attention to her*)   The ones from Christie's are fresher. Let's order the ones from Christie's.

Ophelia *takes off her army boot and beats* **Horatio** *to death. His body disappear into the black asphalt.* **Ophelia** *exists with her arms spread wide.* **Hamlet** *starts playing with his cell phone.* **Ophelia/Medea** *on the floor of the bus station sings to her dead child.*

Ophelia/Medea   May His great Name be blessed forever and ever.
Blessed, praised, glorified, exalted, extolled,
mighty, upraised, and lauded be the Name of the Holy One
Blessed is He.[4]

Hamlet   You read the pain in my eyes and you think you know everything. You think you can read a man from his pain. You think that because you can read a man's pain that he belongs to you, always and forever.

TV (*National Geographic Channel*)   The male bedbug has a penis designed to inject and deliver sperm into the female. This technique is very violent, as the female is pinned down and stabbed several times in the body to ensure insemination. This method has evolved to bypass the female's genital passage, restricting and removing any control the female would usually have over the timing of her conception.

Ophelia   When my body is my master, I'll have none other. (*Screaming.*) When my body is my master, I'll have none other.

Hamlet *switches channels.*

Ophelia (*sips some wine and continues to type*)   The gruesome acts of self-revelation have their point of departure in the

---

[4]Mourner's Kaddish, Judaism 101; Donin, Rabbi Hayim Halevy, *To Pray as a Jew*; Kolatch, Alfred, *The Jewish Book of Why*; Schermon, Rabbi Nosson, *The Complete Artscroll Siddur*. https://www.jewishvirtuallibrary.org/the-mourners-kaddish

benevolence of one's mind towards the lower classes of vulgar descent. I am sure, darling, the dread I have so carefully described to you has no ethical significance for your well-being. I am also sure you'll find the replacement of my emotional imbalance as easily as I will in every creature our minds will desire. The choice so clearly marked by my withering self depends purely on your serotonin level and the desire produced by this particular night. My offer is valid for the time being of your erection and it expires by the time you ejaculate your pitiful paranoias into my expecting visage. Desire constructed as a mathematical function has its advantages in the volatility and permanency of its expectations, which, replicated in fractal proportions, acquire the airy quality of a solid structure fundamentally indistinguishable from any other acidic solution to problems internalized during childhood and postponed for consumption with a glass of Chardonnay or Sauvignon de Blanco, and fish, mildly done in lemon sauce and caviar

Gertrude *passes by, talking on the phone. She has now turned into a machine.*

Gertrude   Didn't the catalogue say satisfaction guaranteed? They send you a defective girl and they think you are going to be stuck with it. . . . Send her back and tell them to send you one like in the picture, with no freckles . . . These days, darling, one has to take care of one's money. Yesterday, I bought some socks made in China. They were defective – I am telling you – aha – aha – so I returned them. One just cannot afford to throw all this money away on defective items these days. – aha – aha – You paid for something, they sent you the wrong thing, you get to send it back and get your money's worth . . . yeah, yeah, that's what I am saying.

Gertrude *disappears. The snow starts falling.*

Hamlet (*on the sly, as if telling a secret*)   Sometimes, when we walk through
each other's eyes like through gates
Sometimes, I am like her
Sometimes, she is who
I am

Ophelia (*typing, frantically*)   The right hand holds the everlasting
love with all of its phantom predicaments of sickening salvation
and rectangular routine of metaphors recycled from corpses of
former lovers and insects fallen on books opened in the middle.
I will promise to cherish my self I found so touchingly located in
your eyes right inside the pupils which I plead you so ardently not
to close when I am coming and in which my grimaces are
magnified to audible figments of our imagination. I also promise to
include the stability you so long desired and confusion interwoven
by occasional fits of my own ego to keep you stable in supply and
demand. I promise to fulfill our Oedipal fantasies and rent my
womb selflessly for an oasis and toilet in which we can relieve our
precious feces of intellectual endeavors. I am sure the arrangement
will satisfy forty percent of our mass leaving the remanding sixty
in burning insatiability of suspicions and physical perpetuity of
gravity and lightness. My left hand offers unrequited love, mine or
yours, we will establish it later. I am sure either way we will adapt
to our roles with the natural grace of slave and master. The desire
is proportional to the waiting time. Darling, she has received the
training of the best whores of Europe, North America and Asia.
The ones you visited on the lonely or drunken nights and in which
you inserted your half-limp penis with hopes of temporary relief
from the nightmare of desire or its lack.

Ophelia *stops. She composes herself.* **Ophelia** *takes out a gun
from her drawer and blows her head off. The sound of the gun
blast and blood all over. She continues typing as if nothing has
happened.*

The malady of death overcomes us. We wish we didn't die and
didn't live. The dread between possessed and possessing
establishes itself with the speed of a thief who stole too much to
feel pleasure and too little to feel anything else and walking away
with a numb smile of contempt, cries hidden behind frozen corners
of self-perpetuation. My thoughts don't flow with the ease your
body promised nor do they boil with grateful insatiability . . .

TV (*National Geographic Channel*)   The male and female
scorpion interlock in an intense embrace, lashing at each other with

their stingers. With their mouths locked, the male will repeatedly stab at the female with his tail. In retaliation, the female will oftentimes consume her mate.

Ophelia *enters. Her wedding dress is in tatters. She has detonation devices strapped to her chest.*

Ophelia   the hunger I feel is not in me
it flows outside and in
in my rapacious arms
you lose yourself
one cannot be saved and stay condemned
the hunger I feel is not in me

She sits in the wheelchair and rolls out, laughing hysterically.

TV News   Today in California, a mother beheaded her baby and ate its brain. *(The anchor girl looks sad for one second, then switches quickly into a broad smile.)* Now onto other news, this one from our lifestyle guru, who will answer the most important question of the season. . . .

'Jingle Bells' starts playing.

Hamlet*'s face on the backdrop blends into the video game he is playing.* **Hamlet** *on the couch and in the video game stands up and takes off his hat and his jacket. He goes backstage and brings a canister of gasoline, which he starts pouring all over.*

Ophelia (*typing as* **Hamlet** *pours the gasoline*)   Far away, far away, darling . . . we definitively managed to convince ourselves of our own existence. Taken to such extreme, I have no choice but to perpetuate this conviction. I beg you not to deny me what rightfully belongs to someone else. I know your commitment to truths and falsities. Served with pieces of lost faiths and those bought on the silent auctions in museums of wax organs and souls. I want you to really understand the promises from my lips are not translatable. I tie your thoughts and mine with such peculiar attention to details. You wanted to feel love or anything for that matter. The theatre of desires is open for public display to spectators curious and oblivious to each other. I saw them yesterday passing through the city when we wept hidden under the bed that refused to be tamed. I walked out with your head under my arm. I stumble, stumble over the words attached to their power. Do not cry darling, the night is coming.

She lights a match. Blackout.

Opheliamaschine

Translated by Theresa Schlesinger

Eine Autowerkstatt, ein Lagerraum oder ein Kinderzimmer,
vollgestopft mit Dingen, gesammelt von einem verlorenen
Reisenden: Michelangelo's David ohne Arme, der einen
Motorradhelm trägt, ein Stapel kaputter afrikanischer Masken, das
Skelett eines toten Dichters, das hysterisch seinen eigenen Schatten
auslacht, eine Babypuppe ohne Glieder, die an einem pinken Lolli
lutscht, Magritte's kaputter Regenschirm, Andy Warhol's altes
Telefon an Gott, ein dreckiger weißer Brautschleier, der irgendwo
zusammen mit anderen Kleidern hängt, Stapel von alten Schuhen
und Perücken.

Eine moderne Einöde mit kaputten Videospielen, Fernseh- und
Computerbildschirmen, die wahllos ohne Ton Szenen unseres
virtuellen Lebens zeigen: Kriegsszenen, Massenmorde, Genozide,
Auschwitz Körper, Pornos, politische Werbung, Wall Street Frauen,
fette Frauen, anorektische Frauen, japanische Schulmädchen,
Frauen mit Burkas, wilde Sufuris, comichafte Explosionen.
Hamlet *und* **Ophelia** *trinken diese tägliche Suppe aus Nachrichten*
und Bildern: ein Mischmasch des menschlichen Kontrasts
zwischen Schönheit und Horror, Unschuld und Gewalt.

Alles ist mit radioaktiver Asche bedeckt.

Hamlet, *trägt Jeans, eine Jacke aus dem 16. Jahrhundert, einen*
Cowboy Hut, sitzt auf dem Sofa und blickt ins Publikum. Er schaut
Fernsehen, zappt mit seiner Fernbedienung gedankenlos durch die
Kanäle. Eine Projektion des Mischmaschs auf der Rückwand der
Bühne.

Hamlet *will die Welt verstehen, aber alles was er tun kann, ist sie*
anzustarren.

Links hinter ihm, **Ophelia,** *die grüne Turnkleidung trägt und hinter*
einem frei stehenden Tisch sitzt, sie tippt etwas auf einer
altmodischen Schreibmaschine. Ein Glas Blutrotwein steht an ihrer
Seite. Sie raucht eine Zigarette und ist offensichtlich auf das
Tippen konzentriert.

Hamlet *und* **Ophelia** *sind die zwei Enden der Welt. Zwischen*
ihnen der Atlantik voll mit verrotteten Leichen, toten Vögeln und
Urin.

Ophelia (*tippt*)   Hamlet, mein Schatz, ich möchte nicht mit dir oder ihr identifiziert werden, deine Spielzeugsoldaten haben meine Seite des Betts eingenommen. Die Ozeane und Kontinente werden schnell für politische Nostalgie und Ausdauer ausgetauscht. Lass die Toten die Toten begraben, die Plage unserer Väter. (*Sie hält inne* und trinkt einen Schluck Wein.)

Hamlet (*geistesabwesend, in Erinnerung an bessere Zeiten*)   Im elenden Würfel

– sechs Betten in sieben Nächten –
dockten sich neu gefangene Larven
an die Küsten ihres eigenen Sägemehls.

Ophelia (*macht ungestört weiter*)   . . . Schreiben ist eine Art intellektuelle Masturbation. Ich schütte mein armes, armseliges Selbst über das weiße Auge meines Computers, stolz darauf, dass ich diese schwierige Kunst der Nachgiebigkeit beherrsche, und trete daher in die neue Ära des solipsistischen Vergnügens ein. Meine Selbstständigkeit erstaunt mich. Oh, diese erogenen Stellen meines Gehirns werden durch größenwahnsinnige Anfälle von Selbstliebe sorgfältig untersucht. Ja, ja genau jetzt sichere ich sie automatisch für später. (*Sie hält inne und nimmt einen Zug ihrer Zigarette.*)

TV (*National Geographic*)   Während ihres Paarungsrituals verschränkt der weibliche weiße Adler seine Krallen mit denen des Männchens und verlangt die totale Unterwerfung, während die zwei unweigerlich zu Boden stürzen. Wenn er versucht sich zu befreien, bevor sie fertig ist, wird sie ihn sich niemals besteigen lassen. Wenn sie nur eine Sekunde zu lang wartet, stürzen sie beide tödlich zu Boden.

Das Geräusch eines vorbeifahrenden Zuges in höchster Geschwindigkeit, der pfeift, als würde er jemand warnen, der auf den Gleisen steht. Der Zug fährt vorbei. Mitternacht am Port Authority. Ding dong, der Ton des Ansagers, der etwas murmelt.

Hamlet *schaut immer noch Fernsehen.*

Ophelia (*nüchtern*)   Die meisten Mädchen am Port Authority sind entweder aus der Bronx oder aus Harlem. Sie tragen gefälschte

Chanel Schals um den Hals und gefälschte Louis Vuitton Taschen
unter ihren Schultern. Sie versuchen modisch und versorgt
auszusehen, als hätten sie einen Mann, für den sie die paar hundert
Dollar scheinbar unnötiger Luxusartikel wert sind. Manche von ihnen
haben Babys oder Kleinkinder dabei, die sie mit leiser Verzweiflung
auf dem Arm halten. Ich bin nie sicher, wer wen mehr braucht: sie
ihre Babys oder ihre Babys sie. Sie sitzen auf dem Boden oder auf
ihren Koffern, warten geduldig auf ihre Busse. Manchmal haben sie
einen Mann dabei und dann leuchten ihre Augen mit sanfter
Genugtuung. Sie wirken zerbrechlich und stark zugleich, als ob sie
jede Minute anfangen könnten zu weinen oder zu fluchen.

Ophelia *fängt wieder an zu tippen. Das Telefon klingelt. Das
Geräusch der vorbeifahrenden Straßenbahn. Ein Kind weint in der
Nachbarwohnung.* **Gertrude** *tritt auf. Sie überquert die Bühne, sie
trägt ein Kleid und brennende Lockenwickler im Haar. Sie stochert
in den Zähnen und redet am Telefon. Ihre Augen leuchten.*

Gertrude   Meine Güte, nein! Sie hatte Sommersprossen?! Also,
hallo, du WEISST, was ich darüber DENKE. Ich meine . . . .
schau, was ich sage ist ganz einfach. Schau dir eine normale
Porzellanpuppe an, hat die Sommersprossen? Hm? Nein, hat sie
nicht. Haben die, die sie dir geschickt haben, Sommersprossen?
Also, . . . schick sie zurück! . . . . Nein, du solltest das nicht tun
müssen! Du solltest NICHT für die Rücksendekosten aufkommen
müssen. Du legst sie einfach wieder in den Karton und schickst sie
zurück. Oh, nein! Du hast dafür gezahlt! . . . Du hast das Bild im
Katalog gesehen, du hast deine Kreditkarte damit belastet und jetzt
solltest du bekommen, wofür du bezahlt hast! . . . Waren da Bilder
von einem Mädchen mit Sommersprossen? Nein! Ok. Mein
Standpunkt . . . habe ich meinen Standpunkt klar gemacht?! . . .
NEIN, weil das eine so genannte MISREPRÄSENTATION ist!
. . . Dafür könnten sie ins Gefängnis kommen, weißt du? . . . Ja, du
kannst viele schöne Mädchen aus China bekommen . . .

*Sie verschwindet hinter der Bühnentür. Ihr Kleid bleibt in der Tür
hängen und sie zieht wütend daran.* **Hamlet** *dreht sich um und
wirft einen Schuh nach ihr, verfehlt sie aber. Ihm wachsen
Fledermausflügel und er schaut weiter Fernsehen.*

Ophelia (*tippt weiter, als ob nichts passiert wäre*)   Das Grauen,
Schatz, das Grauen: ich möchte, dass du es zuschüttest oder es auf
dich nimmst. Du hast die Wahl: Der Wohlstand wartet ungeduldig
darauf, dass unsere jämmerlichen Gene weiter gegeben und durch
zwölf Pfund Kohle und Intellekt unsterblich gemacht werden. Ja, ja,
mein Schatz, ich bin sicher, dass Fortpflanzung eine Quelle
unendlichen Glücks für die Massen sein kann, aber wir sind doch so
viel kultivierter. Du musst verstehen, die Stimmen in meinem Kopf
können von keinem Kinderschrei betäubt werden; du musst wissen,
dass sogar die Schreie, die ich mit einer solchen Grazie erzeuge,
wenn du dankbar dein Recht auf post-koitale Taubheit ausübst . . .
Taubheit . . . (*Pause. Während sie tippt, schaut* **Hamlet** *einen Soft
Porno.*) das Grauen, mein Schatz, ich sprach über das Grauen, nicht
über Taubheit. Ich bin sicher, wenn du dich nur ein bisschen mehr
anstrengst, wirst du es erreichen. Dein Penis wurde sorgfältig
ausgemessen und seine existenziellen Qualitäten wurden mit vollster
Verantwortung für mein eigenes Versagen dein verwundetes Selbst zu
heilen und die Konvention unseres charmanten Treffens zu definieren,
von dem ich hoffe, dass es uns ebenso unerfüllt zurücklässt,
bemessen. Die Länge deines Penis ist proportional zu dem Schmerz,
den ich empfinde, wenn ich in deinen müden Armen eine Zigarette
rauche und dabei die statistische Wahrscheinlichkeit von Lungenkrebs
oder Herzinfakt aufgrund von sexueller Unersättlichkeit und nicht
versorgtem Grauen, berechne. Hamlet, mein Schatz, sprich nicht über
Politik, deine Wünsche, die Welt, Tod und das Blut, das du vergießt,
wenn du wegen der hungernden Kinder weinst.

Ophelia, *in einem Brautkleid, überquert die Bühne, begleitet von*
Horatio *und* **Gertrude**. **Gertrude** *reitet ein Schaukelpferd und
schwenkt ein Schwert hinter ihrem Kopf.* **Horatio** *trägt einen
Smoking, Netzstrumpfhose und rote hohe Schuhe. Ihr Haar ist nach
hinten gebunden. Sie hält eine Platte mit Shrimps und ein
Notizbuch.*

Ophelia (*läuft im Hochzeitskleid die Treppe rauf und
runter*)   Gesegnet seist Du . . . .

Horatio   Dieser Shrimp sah ein bisschen verdorben aus.
Vielleicht sollte ich die Catering Firma anrufen. Wir wollen ja

nicht, dass jemandem schlecht wird. Sie sollten wirklich anfangen Hochzeitsversicherungen für sowas zu verkaufen. Was meinst du?

Ophelia Fragst du dich manchmal, ob du mit der richtigen Person zusammen bist?

Horatio (*schaut von ihrem Notizbuch hoch*) Natürlich bist du das nicht, Schatz. Du könntest nie wirklich mit der richtigen Person zusammen sein. Was ihn richtig macht, ist ja die Tatsache, dass du nicht mit ihm zusammen bist. Was ihn falsch macht, ist die Tatsache, dass du mit ihm zusammen bist. (*Kehrt zurück zum Notizbuch.*) Wo kommt der Shrimp her? La Bella Tosca oder Christie's?

Ophelia Christie's. Du solltest sicher stellen, dass er der Richtige ist. Der Richtige.

Gertrude Oh, der Richtige . . .

Ophelia (*schreit sich das Herz aus der Brust*) Ich will den Richtigen und für immer, zusammen, bis zum Tod . . .

Gertrude Leben, Tod, Liebe oder Lust, das Universum ist unendlich und dehnt sich aus. Wo kamst du her? Wo gehst du hin? *Quo vadis. Panta rhei.* Großartige Fragen, Schatz, aber, egal was dein Vater sagt, deine Miete werden sie dir nicht zahlen. Du solltest sie jetzt aufschreiben und sie in dein geheimes Versteck legen und sie heraus holen, wenn du in Rente bist. Dann werden sie sehr praktisch sein, zwischen dem Golfunterricht, Pilates und den Hitzeschüben. Du solltest wirklich aufhören so zu blinzeln. Du verschmierst dein ganzes Make-Up.

Hamlet (*tritt auf, im Anzug*) Du willst ihn nicht wirklich heiraten, oder?

Horatio (*verdreht die Augen*) Er ist der Richtige. Er ist nicht der Richtige

Gertrude Der richtige für was?

Ophelia Um deine Seele zu heilen . . .

Gertrude *und* **Horatio** *schauen sich an und fangen hysterisch an zu lachen.*

Gertrude Wie der andere?

Horatio Oder der andere.

Gertrude (*philosophisch*) Oder der andere.

Die Kirchenglocken fangen an zu läuten und **Gertrude** *und*
Horatio *verwandeln sich in Avatare; sie gehen, ihre synthetischen
Stimmen lösen sich in absurden Wiederholungen auf: 'der Richtige,
oder ein anderer, welcher, einer, irgendeiner, keiner, der eine, auf
den wir gewartet haben, oder der andere, der eine, auf den sie
gewartet haben, du gewartet hast? Wer hat gewartet? Welcher?*

Hamlet (*spricht vom Bildschirm aus, während die Glocken
läuten*) Sediert euch mit den Schreien
der Wolfskinder
nichts ist echt, aber
Haar steif von der Kotze
heute Nacht –
schlaft ihr ohne zu träumen.
Morgen –
öffnet den Reißverschluss eurer Haut und lasst uns herein
Dr. Tulps Anatomiestunde kann beginnen

*Ding dong – das Geräusch der Bushaltestelle. Die Stimme des
Ansagers nuschelt etwas, unverständlich.*

Ophelia *trägt einen Koffer und einen Kissenbezug voll mit
Puppenköpfen. Sie tritt vorsichtig ein, schaut auf den Busfahrplan
und versucht herauszufinden, wann der Bus abfährt. Sie wird von*
Hamlet *gestoppt. Er trägt eine schwere Goldkette um den Hals.*

Hamlet Hey, wo willst du hin.

Ophelia Einen Freund besuchen.

Hamlet (*checkt sie aus*) Woher kommst du?

Ophelia Huston, Maine.

Hamlet Wo ist das?

Ophelia Das ist ein kleiner Ort; niemand weiß, wo das ist.

Hamlet   Ist das eine Unistadt? Gehst du zur Uni?

Ophelia   Nein.

Hamlet   Was machst du hier? (*Sie ist still, lächelt nervös, fühlt sich offensichtlich unwohl.*) Hehe, Ich weiß, das ist ein Männerding. Er hat dich dort ganz schön reingelegt . . . Hehe . . . Er hat dich dort ganz schön reingelegt. Du solltest hierher nach New York kommen.

Ophelia   Hmm.

Hamlet   Was hast du da drin?

Ophelia   Das hier?

Hamlet   Mhm.

Ophelia   Das sind Köpfe von Schaufensterpuppen. Ich will Friseurin werden.

(*Ding dong*. Der Ansager des Port Authority: 'Der Bus nach Cleveland fährt um 2.30 am Bussteig 5. Bitte vergessen Sie ihr Gepäck nicht.')

Ophelia   Das ist mein Bus.

Er wartet darauf, dass sie etwas sagt, aber sie bleibt stumm, also geht er. Sie kämpft mit dem Kissenbezug und schleift ihn langsam hinter sich her, verschwindet von der Bühne. Er spuckt über seine Schulter und folgt ihr.

'Dream a little Dream of Me' beginnt zu spielen. **Ophelia**, *die hinter ihrem Schreibtisch sitzt, trinkt einen Schluck Wein.* **Hamlet** *verlässt seine Fernbedienung und fängt an ein Videospiel zu spielen. Vertrocknete Herbstblätter beginnen auf sie herab zu fallen. Die Musik hört plötzlich auf, als sich die Tür öffnet.*

Gertrude *tritt auf, sie spricht am Telefon. Sie trägt das selbe Kleid, aber die Hälfte ihres Kopfs ist von den Lockenwicklern befreit. Ihre Haare, wie die der Medusa, fließen in alle vier Weltrichtungen. Sie läuft über die Bühne, redet am Telefon und blättert durch einen Katalog.*

Gertrude . . . welche, denkst du, sollte ich nehmen? Die aus
Russland, Rumänien oder China? Die aus Russland sehen alle gut
aus, alle nett und blond, aber die sagen sie seien beschädigt. Der
ganze russische Wodka, den ihre Mütter getrunken haben . . . Ich bin
nicht ganz sicher bei denen aus Rumänien; sie sehen blass aus, blond
aber zu blass. Sie sind vielleicht unterernährt. Das gleiche mit den
Afrikanischen. Aber die sind so exotisch. Ich würde gut aussehen
mit so einer auf meiner Schulter neben meiner Chanel Tasche. Oder
noch besser, Hermès . . . Wie ist die Garantie? . . . Zwei Jahre? Kann
man eine verlängerte Garantie kaufen? . . . Was, wenn sie stirbt? . . .
Schicken sie eine neue zum Ersatz? Übernehmen sie die
Bestattungskosten? . . . Was ist mit dem Versand? Ich werde nicht
nochmal den Versand zahlen. 25.000 für den ganzen Papierkram –
das war's . . . Ja du hast Recht meine Liebe, die aus Südamerika
sehen nett aus, nicht zu dunkel, nicht zu blass . . . . Mhm. . . . .

Sie geht ab, recht zufrieden mit ihrer Idee.

TV (*vom Bildschirm, Es ist schwer zu sagen, ob es eine Seifenoper
ist oder ein klassischer Roman*)   Diese Zweischneidigkeit ihres
Charakters machte ihm Angst. Jedes Mal, wenn er dachte, sie
gehöre ihm, wurden ihre Augen zu denen einer Unbekannten. Im
einen Moment war sie so vertraut, dass er ihre Stimme in sich drin
hören konnte und dann so fern, dass die plötzliche Einsamkeit, die
in jede Zelle seines Körpers eintrat, physisch schmerzte und ihn
würgte wie das Bewusstsein über den eigenen Tod.

Hamlet *sitzt auf dem Sofa und spielt ein Videospiel. Sein Gesicht
verwandelt sich langsam in* **Ophelia**'*s Gesicht. Sie trägt einen
Armee Helm, den sie in ein schwarzes Kopftuch wickelt.*

Ophelia (*auf dem Bildschirm, als ob sie ein Kinderlied aufsagen
würde*)   Eines Tages

ist mein Fleisch uns davon gelaufen
ließ mich und meine Haut betäubt vor Überraschung
wir schauten uns amüsiert an
wir hatten nichts mehr zu verlieren

Horatio (*liest aus rechtlichen Dokumenten*)   Seit Monaten
bereiten sie sich auf dieses Baby vor. Sie haben alles gemeinsam

gekauft, das Kinderbett, den Kinderwagen, die Kleider. Alles nur
das beste, das teuerste, aus den exklusivsten Katalogen. Er kaufte
ihr ein brandneues Auto, so dass sie ohne auf den Bus zu warten,
zur Uni und zurück kam. Als sie erfuhren, dass es ein Mädchen
werden würde, war er enttäuscht. Er wollte so gern einen Jungen
haben, der weiter führen würde, was er begonnen hatte. Er stellte
sich die Dinge vor, die er ihm beibringen würde. Von seinen
eigenen Gefühlen beschämt, versteckte er seine Enttäuschung,
gewöhnte sich an die Vorstellung eines Mädchens und feuerte
sie während der Schwangerschaft an und ertrug geduldig ihre
Schübe schlechten Humors und willkürlicher Melancholie. Sie
trug sein Baby. Zum ersten Mal war es ihr offiziell erlaubt ihn zu
quälen und sie entdeckte langsam, dass es keine Grenzen zu
ihrem Tun gab. Die Feindseligkeit, die sie ihm gegenüber für all
die Male, wenn sie sein schwaches Ego ermuntern musste,
empfand, verschlimmerte nur ihre Vorstellungen. Sie vernichtete
ihn immer wieder mit wachsender Grausamkeit und er ertrug all
das mit einer Mischung aus Pflichtgefühl, Erstaunen und
Bewunderung.

*Das Geräusch eines Flugzeugs oder Helikopters, der am Himmel
fliegt und der Schatten von Flügeln auf der Bühne. Ophelia breitet
ihre schwarzen Arme aus und fängt an nach oben zu gleiten. Sie
verwandelt sich in einen Raben. Klänge der Großstadt: ein
Krankenwagen, eine Schießerei, lachende Mädchen, jemand
schreit und ein Hund bellt auf der Straße.* **Ophelia** *schaut von oben
zu. Ihr Körper zerfällt in eine Millionen kleine Teilchen, die sie
versucht in einem Einkaufskorb zu sammeln. Die Putzfrau des
Supermarkts schmeißt* **Ophelia** *raus und* **Ophelia** *reißt sich die
Augen aus.*

Hamlet   Licht fällt herein
streichelt die Schatten auf den weißen Laken
riecht nach Blut, Lysol und
dem Urin von gestern.

In welches Fach hast du all deine Schlafstörungen gepackt
und Mosaike, komponiert aus den Schimmelflecken an der Decke,
wo deine Horizonte aufhören?

Ophelia, *im Rollstuhl, geschoben von einer Armee-*
Krankenschwester, tritt auf.

Ophelia   Als Mädchen im Rollstuhl, war ich plötzlich zerrissen:
wem sollte ich meine Treue schwören? Wenn jemand eine Frau
war, war die Antwort einfach. Wenn jemand ein Krüppel war, war
die Antwort einfach. Wenn jemand eine Frau und ein Krüppel war,
war die Antwort einfach. Aber da gab es eine intrinsische
existenzielle Ummöglichkeit, da in der Figur des verkrüppelten
Mannes: war er Feind oder gepeinigter Bruder? Gebunden an sein
Geschlecht oder seinen Rollstuhl? Weil ich meine Politik
gegenüber verkrüppelten Männern nicht bestimmen konnte,
entschied ich präventiv, sie ganz zu vermeiden.

Grundlegend gescheitert, waren verkrüppelte Männer in ihrer
verwundeten Männlichkeit etwas, was ich, mit meiner
verwundeten Weiblichkeit, geneigt war zu vermeiden. Nicht fähig
mit meinen eigenen Widersprüchen umzugehen – zwischen dem
Wunsch begehrt zu werden und dem nach Respekt – benötigte ich
einen Mann mit emotional niedrigen Ansprüchen, einen unendlich
großzügigen, dessen Ego und Verstand so stark und stabil waren,
wie sein niemals-schwacher Schwanz, mit dem er mich immer und
immer wieder von meinem grenzenlosen Sex-Appeal überzeugen
würde, auch für erworbenen Geschmack und stets bezaubernde
Persönlichkeit, die ihn komplett und ohne Vorbehalt erfasste.

Der Rollstuhl dreht sich herum und die **Ophelia** *Puppe verdunstet.*
Die Krankenschwester entstaubt das Kissen und fängt an im Kreis
zu rennen: Sie weiß, dass sie keinen leeren Rollstuhl haben darf,
also stopft sie ihn mit allem, was sie finden kann, voll.

TV: *Talk Show oder Vorabendserie. Eheberatung.* **Ophelia** *und*
Hamlet *sitzen auf der Couch.*

Therapeut   Hallo, danke, dass Sie gekommen sind. Es ist so nett
von ihnen, dass Sie ein Problem haben, welches Sie mit uns teilen
können.

Hamlet   Kein Problem.

Therapeut (*enttäuscht*)   Kein Problem?

Hamlet Oh, nein, es gibt ein Problem. Kein Problem, es mit Ihnen zu teilen.

Therapeut Oh, richtig, wie schön. Also was ist das Problem?

Hamlet Es ist furchtbar, ich kann nicht glauben, was sie getan hat. Sie hat unser Leben ruiniert.

Ophelia Oh, Schatz, was hab ich getan, was hab ich getan, sag es mir doch einfach . . . Oh Schatz (*sie weint*). Wenn du mir einfach sagen würdest, was es ist, ich bin sicher, es würde wieder in Ordnung kommen. Gefährde unsere Liebe und unsere Ehe nicht mit deinem Schweigen.

Therapeut Ja, Kommunikation ist alles. Wenn Sie es uns sagen, werden wir es wissen. Wenn Sie ihre Gefühle mit Ihrer Frau teilen, werden Ihre Gefühle geteilt.

Hamlet Was sie getan hat? Was sie getan hat? Ich kann nicht einmal darüber reden. Schauen Sie, ich zittere immer noch, wenn nur ich daran denke. Ich kann nicht glauben, dass sie das getan hat. Ich kann nicht glauben, dass sie mir das angetan hat . . . .

Ophelia & Therapeut Was habe ich/hat sie getan?

Hamlet Das wollt ihr wissen? Das wollt ihr wissen? In Ordnung, ich erzähle es euch. Gestern morgen, beim Frühstück . . . (*Er flüstert etwas in das Ohr des* **Therapeuten.**)

Therapeut Oh mein Goooooooooooott!

Hamlet Ja, das hat sie getan.

Therapeut Das ist definitiv eine schwierige Situation, aber ich bin sicher, wenn wir sie lösen, wird sie gelöst sein! Scheidungen sind Grund Nummer Eins für Scheidungen. Aber alles andere ist gut?

Ophelia Oh, ja, alles ist gut. Wir führen eine großartige Ehe.

Hamlet Oh, ja, die Arbeit ist gut, das Geld ist gut, die Kinder sind tot.

Therapeut Erst wenn Sie ihre Gefühle nicht mit ihrem objektiven intellektuellen Urteilsvermögen beeinträchtigen, können

Sie sagen, dass Sie einen Zustand wahrer Weisheit erreicht haben. Die Schlussfolgerung, die Sie ziehen, muss immer von vornherein gegeben oder von der empirischen Erfahrung, die Sie angesammelt haben, abgeleitet werden. Sie dürfen nie damit aufhören Aussagen zu treffen, die frei von tiefer intellektueller Objektivität sind. Nur dann können Sie etwas wahrhaftig tiefgründig objektives sagen, wahrhaftig objektiv tiefgründig. (*Er ist von sich selbst überrascht, dass er so clever ist; er lächelt und schüttelt den Kopf, denkt darüber nach, was er gerade gesagt hat, vergisst aber schnell und fängt an in der Nase zu bohren.*)

Ophelia (*hinter ihrem Schreibtisch, tippt*)   Wie seltsam verhält sich doch, wie es scheint, das Angenehme zu seinem Gegensatz, zum Unangenehmen! Beide wollen nicht zu gleicher Zeit im Menschen anwesend sein. Aber wenn einer dem einen nachjagt und es erreicht, ist er fast immer genötigt, auch das andere zu erreichen, als ob die beiden an einer einzigen Spitze verknüpft wären.

TV (*Vortrag*)   Die Frau, deren sexuelles Vergnügen ursprünglich selbstrepräsentativ ist und sich von dem des Mannes unterscheidet, könnte genauso gut keine Klitoris haben: Das Jungfernhäutchen, das für immer (un-)verletzt bleibt, auf dem der Samen für immer in die Welt hinausgeschleudert wird, hat keine Verwendung für das Hysteron. Ist dies die Szene der Gewalt, die man Liebe in der Verwandlung nennt, die in unserer einzigen perfekten Triade enthalten ist? Wenn Frauen schon immer als Instrument der männlichen Selbstdekonstruktion benutzt wurden, ist dies dann die neueste Wendung der Philosophie?

Ophelia (*als Therapeutin*)   Ich möchte gern glauben, dass Sie wissen, was Sie tun und dass Sie nicht nur in der misslichen Lage der selbstzerstörerischen amerikanischen Männlichkeit gefangen sind, die Sie bei Gelegenheit emotional ausgetrocknet hinterlassen wird, intellektuell verhungert und sexuell inkompetent.

Hamlet (*während er ein Videospiel spielt, lässig*)   Willst du, dass ich dich in einem dramatischen Akt der Eifersucht umbringe, der so überwältigend ist, dass ich all meine Sinne verliere? Willst du, dass ich dich während des Orgasmus töte, damit du mit dem Universum im unendlichen Klimax verschmelzen kannst, so dass

du denken könntest, du würdest für immer leben, gefangen in
diesem Moment? Willst du, dass ich dich umbringe, während ich
dir Zärtlichkeiten über meine eigene Verzweiflung in dein Ohr
flüstere? Willst du, dass ich dich umbringe und dir in das sorgfältig
inszenierte Drama Tod folge?

Ophelia *schwebt im Weltraum. Sie versucht Strohhalme zu greifen,
aber die Welt verschwindet am Horizont.* **Ophelia** *versucht zu
gehen, aber es gibt keine Oberfläche zum Gehen. Sie findet die
Fernbedienung und drückt verzweifelt ein paar Mal darauf.
Menschliche und tierische Kadaver treiben den Ganges hinunter.*
Ophelia *wäscht ihr Haar und tritt auf Wüstensand. Ihr Herz blutet.
Ihre Venen sind aus Kabeln.* **Ophelia** *trägt ihre eigene Leiche über
die Wüstengrenze.*

Hamlet   Und ob ich schon wanderte im finsteren Tal,
Ich fürchte kein Unglück; denn du bist bei mir;
Dein Stecken und dein Stab trösten mich,
Du bereitest mir einen Tisch im Angesicht meiner Feinde.

Ophelia (*sitzt in Turnfurben hinter ihrem Schreibtisch. Ruhig und
stoisch, tippt weiter, als ob nichts geschehen wäre*) Bitte, Schatz,
Selbstzerfleischung ist kein notwendiger Handelsvertreter für den
eigenen Marktwert; unsere Reinheit ist rein formal, genau wie
unsere Perversionen, die von unseren Müttern so geschätzt und in
jeder Seifenwerbung angepriesen werden. Schatz, du musst wissen,
dass sie sich automatisch für die Hochzeitsnacht mit Kerzen und
Sehnsüchten, vorsichtig durch das Fernsehen geformt und somit
neu für unsere Generation, aufgehoben hat. Das Grauen, Schatz,
das Grauen. Ich glaube wahrhaftig an Gott und die menschliche
Würde, außer sie liegt in den Gräben mit ihrem Kopf
weggeschossen von jemand anderes Tugend und Hingabe an die
Passion des Lebens, denn ich glaube, dass du derjenige bist, der
mit einer Tiefe, die meinen schwächer werdenden Gliedern
verschlossen ist, in die Tiefe reicht.

Ja, ja, Schatz, du kannst mir ein Gedicht schreiben, oder mich
einfach hart genug ficken; Ich bin sicher, so oder so, dass wir unserer
langjährigen Überzeugung von Unsterblichkeit treu bleiben werden,

erlangt durch die Güte des Herzens und die Verbindung der Seelen, die von ihrem gegenseitigen Hass und ihrer Liebe zueinander erfüllt sind und ihre Tage in der Harmonie der hygienischen Rituale, des postmodernen Diskurses auf verschiedenen intellektuellen Ebenen und der Arbeit verbringen, die uns von materialistischem Überfluss oder Mangel befreien wird, je nachdem, ob die Fortpflanzung ihren statistischen Durchschnitt erreicht oder sich im egoistischen Individualismus der Selbstverehrung ausdrückt. Ich bin mir sicher, dass meine Überzeugung mich wie jeden anderen von mir überzeugen wird, wofür du mir danken wirst, wenn ich dir ein Glas Wein einschenke und dir die Schultern massiere. Die Spitze deines Penis hat ein ontologisches Potenzial, also stecke ich dein Schwert in deine Harnröhre, um zu untersuchen, ob dort ausreichend Platz ist, um meine Angst und die all anderen zu aufzunehmen, die in Anbetracht der Globalisierung unserer sexuellen Gewohnheiten von den zukünftigen Vätern Amerikas und fünf anderer Kontinente unbeabsichtigt hinterlassen wurden. Der Vater meiner Großmutter kam auf mysteriöse Weise irgendwo zwischen Prag und Wien ums Leben, genau so wie es uns ergehen wird.

Horatio *tritt auf mit einer Silberplatte mit Shrimp.*

Horatio (*zu* **Hamlet**, *der immer noch auf der Couch sitzt*)   Shrimp?

Hamlet   Nein danke, ich bin auf Diät.

Horatio *fällt plötzlich etwas ein und er erhebt seine Faust und schreit: 'Freiheit!' Er wird von dem Panzer überfahren und sein Körper verschwindet im Schwarzen Asphalt. Eine Gruppe lächelnder Kinder rennt über den Bürgersteig, sie lachen und halten sich an den Händen. Die schwarzen Raben picken an* **Horatio**'s *Fleisch. Das Geräusch der Bushaltestelle. Ding dong.*

Der Ansager   Der Bus von Paris nach New York, über London und Tokyo, fährt von Steig 5. Der Bus von Paris nach New York, über London und Tokyo, fährt von Steig 5.

Die Ansage wird ein paar Mal wiederholt, als ob der Mechanismus hängen geblieben wäre. Sobald die Ansage beginnt, tritt **Ophelia**

auf, die ein Hochzeitskleid mit Blutflecken und ein Kopftuch trägt.
Sie versucht den richtigen Steig zu finden. **Horatio**, *der eine*
silberne Platte mit einem menschlichen Kopf, umrundet von
Shrimp, trägt, folgt ihr.

Ophelia *tritt auf.*

Ophelia (*wütend*)   Der Richtige, der Richtige. Ich bin die
Richtige. Ich bin die, auf die ich gewartet habe. Ich bin die
Richtige. Eine, die einzige, welche. Die Richtige, die Heilige, die
Rechtmäßige, **die Gesegnete.**

Horatio (*hört ihr nicht zu*)   Die von Christie's sind frischer. Lass
uns die von Christie's bestellen.

Ophelia *zieht ihren Armee Stiefel aus und schlägt* **Horatio** *tot.*
Sein Körper verschwindet im schwarzen Asphalt. **Ophelia** *tritt ab*
mit ihren Armen weit ausgestreckt **Hamlet** *beginnt auf seinem*
Handy zu spielen. **Ophelia/Medea** *singt zu ihrem toten Kind auf*
dem Boden der Bushaltestelle.

Ophelia/Medea   Sein großer Name sei gepriesen in Ewigkeit und
Ewigkeit der Ewigkeiten.

Gepriesen sei und gerühmt, verherrlicht, erhoben, erhöht, gefeiert,
hocherhoben und gepriesen sei der Name des Heiligen,
gelobt sei er.

Hamlet   Du hast den Schmerz in meinen Augen gelesen und du
denkst, du weißt alles. Du denkst, du kannst einen Mann anhand
seines Schmerzes lesen. Du denkst das, weil du am Schmerz eines
Mannes erkennen kannst, dass er zu dir gehört, immer und für
immer.

TV (*National Geographic Kanal*)   Die männliche Bettwanze hat
einen Penis, der dazu bestimmt ist, Sperma in das Weibchen zu
injizieren und abzugeben. Diese Technik ist sehr gewalttätig, denn das
Weibchen wird dabei festgenagelt und mehrere Male in den Körper
gestochen, um die Befruchtung zu gewährleisten. Diese Methode hat
sich entwickelt, um die weibliche genitale Passage zu umgehen, so
dass jedwede Kontrolle, die das Weibchen sonst über den Zeitpunkt
der Empfängnis hätte, eingeschränkt und entzogen wird.

Ophelia   Wenn mein Körper mein Herr ist, werde ich keinen anderen haben. (*Schreit.*) Wenn mein Körper mein Herr ist, werde ich keinen anderen haben.

Hamlet *wechselt den Sender.*

Ophelia (*trinkt etwas Wein und tippt weiter*)   Die grausamen Akte der Selbstoffenbarung haben ihren Ausgangspunkt in der Güte des eigenen Verstands gegenüber den niedrigeren Klassen vulgären Ursprungs. Ich bin sicher, Schatz, das Grauen, dass ich dir so sorgfältig beschrieben habe, hat keine ethische Signifikanz für dein Wohlergehen. Ich bin mir auch sicher, dass du einen Ersatz finden wirst für mein emotionales Ungleichgewicht, so einfach wie ich in jeder Kreatur, die unser Verstand begehrt. Die deutlich markierte Entscheidung meines verblühenden Selbst hängt völlig von deinem Serotonin Level ab und von dem Wunsch, produziert von dieser speziellen Nacht. Mein Angebot ist für den Moment deiner Erektion gültig und es läuft aus, sobald du deine erbärmliche Paranoia in mein erwartendes Gesicht ejakulierst. Begehren, konstruiert als eine mathematische Funktion, hat ihre Vorteile in der Unbeständigkeit und Dauerstellung seiner Erwartungen, die, wiederholt in fraktalen Verhältnissen, die luftige Qualität einer soliden Struktur benötigen, die nicht unterscheidbar ist, von irgend einer säuerlichen Lösung zu Problemen, die während der Kindheit internalisiert werden und für den Verbrauch verschoben wurden mit einem Glas Chardonnay oder Sauvignon de Blanco und Fisch, mild gekocht in Zitronensauce und Kaviar.

Gertrude *geht vorbei, sie redet am Telefon. Sie ist mittlerweile zur Maschine geworden.*

Gertrude   Stand im Katalog nicht Zufriedenheit garantiert? Sie schicken dir ein beschädigtes Mädchen und denken, dass du darauf festsitzt . . . Schick sie zurück und sag ihnen, sie sollen dir eine wie auf dem Bild schicken, ohne Sommersprossen . . . Heutzutage, Schatz, muss man auf sein Geld aufpassen. Gestern habe ich Socken aus China gekauft. Sie waren beschädigt – ich sag's dir – aha – aha – also hab ich sie zurück gegeben. Man kann sich das nicht leisten, all das Geld für beschädigte Artikel weg zu schmeißen heutzutage – aha – aha – Du hast für etwas gezahlt, sie

haben dir das Falsche geschickt, du solltest es zurück schicken
können und dein Geld zurück bekommen . . . ja, ja, das sag ich ja.

Gertrude *verschwindet. Der Schnee beginnt zu fallen.*

Hamlet (*verstohlen, als ob er ein Geheimnis erzählen
würde*)   Manchmal, wenn wir durch
die Augen des anderen gehen wie durch Tore
Manchmal bin ich wie sie
Manchmal ist sie, wer
ich bin

Ophelia (*tippt, fieberhaft*)   Die rechte Hand hält die ewige Liebe
mit all ihren Phantom Zwickmühlen abscheulicher Erlösung und
rechtwinkliger Routine der Metaphern, die von Leichen früherer
Liebhaber recycelt und von Insekten, die auf Bücher, in der Mitte
geöffnet, fielen, Ich verspreche mein Selbst zu lieben, das ich so
berührend in deinen Augen lokalisiert gefunden habe, genau in den
Pupillen, die ich so leidenschaftlich anflehe, dass du sie nicht
schließt, wenn ich komme, und in denen meine Grimassen
vergrößert werden in hörbare Hirngespinste unserer Vorstellung.
Ich verspreche weiterhin Beständigkeit, die du schon so lange
begehrst, und Verwirrung, verwoben mit gelegentlichen Anfällen
meines eigenen Egos, einzubinden, um dich stabil zu halten in
Versorgung und Nachfrage. Ich verspreche deine ödipalen
Fantasien zu erfüllen und meinen Mutterleib selbstlos zu vermieten
für eine Oase und Toilette in der wir uns von unseren wertvollen
Fäkalien intellektuellen Bestrebens erleichtern können. Ich bin
sicher das Arrangement wird vierzig Prozent unserer Masse
befriedigen, was die verbleibenden sechzig Prozent in brennender
Unersättlichkeit von Verdachten und körperlicher Ewigkeit der
Schwerkraft und Leichtigkeit hinterlässt. Meine linke Hand bietet
unerwiderte Liebe, meine oder deine, wir werden es später
feststellen. Ich bin sicher, so oder so, werden wir uns an unsere
Rollen mit der natürlichen Grazie eines Sklaven und Herren
anpassen. Das Begehren ist proportional zur Wartezeit. Schatz, sie
hat das Training für die besten Huren in Europa, Nordamerika und
Asien erhalten. Die, die du in den einsamen oder betrunkenen
Nächten besucht hast und in die du deinen halbschlaffen Penis

eingeführt hast, in der Hoffnung auf temporäre Erleichterung von den Albträumen von Begehren oder Mangel desselben.

Ophelia *hört auf. Sie beruhigt sich.* **Ophelia** *nimmt ein Gewehr aus ihrer Schublade und schießt sich den Kopf weg. Das Geräusch des explodierenden Gewehrs und Blut überall. Sie tippt weiter, als sei nichts geschehen.*

Das Übel Tod kommt über uns. Wir wünschen uns nicht zu sterben und nicht zu leben. Das Grauen zwischen besessen und besitzen etabliert sich mit der Geschwindigkeit eines Diebes, der zu viel gestohlen hat, um Vergnügen zu spüren und zu wenig, um irgendetwas anderes zu spüren und mit einem tauben Lächeln der Verachtung davonläuft, er weint versteckt hinter gefrorenen Ecken vonSelbstperpetuierung. Meine Gedanken fließen nicht mit der Leichtigkeit deines versprochenen Körpers, noch kochen sie mit dankbarer Unersättlichkeit . . .

TV (*National Geographic Kanal*)   Das männliche Skorpion verzahnt sich mit dem weiblichen in einer intensiven Umarmung sie peitschen sich gegenseitig mit ihrem Stachel. Ihre Münder verzahnt, wird das Männchen das Weibchen wiederholt mit seinem Schwanz stechen. Als Vergeltung wird das Weibchen den Partner oftmals verzehren.

Ophelia *tritt auf. Ihr Hochzeitskleid ist in Fetzen. Sie hat ein Zündungsapparat an die Brust geschnallt.*

Ophelia   der hunger, den ich spüre, ist nicht meiner
er fließt außen und innen
in meinen habgierigen Armen
verlierst du dich
man kann nicht gerettet werden und verurteilt bleiben
der hunger, den ich spüre, ist nicht meiner

Sie sitzt im Rollstuhl und rollt heraus, hysterisch lachend.

Fernsehnachrichten   Heute in Kalifornien köpfte eine Mutter ihr Baby und aß sein Gehirn. (*Die Nachrichtensprecherin sieht für eine Sekunde traurig aus und wechselt dann schnell zu einem* *breiten Lächeln.*) Und jetzt beantwortet unser Lifestyle Guru die wichtigsten Fragen der Jahreszeit . . .

'Jingle Bells' beginnt zu spielen.

Hamlet'*s Gesicht auf der Leinwand geht in das Videospiel über, das er spielt.*

Hamlet *auf der Couch und im Videospiel steht auf und setzt seinen Hut ab und zieht die Jacke aus. Er geht hinter die Bühne und bringt einen Kanister Benzin, den er beginnt überall auszuschütten.*

Ophelia (*tippt, während* **Hamlet** *das Benzin ausschüttet*)   Weit weg, weit weg, Schatz . . . wir haben es auf jeden Fall geschafft uns von unserer eigenen Existenz zu überzeugen. So extrem, dass ich keine andere Wahl habe, als diese Überzeugung aufrechtzuerhalten. Ich bitte dich mir nicht zu verweigern, was rechtmäßig jemand anderem gehört. Ich kenne deinen Einsatz für Wahrheiten und Irrtümer. Serviert mit Stücken verlorenen Glaubens und denen, die bei stillen Auktionen im Museum für Wachsorgane und Seelen gekauft wurden. Ich will, dass du wirklich verstehst, die Versprechen meiner Lippen sind nicht übersetzbar. Ich binde deine Gedanken und meine mit solch eigenartiger Detailaufmerksamkeit. Du wolltest Liebe spüren oder eigentlich irgendetwas.

Das Theater des Begehrens ist öffentlich zugänglich für neugierige und nichts ahnende Zuschauer. Ich habe sie gestern durch die Stadt gehen sehen, als wir versteckt unter dem Bett, das sich weigerte gezämt zu werden, weinten. Ich lief mit deinem Kopf unter meinem Arm heraus. Ich stolpere, stolpere über die Worte, verbunden mit ihrer Stärke. Weine nicht Schatz, die Nacht kommt.

Sie zündet ein Streichholz an. Blackout.

Ophéliemachine

Translated by Romain Pasquer

Un concessionnaire de voiture, un local de rangement ou une salle de jeux pour enfants, remplie d'objets rassemblés là par un voyageur perdu: Le David *de Michel-Ange sans bras portant un casque de moto, une pile de masques Africains brisés, le squelette d'un poète mort riant hystériquement face à son ombre, une poupée démembrée suçant une sucette rose, le parapluie cassé de Magritte, le vieux téléphone en accès direct avec Dieu d'Andy Warhol, un voile blanc sale de mariage suspendu quelque part avec d'autres vêtements, des piles de vieilles chaussures et de perruques.*

C'est un terrain vague moderne, fait de jeux de consoles cassés, d'écrans de TV, et d'écrans d'ordinateurs sur lesquels défilent des scènes aléatoires de nos vies virtuelles, sans aucuns sons : scènes de guerre, meurtres de masse, génocides, corps d'Auschwitz, porno, annonces de campagnes politiques, femmes de Wall Street, femmes obèses, femmes anorexiques, écolières japonaises, femmes en burkas, safaris sauvages, explosions de bande dessinée. **Hamlet** *et* **Ophélie** *boivent chaque jour cette soupe d'informations et d'images : un méli-mélo des contrastes de la vie humaine entre beauté et horreur, innocence et violence.*

Tout est recouvert par une couche de cendre radioactive.

Hamlet, *habillé en jeans, une veste du sixième siècle, avec un chapeau de cowboy, il est assis sur un canapé faisant face au public. Il regarde la télévision, avec la télécommande il change les chaînes sans réfléchir. A l'arrière-plan de la scène, une projection du méli-mélo.* **Hamlet** *veut comprendre le monde, mais il ne peut qu'y poser un regard fixe et vide.*

À gauche de la scène, derrière lui, **Ophélie**, *habillée en vert-camouflage de l'armée, assise devant un bureau suspendu, elle écrit quelque chose sur une vieille machine à écrire. Un verre de vin rouge sang est posé sur le côté. Elle fume une cigarette et porte toute son attention à ce qu'elle écrit.*

Hamlet *et* **Ophélie** *se trouvent aux deux extrémités du monde. Entre eux, l'Océan Atlantique plein de corps pourrissants, d'oiseaux morts et d'urine.*

Ophélie (*en train d'écrire*)   Hamlet, mon chéri, je ne veux pas m'identifier à toi ou à elle, tes soldats en plastique ont envahi mon côté du lit. On peut facilement troquer les océans et les continents pour de la nostalgie politique ou de l'endurance. Laisse les morts enterrer les morts, la plaie de nos pères. (*Elle fait une pause et boit une gorgée de vin.*)

Hamlet (*la tête ailleurs, se rappelant des temps meilleurs*)   Dans le dé maudit
– six lits par sept chevaliers –
Des larves nouvellement écloses se sont amarrées
Sur les rivages de leur propre sciure.

Ophélie (*continuant, imperturbable*)   . . . écrire est une forme de masturbation intellectuelle. Je renverse mon moi, cet être pauvre et pathétique, sur l'œil blanc de mon ordinateur, fière de maitriser cet art difficile de l'autocomplaisance, et de pouvoir ainsi entrer dans la nouvelle ère des plaisirs solipsistes. Mon autosuffisance m'étonne moi-même. Oh, ces points érogènes de mon cerveau, examinés consciencieusement dans des élans mégalomaniaques de narcissisme. Oui, oui tout de suite, je vais la sauvegarder automatiquement pour plus tard. (*Elle fait une pause et prend une bouffée de sa cigarette.*)

TV (*Chaine National Geographic*)   Lors du rituel d'accouplement, la femelle aigle à tête blanche accroche ses serres à celles du mâle, demandant sa soumission totale alors qu'ils plongent vers le sol, figés. S'il essaye de se libérer avant qu'elle ne soit prête, elle ne le laissera pas s'accoupler avec elle. Si elle attend ne serait-ce que quelques secondes de trop, ils s'écraseront tous les deux au sol dans une chute fatale.

Le bruit d'un train qui passe en se déplaçant à pleine vitesse, sifflant comme s'il essayait de prévenir une personne se trouvant sur les rails. Le train passe. Minuit à Port Authority. Ding dong, le son de l'annonceur, marmonnant quelque chose, **Hamlet** *regarde continuellement la TV*

Ophélie (*dans la continuité*)   La plupart des filles à Port Authority sont soit du Bronx soit de Harlem. Elles couvrent leurs têtes de fausses écharpes Chanel, et portent de faux sacs Louis Vuitton sous leurs épaules. Elles essayent de donner l'impression qu'elles sont à la mode et entretenues, comme si elles avaient un homme pour lequel elles ne valent pas plus que ces quelques centaines de dollars de faux articles de luxe inutiles. Certaines ont de jeunes bébés ou des bambins avec elles, elles les portent avec un désespoir silencieux. Je ne sais jamais qui a le plus besoin de l'autre, elles sont leurs bébés, ou eux sont leurs bébés. Elles s'assoient sur le sol ou sur leur valise, attendant patiemment leur bus. Parfois, elles sont avec un homme, alors leurs yeux brillent d'une douce satisfaction. Elles ont l'air tout à la fois fragiles et dures, comme si elles pouvaient commencer à pleurer ou à jurer à tout moment.

Ophélie *se remet à taper à la machine. Le téléphone sonne. Le bruit du tram qui passe. Un enfant pleure dans l'appartement voisin.* **Gertrude** *entre. Elle traverse la scène, elle porte une robe et des rollers comme embrasés sur sa tête. Elle se cure les dents et parle au téléphone. Ses yeux sont embrasés.*

Gertrude   Oh mon dieu, non ! Elle a des taches de rousseur ? Mais, Allo, tu SAIS ce que JE PENSE de ça. Enfin. . . tout ce que je dis ce n'est pas plus compliqué que ça. Quand tu regardes une poupée chinoise normale, est-ce qu'elle a des taches de rousseur ? Alors ? Non, elle n'en a pas. Est-ce que celles qu'on t'envoie elles ont des taches de rousseur ? Donc. . . renvoie-la ! . . . Non, tu n'aurais pas dû faire ça ! Tu NE devrais PAS avoir à payer les frais de port pour le retour. Tu la remets direct dans le carton et tu la renvoies. Oh non ! Tu as payé pour ça ! . . . Tu as vu la photo dans le catalogue, tu l'as payé avec ta carte bleue et maintenant tu devrais recevoir ce que tu as payé ! . . . Est-ce qu'il y avait des photos d'une fille avec des taches de rousseur ? Non ! Ok. C'est bien ce que je voulais dire . . . Tu as compris ? . . . NON, parce que c'est ce qu'on appelle de la FALSIFICATION ! . . . On peut les envoyer en prison pour ça, tu le sais ? . . . Oui tu peux en avoir des tas de jolies filles de Chine . . .

Elle disparait derrière la porte de la scène. Sa robe se coince dans la porte et elle la tire avec énervement. **Hamlet** *se retourne vers*

elle et balance une chaussure vers elle, mais il la rate. Il lui pousse
des ailes de chauve-souris et il se remet à regarder la télévision.

Ophélie (*continue de taper à sa machine comme si rien n'était*
arrivé) L'angoisse, chéri, l'angoisse ; je veux que tu le remplisses
ou que tu t'en charges. C'est ton choix : la prospérité attend avec
impatience que nos pauvres gênes soient transmis, et immortalisés
dans cinq kilos de carbone et d'intellect. Oui, oui, chéri, je suis
sûre que la procréation peut être une source de joie infinie pour les
masses, mais nous nous sommes tellement plus raffinés. Tu dois
comprendre, les voix dans ma tête ne peuvent pas être assourdies
par les cris d'un enfant. Tu dois le savoir, même les cris que je
produis avec une telle grâce quand tu exerces par clémence ton
droit à l'engourdissement post-coïtal . . . l'engourdissement. . .
(*Pause. Pendant qu'elle écrit,* **Hamlet** *regarde du porno soft.*)
l'angoisse, chéri, l'angoisse dont je parlais, pas l'engourdissement.
Je suis sûre que si tu y mets un peu plus du tien, tu l'atteindras. J'ai
soigneusement mesuré ton pénis, et j'ai également évalué ses
qualités existentielles en acceptant de prendre toute la
responsabilité dans mon échec à soigner ton être blessé, définissant
ainsi le cadre de notre charmante rencontre qui je l'espère nous
laissera tout deux autant insatisfaits. La longueur de ton pénis est
proportionnelle à l'angoisse que je ressentirai en fumant une
cigarette dans tes bras fatigués, et en contemplant les probabilités
statistiques d'un cancer du poumon ou d'une attaque cardiaque
causés par une insatiabilité sexuelle, et des angoisses qu'on
n'aurait pas correctement traitées. Hamlet, chéri, ne parle pas de
politique, de tes désirs, du monde, de la mort et du sang que tu as
perdu en pleurant devant des enfants affamés.

Ophélie, *portant une robe de mariée, traverse, accompagnée*
par **Horatio** *et* **Gertrude**. **Gertrude** *conduit un cheval à*
bascule, agitant une épée derrière sa tête. **Horacio** *porte un*
smoking, des bas en résille, et des talons rouges. Ses cheveux
sont tirés en arrière. Elle porte un plateau de crevettes et un
cahier de note.

Ophélie (*en train de monter et redescendre les escaliers en robe de*
mariée) Béni sois-tu . . .

Horatio   Cette crevette a l'air un peu chétive. Peut-être que je devrais appeler l'entreprise de restauration. Tu ne veux pas que quelqu'un tombe malade. Ils devraient vraiment commencer à vendre des assurances de mariage pour ce genre de choses. Qu'est-ce que tu en penses ?

Ophélie   Tu t'es déjà demandé si tu étais avec la bonne personne ?

Horatio (*levant les yeux de son cahier de notes*)   Bien sûr que tu ne l'es pas, chéri. Tu ne pourras jamais *être* véritablement avec la bonne personne. Ce qui fait que c'est le bon c'est que tu n'es pas avec lui. Ce qui fait que ce n'est pas le bon c'est le fait qu'il soit avec toi. (*Retournant à son cahier de notes.*) D'où viennent les crevettes ? La Bella Tosca, ou Christie's ?

Ophélie   Christie's. Tu devrais t'assurer que c'est le bon. Le bon.

Gertrude   Oh, le bon . . .

Ophélie (*pleurant de tout son cœur*)   Je veux l'avoir, le bon, et toujours, ensemble, jusqu'à la mort . . .

Gertrude   La vie, la mort, l'amour et le plaisir, l'univers est infini et il continue de s'étendre. D'où es-tu venu ? Où vas-tu ? *Quo vadis. Panta Rei.* De grandes questions, chéri, mais, malgré ce que ton père peut dire, elles ne payeront pas ton loyer. Tu devrais les poser par écrit maintenant, les mettre dans ta cachette secrète, et les ressortir quand tu seras à la retraite. Elles te seront vraiment utiles à ce moment-là, entre les leçons de golf, le Pilate, et les bouffées de chaleur. Tu devrais vraiment arrêter de cligner des yeux comme ça. Ton maquillage s'étale sur tout ton visage.

Hamlet (*rentre, en smoking*)   Tu ne vas tout de même pas te marier avec *lui*, rassure-moi ?

Horatio (*levant les yeux au ciel*)   C'est le bon. Ce n'est pas le bon.

Gertrude   Le bon pour quoi ?

Ophélie   Pour guérir ton âme . . .

Gertrude *et* **Horatio** *se regardent et se mettent à rire de façon hystérique.*

Gertrude   Comme l'autre ?

Horatio   Ou l'autre

Gertrude (*philosophiquement*)   Ou un autre encore.

Des cloches d'Église se mettent à sonner et elles se transforment en avatars ; elles partent, leurs voix synthétisées se dissolvant dans d'absurdes répétitions. « Le bon, ou un autre, lequel, quelqu'un, n'importe qui, personne, celui que nous avons attendu, ou l'autre, celui qu'ils ont attendu, que tu as attendu ? Qui a été attendu ? Lequel ? »

Hamlet (*parlant depuis l'écran alors que les cloches sonnent*)   Anesthésie-toi avec les cris des enfants du loup.
Rien n'est réel sauf
Cheveux raides de vomis
Ce soir –
Tu vas dormir sans rêver.
Demain –
Défais ta peau et laisse-nous rentrer
La leçon d'anatomie du Dr. Tulp peut commencer.

Ding dong – *le bruit de la station de bus. La voix de l'annonceur marmonne, elle est inintelligible.*

Ophélie *transporte une valise et une taie d'oreiller pleines de têtes de mannequins. Elle rentre prudemment, elle regarde les horaires du bus et essaye d'en déduire à quelle heure le bus part. Elle est stoppée par* **Hamlet**. *Il porte une chaine en or lourde autour de son cou.*

Hamlet   Hey, tu vas où ?

Ophélie   Rendre visite à un ami.

Hamlet (*il l'observe*)   D'où viens-tu ?

Ophélie   Huston, Maine

Hamlet   C'est où ?

Ophélie   C'est une petite ville. Personne ne sait où c'est.

Hamlet   C'est une ville universitaire ? Tu es à l'université ?

Ophélie   Non.

Hamlet   Qu'est-ce que tu fais là-bas ? (*Elle est silencieuse, esquissant un sourire, clairement mal à l'aise.*) Haha, je sais, c'est une histoire de mec. Il t'a monté la tête là-bas. Haha Il t'a complètement monté la tête là-bas. Tu devrais venir ici, à New-York.

Ophélie   Hmmm.

Hamlet   Qu'est-ce que tu as là-dedans ?

Ophélie   Ça?

Hamlet   Hein-hein.

Ophélie   Ce sont des têtes de mannequins. Je suis en apprentissage pour devenir coiffeuse.

(*Ding dong*. L'annonceur de Port Authority : « le bus de deux heures et demi (du matin) vers Cleveland va partir Porte 5. Merci de ne pas oublier vos bagages derrière vous. »)

Ophélie   C'est mon bus.

Il attend qu'elle dise quelque chose, mais elle reste silencieuse, alors il s'en va. Elle se déplace difficilement avec sa taie d'oreiller et elle la traine lentement derrière elle, disparaissant à l'arrière en dehors de la scène. Il crache par-dessus son épaule et la suit.

« Dream a Little Dream of Me » commence à jouer. **Ophélie,** *assise face à son bureau, prend une gorgée de vin.* **Hamlet** *abandonne sa télécommande et se met à jouer à un jeu vidéo. Des feuilles d'automne sèches commencent à leur tomber dessus. La musique s'arrête brutalement quand les portes s'ouvrent.*

Gertrude *entre, elle parle au téléphone. Elle porte la même robe, mais la moitié de sa tête n'a plus de bigoudis. Ses cheveux, tels*

*ceux de Méduse, volent dans les quatre directions du monde. Elle
traverse la scène, parlant au téléphone et feuilletant le catalogue.*

Gertrude   Tu penses que je devrais prendre lequel ? Celui de
Russie, Roumanie, ou de Chine ? Ceux de Russie ont l'air bien, tous
gentils et blonds, mais on dit qu'ils sont abimés. Toute cette vodka
russe que leurs mères boivent . . . Je ne suis pas sûre pour ceux de
Roumanie ; ils sont pâles, blonds mais trop pâles. Ils sont peut-être
mal-nourris. C'est la même chose avec ceux d'Afrique. Mais ils
sont si exotiques. J'aurais l'air bien avec un sur mon épaule à côté
de mon sac Chanel. Ou encore mieux, Hermès . . . Tu sais combien
de temps dure la garantie pour eux ?. . . Deux ans ? Tu peux prendre
une extension de garantie ? . . . Et si ça meurt ? . . . . Est-ce qu'ils en
envoient un autre pour le remplacer ? Est-ce qu'ils couvrent le coût
des funérailles ? Et le transport ? Je ne vais pas encore payer pour
les frais d'envois. Vingt-cinq mille pour toute la paperasse – c'est
ça. . . . Oui, tu as raison mon cher, ceux d'Amérique du Sud ont l'air
pas mal du tout, pas trop foncés, pas trop pâles . . . Hein-hein . . . .

Elle part, assez satisfaite par cette idée

TV (*depuis l'écran, Il est difficile de deviner s'il s'agit d'un soap
opéra ou d'un une adaptation d'un roman classique*)   Cette
dualité dans sa nature lui a fait peur. Chaque fois qu'il était sûr de
la posséder, ses yeux devenaient ceux d'une étrangère. Un moment
elle était si familière qu'il pouvait entendre sa voix à l'intérieur de
lui, et si distante que la soudaine solitude qui pénétrait chaque
cellule de son corps le blessait physiquement et l'étouffait comme
la conscience de sa mort.

Hamlet *est assis sur le canapé, il joue à un jeu vidéo. Son visage
se transforme lentement en celui d'***Ophélie***. Elle porte un casque
de l'armée, qu'elle recouvre avec une écharpe noire.*

Ophélie (*depuis l'écran, comme si elle chantait une comptine pour
enfant*)   Un jour
Ma peau nous a abandonnés
Me laissant moi et ma peau dans une stupeur de surprise
Nous nous sommes regardées, amusées
Nous n'avions plus rien à perdre

Horatio (*lit des documents juridiques*)   Depuis des mois ils se sont préparés pour ce bébé. Ils avaient tout acheté ensemble, le berceau, la poussette, les habits. Ils n'avaient choisi que le meilleur, le plus cher, dans les catalogues les plus exclusifs. Il lui avait acheté une toute nouvelle voiture pour qu'elle puisse aller à l'université et en revenir sans avoir à prendre le bus. Quand ils ont appris que ce serait une fille. Ça l'a déçu. Il voulait vraiment avoir un garçon pour continuer ce qu'il avait commencé. Il s'était imaginé tout ce qu'il pourrait lui enseigner. A cause de la honte qu'il ressentait face à ses propres sentiments, il les a cachés, il s'est fait à l'idée que ce serait une fille, et s'en est réjoui pendant la grossesse, supportant patiemment ses élans de mauvaises humeurs et ses mélancolies impromptues. Elle portait son bébé. Pour la première fois, elle était officiellement autorisée à le torturer, et elle découvrit lentement qu'il n'y avait pas de limites à ce qu'elle pouvait faire. Toute la rancœur qu'elle ressentait envers lui pour toutes ces fois où elle avait dû se plier à son ego fragile, ne fit qu'exacerber son imagination. Elle l'écrasa encore et encore avec à chaque fois une cruauté plus raffinée, et il supporta tout avec un mélange de sens du devoir, de sidération et d'émerveillement.

Le bruit d'un avion ou d'un hélicoptère volant au-dessus et l'ombre des ailes passe sur la scène. **Ophélie** *étend ses bras noirs et se met à flotter dans les airs. Elle se transforme en corbeau. Les bruits d'une grande ville : une ambulance, une fusillade, des filles rigolent, une personne crie et un chien aboie dans la rue.* **Ophélie** *surplombe et observe la scène. Son corps se brise en un million de petits morceaux qu'elle essaye de rassembler dans un panier de courses. La femme de ménage du supermarché la jette dehors, et elle s'arrache les yeux.*

Hamlet   Les lumières s'invitent
caressant les ombres des rues blanches
dégageant une odeur de sang, eau de javel et
d'urine de la veille

Dans quel tiroir as-tu mis toutes tes insomnies
Et les mosaïques composées par les tâches de moisissures au plafond
Où est-ce que ton horizon s'arrête ?

Ophélie *entre en fauteuil roulant, poussée par une infirmière de l'armée.*

Ophélie En tant que fille en fauteuil roulant, j'ai été soudainement déchirée : à qui devrais-je promettre mes alliances ? Si cette personne était une femme, la réponse était simple. Si cette personne était un estropié, la réponse était simple. Mais, il y avait une impossibilité existentielle intrinsèque dans la figure de l'homme estropié : était-ce un ennemi ou un frère martyre ? Est-il Enchaîné à son sexe ou à son fauteuil roulant ? Puisque je ne pouvais me décider sur ma politique face aux hommes estropiés, j'ai décidé de tous les éviter, par précaution. Fondamentalement baisés dans leur masculinité, les hommes estropiés représentaient pour moi, avec ma féminité blessée, quelque chose que j'étais encline à éviter. Incapable de gérer mes propres contradictions – entre l'envie d'être désirée et celle d'être respectée – j'avais besoin d'un homme me demandant peu d'investissements émotionnels, qui serait infiniment généreux, dont l'égo et l'esprit seraient forts et solides comme sa bite infatigable, avec laquelle il me convaincrait encore et encore de mon sex-appeal sans limites, même pour des gouts raffinés, et une personnalité toujours plus fascinante qui le capturait totalement et sans réserve.

*Le fauteuil roulant tourne sur lui-même et le mannequin d'***Ophélie** *s'évapore. L'infirmière époussette l'oreiller et commence à tourner en rond : elle sait qu'elle ne peut pas se retrouver avec un fauteuil roulant vide alors elle le remplit avec tout ce qu'elle trouve.*

TV : *Talk show ou prime time. Thérapie de couple.* **Ophélie** *et* **Hamlet** *assis sur le canapé.*

Thérapeute Salut, merci d'être venu. C'est si gentil à vous d'avoir un problème à régler.

Hamlet Pas de problème.

Thérapeute (*déçu*) Pas de problèmes ?

Hamlet Oh non, il y a un problème. Pas de problèmes que nous soyons venus partager le problème avec vous.

Thérapeute   Ah d'accord, formidable. Alors, quel est le problème ?

Hamlet   C'est horrible. Je n'arrive pas à croire ce qu'elle a pu faire. Elle a détruit nos vies.

Ophélie   Oh, chéri, qu'est-ce que j'ai fait, si seulement tu me le disais... oh chéri (*pleure*). Si tu pouvais juste me dire ce que c'est, je suis sûre que nous irions mieux. Ne mets pas en danger notre amour et notre mariage avec ton silence.

Thérapeute   Oui, c'est juste une question de communication. Si vous pouviez nous le dire, alors nous saurions. Si vous pouviez parler de vos sentiments avec votre femme, vos sentiments seraient partagés.

Hamlet   Ce qu'elle a fait ? Ce qu'elle a fait ? Je ne peux même pas en parler. Voyez-vous même, j'en tremble encore rien que d'y penser. Je ne peux pas croire qu'elle ait fait ça. Je ne peux pas croire qu'elle m'ait fait ça à moi . . .

Ophélie & Thérapeute   Qu'est-ce qu'elle a / (*j'ai*) fait ?

Hamlet   Vous voulez savoir ? Vous voulez savoir ? Très bien, je vais vous le dire. Hier matin, au petit-déjeuner. . . (*Il chuchote à l'oreille du* **Thérapeute**.)

Thérapeute   Oh, mon dieuuuuuuuu !

Hamlet   Oui, c'est ce qu'elle a fait.

Thérapeute   C'est sans aucun doute une situation difficile, mais je suis sûr que si nous trouvons une solution, cela sera résolu. Les divorces sont la principale raison des divorces. Mais, sinon tout va bien ?

Ophélie   Oh oui, tout va bien. Nous avons un très beau mariage.

Hamlet   Oh oui, le boulot va bien, l'argent va bien, les enfants sont morts.

Thérapeute   Ce n'est qu'à partir de ce moment-là que vous pouvez dire que vous avez véritablement atteint un état de sagesse, quand vous ne laissez plus vos émotions interférer avec votre jugement intellectuel impartial et objectif. La conclusion que vous tirez doit toujours être donnée a priori ou déconnectée de l'expérience empirique que vous avez accumulée. Vous ne devez jamais vous contentez de déclarations qui sont dépourvues d'une profonde impartialité intellectuelle. Ce n'est qu'à partir de ce moment-là que vous pouvez dire quelque chose de véritablement et profondément impartial, véritablement impartialement profond. (*Il se surprend lui-même d'être si intelligent ; il sourit et hoche la tête, méditant sur ce qu'il vient de dire, mais rapidement il oublie, et commence à se curer le nez.*)

Ophélie (*derrière son bureau, tapant*)   Quelle chose étrange, mes amis, paraît être ce qu'on appelle le plaisir ! Et quel singulier rapport il a naturellement avec ce qui passe pour être son contraire, la douleur ! Ils refusent de se rencontrer ensemble chez l'homme ; mais qu'on poursuive l'un et qu'on l'attrape, on est presque toujours contraint d'attraper l'autre aussi, comme si, en dépit de leur dualité, ils étaient attachés à une seule tête.

TV (*conférence*)   La femme dont le plaisir sexuel se représente originairement d'une façon différente de celui de l'homme, pourrait tout aussi bien ne pas avoir de clitoris : l'hymen qui reste toujours (*in*)violé, et sur lequel la semence est pour toujours renversée et disséminée au loin, n'est d'aucune utilité pour l'hysteron. Est-ce que cette scène de violence qu'on appelle l'amour en transformation est contenue dans notre triade parfaite. Si les femmes ont toujours été utilisées comme l'instrument de l'auto-déconstruction masculine, est-ce que cette philosophie en est le nouveau renversement ?

Ophélie (*parle en tant que thérapeute*)   J'aime à croire que vous savez ce que vous faites et que vous n'êtes pas tout simplement pris au piège des impasses de la masculinité américaine autodestructrice, qui vous laissera au final émotionnellement vidé, intellectuellement affamé et sexuellement incompétent.

Hamlet (*joue à un jeu vidéo, nonchalamment*)   Est-ce que tu veux que je te tue dans un acte dramatique de jalousie si accablant que j'en perde la raison ? Est-ce que tu veux que je te tue pendant que tu jouis pour que tu puisses te fondre avec l'univers dans un

climax éternel, pour que tu puisses croire que tu vas vivre
éternellement ainsi capturée dans ce moment ? Est-ce que tu veux
que je te tue pendant que je te chuchote à l'oreille des nullités
douces à propos de mon propre désespoir ? Veux-tu que je te tue, et
moi également pour te suivre dans le drame de la mort si
minutieusement mise en scène ?

Ophélie *flotte dans l'espace. Elle essaye de se raccrocher à ce
qu'elle peut, mais le monde disparait à l'horizon.* **Ophélie** *essaye
de marcher mais il n'y a aucune surface sur laquelle marcher. Elle
attrape la télécommande et appuie désespérément dessus plusieurs
fois. Des carcasses d'animaux flottent sur le fleuve du Gange.*
Ophélie *lave ses cheveux et marche sur le sable du désert. Son
cœur saigne. Ses veines sont faites de câbles.* **Ophélie** *porte son
propre corps par-delà la frontière du désert.*

Hamlet   Quand je marche dans la vallée de l'ombre de la mort,
Je ne crains aucun mal : car tu es avec moi ;
Ta houlette et ton bâton me rassurent.
Tu dresses devant moi une table, En face de mes adversaires.

Ophélie (*assise derrière son bureau en tenue vert militaire. Calme
et stoïque, continuant à écrire, comme si rien ne s'était
passé*)   S'il te plait, chéri, l'autocritique n'est pas nécessairement
ce qui fait la valeur de quelqu'un sur le marché. Notre pureté est
purement formelle tout comme nos perversions tellement chéries
par ta mère, et promues dans toutes les publicités pour savon.
Chéri, tu dois savoir qu'elle préserve automatiquement sa virginité
pour la nuit de noce avec des bougies et des désirs soigneusement
sculptés par la TV, d'où leur nouveauté pour notre génération.
L'angoisse, chéri, l'angoisse. Je crois véritablement en dieu et la
dignité humaine, sauf quand celle-ci se trouve dans les tranchées
avec sa tête explosée par la vertu et l'engagement profond d'un
autre pour la vie. Tout comme je crois que tu es celui qui peut
atteindre le cœur avec profondeur au plus près de mes membres
faiblissants. Oui, oui, chéri, tu peux m'écrire un poème, ou juste
me baiser suffisamment ; je suis sure que dans les deux cas, nous
resterons fidèles à notre vieille conviction de l'immortalité
accomplie par la bonté du cœur, et l'union de nos âmes libérées de

leur haine mutuelle et de l'amour que nous avons l'un pour l'autre,
passant leurs jours dans l'harmonie de leurs rituels hygiéniques,
discours post-moderne faits de niveaux intellectuels divers et de
travail qui nous libèrera des abondances ou pénuries matérielles
selon que la procréation ait atteint sa moyenne statistique ou
qu'elle se soit exprimée dans l'individualisme égoïste de l'auto-
adoration. Je suis sûre que ma conviction me donnera une
confiance en moi-même comme cela serait le cas pour n'importe
qui d'autre, et dont tu me remercieras quand je te servirai un verre
de vin et que je te masserai les épaules. Le bout de ton pénis a un
potentiel ontologique, donc je plonge ton épée dans ton urètre afin
d'examiner si l'espace y est suffisamment spacieux pour absorber
mon angoisse et toutes celles laissées accidentellement par les
futurs pères de l'Amérique et des cinq autres continents au vu de la
mondialisation de nos pratiques sexuelles. La grand-mère de mon
père a péri mystérieusement quelque part entre Prague et Vienne, et
il nous arrivera exactement la même chose.

Horatio *entre avec une assiette de crevettes.*

Horatio (*à* **Hamlet**, *qui est toujours assis sur le
canapé*)   Crevettes ?

Hamlet   Merci, je suis au régime

Horatio *se souvient soudainement de quelque chose et lève son
poing, criant : « Liberté ! » Il court auprès du tank et son corps
disparait dans l'asphalte noir. Un groupe d'enfants souriant court
sur le trottoir, riant et se tenant les mains. Le corbeau noir picore
la peau d'*Horatio. *Le bruit de la station de bus. Ding dong.*

L'Annonceur   Le bus de Paris à New York, passant par Londres
et Tokyo, partira depuis la porte 5.

Le bus de Paris à New York, passant par Londres et Tokyo, partira
depuis la porte 5.

*L'annonce est répétée quelques fois comme si le mécanisme était
cassé. Quand l'annonce débute,* **Ophélie** *entre et porte une robe de
mariée tachée de sang et un foulard. Elle essaie de trouver la
bonne porte. Elle est suivie par* **Horatio**, *qui transporte une*

*assiette avec une tête humaine d'homme dessus, entourée de
crevettes.*

Ophélie *entre.*

Ophélie (*en colère*)   La seule, la seule. Je suis la seule. Je suis
celle que j'ai tant attendu. Je suis la seule. Unique, seulement une,
laquelle. La seule, la sainte, fondamentalement la seule, celle qui
est bénie.

Horatio (*ne faisant pas attention à elle*)   Celles de Christie's sont
plus fraiches. Commandons celles de Christie's.

Ophélie *enlève sa botte de l'armée et bat à mort* **Horatio**. *Son
corps disparait dans l'asphalte noir.* **Ophélie** *existe avec ses bras
grands ouverts.* **Hamlet** *commence à jouer avec son téléphone.*
Ophélie/Médée *sur le sol de la station de bus chante à son enfant
mort.*

Ophélie/Médée   Puisse son grand Nom être béni à jamais et dans
tous les temps des mondes.
Béni et loué et glorifié et exalté, et élevé
Vénéré et élevé et loué soit le nom du Saint,
Béni soit-il.

Hamlet   Tu lis la peine dans mes yeux et tu crois tout savoir. Tu
penses pouvoir lire un homme au travers de sa peine. Tu penses
que parce que tu peux lire la peine d'un homme, il t'appartient,
pour toujours.

TV (*Chaine National Geographic*)   Le male punaise de lit a un
pénis conçu pour injecter et délivrer le sperme à l'intérieur de la
femelle. Cette technique est très violente, la femelle est clouée au
sol et son corps est poignardé plusieurs fois pour assurer
l'insémination. Cette méthode a évolué pour éviter le passage par
l'appareil génital femelle, diminuant et enlevant tout contrôle que
la femelle aurait normalement sur les étapes de la conception.

Ophélie   Quand mon corps sera mon maitre, je n'en aurai aucun
autre. (*Crie en le disant.*) Quand mon corps sera mon maitre, je
n'en aurai aucun autre.

Hamlet *change de chaines.*

Ophélie (*boit du vin et continue à écrire*)   Les actes répugnants d'autorévélations trouvent leur origine dans l'esprit des personnes qui manifestent une générosité pour les classes plus populaires issues d'ascendance vulgaire. J'en suis sure, chéri, l'angoisse que je t'ai si précisément décrite n'a aucune conséquence éthique sur ton bien-être. Je suis aussi certaine que tu pourras remplacer mon déséquilibre émotionnel aussi facilement que je le ferais pour chaque créature que nos esprits désireront. Le choix, si clairement pris par mon moi atrophié dépend uniquement de ton niveau de sérotonine et du désir produit par cette nuit particulière. Mon offre reste valide le temps de ton érection et elle expire au moment où tu éjacules tes paranoïas pitoyables sur mon visage qui les attend. Le désir conçu comme une fonction mathématique a ses avantages de par sa volatilité et la permanence de ses prévisions, lequel répliqué dans des proportions fractales, acquière la qualité légère d'une structure solide fondamentalement indiscernable de tout autre solution acide aux problèmes internalisés pendant l'enfance et remis à plus tard pour être consommés avec un verre de Chardonnay ou de Sauvignon de Blanco, et du poisson, légèrement cuit dans une sauce de citron et caviar.

Gertrude *passe en parlant au téléphone. Elle s'est métamorphosée en machine.*

Gertrude   Le catalogue n'avait-il pas dit que la satisfaction était garantie ? Ils vous envoient une fille défectueuse et ils pensent que vous allez rester coincés avec . . . Renvoie la et dis-leur de t'en envoyer une comme sur la photo, sans taches de rousseur . . . De nos jours, chéri, on se doit de faire attention à l'argent qu'on dépense. Hier, j'ai acheté des chaussettes faites en Chine. Elles étaient défectueuses- je te le dis- Ah ah – Ah ah – donc je les ai renvoyés. Ces temps-ci on ne peut pas se permettre de dépenser autant d'argent sur des objets défectueux. – ah ah – ah ah – Tu as payé pour quelque chose, ils t'envoient le mauvais produit, tu dois pouvoir le renvoyer et en avoir pour ton argent. . . oui, oui, c'est ce que je dis.

Gertrude *disparait. La neige commence à tomber.*

Hamlet (*en cachette, comme s'il disait un secret*)   Parfois, quand nous traversons
Les yeux de l'un et de l'autre comme on traverse des portes
Parfois, je suis comme elle
Parfois, elle est qui
Je suis

Ophélie (*écrivant, frénétiquement*)   La main droite tient l'amour éternel avec toutes ses impasses fantomatiques de délivrance écœurante et la routine rectangulaire des métaphores recyclées des corps des amants et des insectes tombés des livres ouverts en leur milieu. Je promettrai de me chérir tel que je me suis trouvée de façon si touchante dans tes yeux à l'intérieur des pupilles que je te supplie si ardemment de ne pas fermer quand je suis en train de jouir et dans lesquelles mes grimaces y sont magnifiées en des produits audibles de notre imagination. Je promets aussi d'inclure la stabilité que tu as si longtemps désirée et la confusion entrelacée par d'occasionnels coups de poings de mon ego pour te maintenir dans une offre et une demande stable. Je promets de satisfaire nos fantaisies œdipiennes et de louer mon ventre charitablement pour une oasis et des toilettes dans lesquelles nous puissions nous soulager de nos précieuses fèces issues de nos aventures intellectuelles. Je suis sûre que l'arrangement satisfera quarante pourcents de notre masse, et laissera les soixante restant dans des suspicions d'une brûlante insatiabilité et dans une perpétuité physique de gravité et de légèreté. Ma main gauche offre un amour sans retour, le mien ou le tien, nous en déciderons plus tard. Je suis sûre que dans les deux cas nous nous adapterons à nos rôles avec la grâce naturelle du maitre et de l'esclave. Le désir est proportionnel au temps d'attente. Chéri, elle a été formée par les meilleures putes d'Europe, d'Amérique du Nord et d'Asie. Celles à qui tu as rendu visite pendant tes nuits alcoolisées ou solitaires, et durant lesquelles tu as rentré ton pénis à demi mou avec l'espoir de vivre un soulagement temporaire du cauchemar du désir ou de son manque.

Ophélie *s'arrête. Elle se reprend.* **Ophélie** *sort un pistolet de son tiroir et se fait exploser la tête. Le bruit du coup de feu et du sang répandu partout. Elle continue à écrire comme si de rien n'était.*

La maladie de la mort triomphe de nous. Si seulement nous ne mourrions pas et ne vivions pas. L'angoisse entre être possédé et posséder s'installe à la vitesse d'un voleur qui aurait volé beaucoup trop pour ressentir du plaisir et pas assez pour ressentir quelque chose d'autre, et qui en partant avec un sourire hébété de mépris pleurerait caché derrière des coins glacés se renouvelant perpétuellement. Mes pensées ne filent pas avec la facilité que ton corps avait promis pas plus qu'elles ne bouillent avec une insatiabilité reconnaissante . . .

TV (*Chaine de National Geographic*)   Le mâle et la femelle scorpion s'entrelacent dans une étreinte intense, se fouettant mutuellement avec leurs dards. Alors que leurs deux bouches sont collées, le mâle va poignarder de façon répétée la femelle avec sa queue. En représailles, souvent la femelle consommera son partenaire.

Ophélie *entre. Sa robe de mariage est en lambeaux. Elle a des explosifs accrochés à sa poitrine.*

Ophélie   La faim que je ressens n'est pas en moi
Ça coule en dehors et au dedans
Dans mes bras voraces
Tu te perds
On ne peut pas être sauvé et rester condamné
La faim que je ressens n'est pas en moi

Elle s'assoie dans le fauteuil roulant et sort en riant hystériquement.

News TV   Aujourd'hui en Californie, une mère a décapité son bébé et a mangé son cerveau. (*La présentatrice a l'air triste le temps d'une seconde, puis retrouve rapidement son grand sourire.*) Maintenant la suite des informations, celle-ci nous vient de notre guru de l'hygiène de vie, qui va répondre à la question la plus importante de la saison . . .

« Jingle Bells » commence à jouer

*Le visage d'***Hamlet*** sur la toile de fond se mélange au jeu vidéo avec lequel il joue.*

Hamlet *sur le canapé et dans le jeu vidéo se lève et enlève son chapeau et sa veste. Il part dans les coulisses et ramène une bonbonne d'essence qu'il commence à répandre sur le sol.*

Ophélie (*écrit pendant qu'***Hamlet** *répand l'essence*)   Au loin, au loin, chéri . . . Nous avons certainement réussi à nous convaincre nous-mêmes de notre propre existence. Pris dans une telle extrémité, je n'ai pas d'autres choix que de perpétuer cette conviction. Je te supplie de ne pas me refuser ce qui appartient de droit à quelqu'un d'autre. Je connais ton attachement aux vérités et aux mensonges. Servis avec des morceaux de croyances perdues et celles achetées pendant des enchères silencieuses dans des musées d'âmes et d'organes en cire. Je veux vraiment que tu comprennes que les promesses de mes lèvres ne sont pas traduisibles. J'attache tes pensées aux miennes avec une si grande attention pour les détails. Tu voulais ressentir l'amour ou quelque chose qui compte. Le théâtre des désirs est ouvert pour les spectateurs curieux et ignorants d'eux mêmes. Je les ai vu hier passant à travers la ville alors que nous pleurions cachés sous ce lit qui refusait d'être apprivoisé. Je suis sortie avec la tête sous mon bras. J'ai trébuché, trébuché sur les mots attachés à leurs pouvoirs. Ne pleure pas chéri, la nuit vient.

Elle allume une allumette. Coupure de courant / noir

Opheliamachine

Traduzione dall'inglese di Maria Pia Pagani

Una concessionaria di automobili, una rimessa o una sala giochi
per bambini, piena di oggetti ammucchiati da un viaggiatore
smarrito: un David *di Michelangelo senza braccia che indossa un*
casco da motociclista, una pila di maschere africane sfasciate, lo
scheletro di un poeta morto che sbeffeggia istericamente la propria
ombra, una bambola con gli arti mancanti che succhia un lecca-
lecca rosa, l'ombrello rotto di Magritte, un vecchio telefono di
Andy Warhol per parlare con Dio, un velo da sposa sporco che
spenzola da qualche parte con altri indumenti, cataste di scarpe
vecchie e parrucche.

È una moderna terra desolata, con console di videogiochi rotte,
schermi TV e schermi di computer che mostrano a casaccio scene
mute delle nostre vite virtuali: scene di guerra, omicidi di massa,
genocidi, corpi di Auschwitz, porno, annunci politici, donne di
Wall Street, donne grasse, donne anoressiche, studentesse
giapponesi, donne in burka, safari selvaggi, esplosioni di fumetti.
Amleto *e* **Ofelia** *si sorbiscono questa zuppa quotidiana di notizie e*
immagini: un marasma dell'umano contrasto tra bellezza e orrore,
innocenza e violenza.

Tutto è coperto da cenere radioattiva.

Amleto *in jeans, con giacca del XVI secolo e stivali da cowboy, è*
seduto sul divano di fronte al pubblico. Guarda la TV, lanciando
con noncuranza i canali con il suo telecomando. Sul fondale scorre
una proiezione di quel marasma. **Amleto** *vuole capire il mondo,*
ma tutto quel che può fare è guardarlo fisso.

Su un ponteggio a sinistra, dietro di lui, c'è **Ofelia** *in mimetica*
militare verde. È seduta dietro una scrivania galleggiante, e sta
battendo qualcosa con una macchina da scrivere vecchio stile. Si
tiene accanto un bicchiere di vino color rosso sangue. Fuma una
sigaretta ed è tutta concentrata nel dattilografare.

Amleto *e* **Ofelia** *sono alle due estremità del mondo. Tra loro,*
l'Oceano Atlantico pieno di cadaveri in decomposizione, carcasse
di uccelli e urina.

Ofelia (*intenta a dattilografare*)   Amleto, mio caro, io non
desidero identificarmi con te o con lei; i tuoi soldatini giocattolo

hanno invaso un lato del mio letto. L'oceano e i continenti si
scambiano facilmente per nostalgia politica e tolleranza. Lasciate
che i morti seppelliscano i morti, la piaga dei nostri padri. (*Fa una
pausa e beve un sorso di vino.*)

Amleto (*distrattamente, ricordando tempi migliori*)
Nel maledetto gioco dei dadi
– sei letti per sette notti –
le larve appena formate attraccano
alle rive della loro stessa legnosa polvere.

Ofelia (*continuando indisturbata*)   . . .la scrittura è una forma di
masturbazione intellettuale. Io riverso il mio povero e patetico ego
sull'occhio bianco del mio computer, orgogliosa di padroneggiare
questa difficile arte dell'auto-indulgenza, per entrare così nella
nuova era del piacere solipsista. La mia auto-sufficienza mi
stupisce. Oh, quei punti erogeni sul mio cervello esaminati
attentamente in crisi megalomani di auto-adorazione! Sì, sì, subito:
salverò automaticamente me stessa per il dopo. (*Fa una pausa e
aspira dalla sigaretta.*)

TV (*National Geographic Channel*)   Durante il rituale di
accoppiamento, l'aquila bianca femmina blocca con i suoi artigli il
maschio chiedendogli la completa sottomissione e scaraventandolo
inerte a terra. Se lui prova a liberarsi prima che lei sia pronta, lei non
si lascerà montare. Se lei sarà costretta ad aspettare qualche secondo
di troppo, si faranno reciprocamente a pezzi fino alla morte.

*Si sente il rumore di un treno in corsa a tutta velocità, che fischia
come se cercasse di mettere in guardia qualcuno che sta sui binari.
Il treno passa. Port Authority Bus Terminal, è mezzanotte.* Ding
dong, *il suono dell'annunciatore che borbotta qualcosa.* **Amleto**
continua a guardare la TV.

Ofelia (*prosaica*)   Al Port Authority Bus Terminal, la maggior
parte delle ragazze proviene dal Bronx o da Harlem. Usano foulard
di Chanel taroccati e borse di Louis Vuitton altrettanto taroccate.
Cercano di essere alla moda e di curarsi, come se avessero un
uomo per il quale valgano quei duecento dollari di lusso
all'apparenza inutile. Alcune di loro hanno bambini piccoli o

neonati appresso, e li tengono con quieta disperazione. Io non sono mai sicura di chi abbia più bisogno: se loro dei loro bambini, o i loro bambini di loro. Si siedono per terra o sulle loro valigie, aspettando pazientemente l'autobus. Qualche volta sono insieme a un uomo, e allora i loro occhi brillano di una dolce soddisfazione. Sembrano sia fragili che tenaci, potrebbero mettersi a piangere o a imprecare in qualsiasi momento.

Ofelia *si rimette a dattilografare. Suona il telefono. Si sente il rumore di un tram in marcia. Nell'appartamento confinante c'è un bambino che piange. Entra* **Gertrude**. *Attraversa il palcoscenico in vestaglia e bigodini rosso fuoco. Tiene in bocca uno stuzzicadenti e parla al telefono. I suoi occhi sono raggianti.*

Gertrude   Oh mio Dio, no! Quella aveva le lentiggini?! Beh, tu SAI cosa ne PENSO IO. Voglio dire . . . Guarda che tutto quello che sto dicendo è molto semplice. Osserva una normale bambolina cinese: ha le lentiggini? Eh? No, non le ha. Ti hanno mandato l'unica che ha le lentiggini? E allora . . . Rimandala indietro!. . . No, non dovresti! NON dovresti pagare le spese di reso. Ficcala in quel box e rimandala indietro. Oh, no! Hai pagato! Hai visto la foto sul catalogo, l'hai addebitata sulla tua carta di credito e adesso dovresti avere ciò per cui hai pagato!. . . C'erano foto di una ragazza con le lentiggini? No! Ok. La mia opinione è. . . Posso avere una mia opinione?!. . . NO, perché questa si chiama FALSA DICHIARAZIONE!. . . Possono finire in galera per questo, lo sai? Yeah, puoi procacciarti un sacco di belle ragazze dalla Cina . . .

Scompare dietro una porta del palcoscenico. La sua vestaglia rimane impigliata nella porta, e la tira con rabbia. **Amleto** *si gira e le tira dietro una scarpa, ma manca il colpo. Gli spuntano un paio di ali da pipistrello e torna a guardare la TV.*

Ofelia (*continua a dattilografare come se niente fosse*)   Il terrore, caro, il terrore; voglio che ti riempia o che tu lo prenda in carico. A te la scelta: la prosperità attende con impazienza i nostri poveri geni per scomparire, ed essere immortalata in dodici libbre di carbone e di intelletto. Sì, sì, caro, sono certa che la procreazione possa essere fonte di infinita gioia per le masse, ma noi siamo molto più raffinati. Cerca di capire, le voci nella mia testa non

possono essere sommerse dal pianto di un bambino; devi sapere
che persino le urla che produco con tanta grazia quando tu eserciti
pietosamente il tuo diritto all'intorpidimento post-coitale . . .
L'intorpidimento. . . (*Pausa. Mentre lei dattilografa,* **Amleto**
guarda dei porno soft.) Il terrore, caro, il terrore; di questo stavo
parlando, non dell'intorpidimento. Sono sicura che se provassi a
fartelo venire un po' più duro, ce la faresti. Il tuo pene è stato
misurato con attenzione e le sue qualità esistenziali sono state
accertate con piena responsabilità, vista la mia incapacità di curare
il tuo ego ferito e definire i patti del nostro affascinante incontro,
che spero ci lascerà ugualmente insoddisfatti. La lunghezza del tuo
pene è proporzionale all'angoscia che proverò fumando una
sigaretta tra le tue braccia stanche, contemplando la probabilità
statistica di un tumore al polmone o di un attacco di cuore causato
da insaziabilità sessuale, con tutta la paura di non avere le cure
appropriate. Amleto, caro, non parlare di politica, dei tuoi desideri,
del mondo, della morte e del sangue che hai versato piangendo per
i bambini che muoiono di fame.

Ofelia, *indossando un abito da sposa, attraversa il palcoscenico
accompagnata da* **Gertrude** *e da* **Orazio**. **Gertrude** *cavalca un
cavallo a dondolo e brandisce una spada.* **Orazio** *indossa un abito
da sera, calze a rete e tacchi rossi. Ha i capelli tirati indietro,
sorregge un piatto di gamberetti e un block-notes.*

Ofelia (*cammina su e giù per le scale in abito da sposa*)   Che tu
sia benedetto . . .

Orazio   Questi gamberetti sembrano un po' avariati. Forse dovrei
chiamare il catering. Tu non vuoi che nessuno vomiti.
Bisognerebbe proprio cominciare a stipulare un'assicurazione di
nozze per cose di questo genere. Che ne pensi?

Ofelia   Ti sei mai chiesto se stai con la persona giusta?

Orazio (*alzando gli occhi dal suo block-notes*)   Certo che no,
tesoro. Non puoi mai *stare* davvero con la persona giusta. Ciò che
lo rende giusto, è il fatto che tu non stai con lui. Ciò che lo rende
sbagliato, è il fatto che tu stai con lui. (*Tornando al block-notes.*)
Da dove arrivano i gamberetti? La Bella Tosca o Christie's?

Ofelia   Christie's. Devi assicurarti che lui sia l'unico. L'unico.

Gertrude   Oh, l'unico . . .

Ofelia (*consumandosi gli occhi dal piangere*)   Voglio che sia l'unico e per sempre, insieme, fino alla morte . . .

Gertrude   Vita, morte, amore o lussuria, l'universo è infinito e in espansione. Da dove venite? Dove state andando? *Quo vadis. Panta rei.* Grandi questioni, tesoro. Ma, a dispetto di quel che dice tuo padre, non ti pagheranno l'affitto. Dovresti prendere appunti adesso, riporli nel tuo nascondiglio segreto, e tirarli fuori quando sarai in pensione. Ti saranno davvero utili allora, tra lezioni di golf, pilates e vampate di calore. Dovresti proprio smetterla con queste occhiatacce. Il tuo trucco è tutto sbavato.

Amleto (*entra in smoking*)   Non avrai mica intenzione di sposare *lui*, vero?

Orazio (*alzando gli occhi*)   È l'unico. Non è l'unico.

Gertrude   L'unico per fare cosa?

Ofelia   Per guarire la vostra anima . . .

Gertrude *e* **Orazio** *si guardano e cominciano a ridere istericamente.*

Gertrude   Come quell'altro?

Orazio   O quell'altro ancora.

Gertrude (*filosoficamente*)   O un altro ancora.

Le campane cominciano a suonare e **Gertrude** *e* **Orazio** *si trasformano in avatar. Si interrompono e, al sintetizzatore, la loro voce si dissolve in ripetizioni assurde: «L'unico, o l'altro, quale?, Qualcuno, chiunque, nessuno, quello che stavamo aspettando, o l'altro ancora, quello che stavano aspettando, voi stavate aspettando? Chi sta aspettando? Quale?»*

Amleto (*parlando dallo schermo, come le campane che battono i rintocchi*)   Acquietatevi con le grida del lupo dei bambini nulla è reale, se non

i capelli impiastricciati dal vomito.
Stasera –
dormirai senza sognare.
Domani –
squarcia la tua pelle e lascia che per noi
cominci la lezione di anatomia del dottor Tulp.

Ding dong – *il suono della stazione degli autobus. La voce
dell'annunciatore borbotta qualcosa di incomprensibile.*

Ofelia *sta portando una valigia e un finto cuscino pieno di teste di
manichini. Entra con fare circospetto, guardando l'orario degli
autobus e cercando di capire a che ora parte una corsa. È fermata
da* **Amleto***, che porta al collo una pesante catena d'oro.*

Amleto   Ehi, dove stai andando?

Ofelia   A trovare un amico.

Amleto (*dandole un'occhiata*)   Di dove sei?

Ofelia   Huston, Maine.

Amleto   Dove?

Ofelia   È una piccola città, nessuno sa dove si trova.

Amleto   È una città universitaria? Sei in un college?

Ofelia   No.

Amleto   Che ci stai a fare laggiù? (*Lei tace, sorride in modo
fiacco ed è chiaramente a disagio.*) Eh, lo so, è roba da ragazzi.
Dai, che ti ha sfinita ben bene. Eh-eh. Dai, che ti ha conciata per le
feste. Dovresti venire qui, a New York.

Ofelia   Hmm.

Amleto   Cos'hai lì dentro?

Ofelia   Qui?

Amleto   Uh-huh.

Ofelia   Queste sono teste di manichini. Mi sto esercitando a fare
la parrucchiera.

Ding dong. *L'annunciatore del Port Authority Bus Terminal: «Alle 2.30 l'autobus per Cleveland è in partenza dalla pensilina 5. Per favore, non dimenticate i vostri bagagli».*

Ofelia   Ecco il mio autobus.

Lui aspetta che lei dica qualcosa. Ma lei tace, e così lui se ne va. Lei lotta con il finto cuscino e lentamente se lo trascina dietro, scomparendo dietro le quinte. Lui si volta a sputare e la segue.

'Dream a Little Dream of Me', comincia la registrazione. **Ofelia,** *seduta alla sua scrivania, beve un sorso di vino.* **Amleto** *molla il suo telecomando e comincia la registrazione di un videogame. Su di loro cominciano a cadere delle foglie autunnali rinsecchite. Non appena si apre la porta, la musica si ferma di colpo.*

Entra **Gertrude,** *parlando al telefono. Indossa la stessa vestaglia, ma ha metà chioma fuori dalla retina che trattiene i bigodini. I suoi capelli, come quelli della Medusa, sono sparpagliati ai quattro venti. Cammina per il palcoscenico mentre parla al telefono e sfoglia il catalogo.*

Gertrude   . . . quale pensi che debba prendere? Quelle dalla Russia, dalla Romania o dalla Cina? Quelle dalla Russia sembrano buone, tutte bionde e carine, ma dicono che siano guaste. Con tutta la vodka che hanno bevuto le loro madri . . . Di quelle dalla Romania non sono sicura: sembrano pallide, bionde ma troppo pallide. Potrebbero essere malnutrite. Lo stesso per quelle dall'Africa. Ma sono così esotiche! Vorrei fare bella figura, come quando sfoggio la mia borsa Chanel. O, meglio ancora, Hermès . . . Che garanzia c'è su di loro?. . . Due anni? Puoi ottenere una garanzia più lunga?. . . Cosa succede se una muore? Ne mandano una nuova per rimpiazzarla? Le spese del funerale le coprono loro?. . . E le spese di spedizione? Io non ho intenzione di pagarle di nuovo. Venticinquemila dollari per tutte le pratiche burocratiche, affare fatto . . . Sì, hai ragione, tesoro: quelle dal Sud America sembrano così belle, non troppo scure e nemmeno troppo pallide . . . Uh-huh . . .

Se ne va, tutta contenta per la sua idea.

TV *(dallo schermo, ma è difficile dire se si tratta di una soap opera o di un romanzo classico)*   Questo dualismo della natura di

lei, lo spaventava. Ogni volta che era sicuro di possederla, gli occhi
di lei diventavano quelli di un'estranea. Per lui era così familiare
che poteva sentire la sua voce dentro, e così distante che
un'improvvisa solitudine invadeva ogni cellula del suo corpo,
ferendolo fisicamente e soffocandolo come la consapevolezza della
sua morte.

Amleto *è seduto sul divano e sta giocando con un videogame.*
La sua faccia si trasforma lentamente in quella di **Ofelia**. *Lei*
indossa un casco militare, che ha coperto con un velo nero.

Ofelia (*dallo schermo, come se recitasse una filastrocca per*
bambini)   Un giorno
la mia carne ci ha piantato in asso,
lasciando me e la mia pelle in uno stupito torpore.
Ci guardavamo divertiti,
non avevamo nient'altro da perdere.

Orazio (*leggendo alcuni documenti legali*)   Si stavano
preparando da mesi per questo bambino. Stavano comprando
tutto insieme: il presepe, il passeggino, gli indumenti. Tutto
era il migliore, il più costoso, dai cataloghi più esclusivi. Lui
le aveva comprato una macchina nuova di zecca per farla andare
e tornare dall'università senza dover aspettare l'autobus. Quando
seppero che era una femmina, lui ci rimase male. Desiderava
molto avere un maschio, per portare avanti ciò che aveva
cominciato. Fantasticava sulle cose che gli avrebbe insegnato.
Vergognandosi dei suoi sentimenti, nascose la sua delusione e si
abituò all'idea di una femmina: la incoraggiò durante la
gravidanza, sopportando pazientemente i suoi accessi di malumore
e la sua accidentale malinconia. Lei stava portando in grembo la
sua creatura. Per la prima volta le fu ufficialmente permesso di
torturarlo, e pian piano scoprì che non c'era alcun limite a quel che
poteva fare. Il risentimento che provava contro di lui per tutte le
volte in cui aveva dovuto adattarsi agli umori del suo fragile ego
maschile, non aveva fatto che esasperare la sua immaginazione.
Man mano lo schiacciò con una sempre più raffinata crudeltà, e lui
sopportava tutto con un misto di senso del dovere, soggezione e
stupore.

*Il rumore di un aeroplano o di un elicottero in volo, e l'ombra
delle ali sul palcoscenico.* **Ofelia** *spiega le sue ali nere e comincia
a fluttuare. Si trasforma in un corvo. I suoni della grande città:
un'ambulanza, una sparatoria, ragazze che ridono, qualcuno che
grida, un cane che abbaia per la strada.* **Ofelia** *osserva tutto
dall'alto. Il suo corpo si frantuma in migliaia di piccoli pezzi, che
svolazzando cerca di raccogliere in un carrello della spesa. La
donna delle pulizie del supermercato butta fuori* **Ofelia** *a calci, e*
Ofelia *le cava gli occhi.*

Amleto   Gocce di luce
per accarezzare le ombre sui fogli bianchi
che odorano di sangue, disinfettante e
urina di ieri.
In quale cassetto hai riposto tutte le tue insonnie
e i mosaici formati dalle macchie di muffa sul soffitto
dove finisce il tuo orizzonte?

Ofelia *entra su una sedia a rotelle, spinta da un'infermiera
dell'esercito.*

Ofelia   Eccomi su una sedia a rotelle, mi sono improvvisamente
fracassata: con chi potrei stringere un patto di alleanza? Se si
fosse trattato di una donna, la risposta sarebbe stata facile. Se
si fosse trattato di una invalida, la risposta sarebbe stata facile.
Se si fosse trattato di una donna e di una invalida, la risposta
sarebbe stata facile. Ma nella figura del maschio invalido c'è
un'intrinseca impossibilità esistenziale: è un nemico o un fratello
martire? È frenato dal suo sesso o dalla sua sedia a rotelle? Dal
momento che non posso stabilire una mia linea politica verso i
maschi invalidi, ho preventivamente deciso di evitarli del tutto.
Fondamentalmente oppressi dalla loro virilità ferita, i maschi
invalidi sono qualcosa che io – con la mia femminilità ferita – sono
per natura incline a evitare. Incapace di affrontare le mie stesse
contraddizioni – che oscillano tra il voler essere desiderata e il
voler essere rispettata – ho bisogno di un uomo emotivamente a
bassa manutenzione, generoso all'infinito, il cui ego e la cui mente
siano forti e vigorosi come il suo cazzo che non vacilla mai, con
cui potrebbe convincermi più e più volte del mio sconfinato

sex-appeal, e persino dei gusti acquisiti e della mia affascinate personalità che lo ha catturato in modo totale, senza riserve.

La sedia a rotelle si gira, e il manichino di **Ofelia** *sparisce. L'infermiera spolvera il cuscino e comincia a correre in tondo: sa che non può avere una sedia a rotelle vuota, e così la riempie con tutto quel che può.*

TV: *talk-show o serie prime-time. Consulenza matrimoniale.* **Amleto** *e* **Ofelia** *sono seduti sul divano.*

L'analista   Salve, benvenuti. È molto importante per voi avere un problema da condividere.

Amleto   Nessun problema.

L'analista (*deluso*)   Nessun problema?

Amleto   Beh, un problema c'è. Noi non abbiamo nessun problema nel condividere il problema con lei.

L'analista   Bene, ottimo. Allora, qual è il problema?

Amleto   È terribile, non posso credere a ciò che ha fatto. Ha rovinato le nostre vite.

Ofelia   Oh, tesoro, cosa ho fatto! Cosa ho fatto! Se mi hai appena detto . . . Oh, tesoro (*piange*). Se solo tu potessi dirmi *cosa*, sono certa che tutto filerebbe nel modo giusto. Non mettere in pericolo il nostro amore e il nostro matrimonio con il tuo silenzio.

L'analista   Sì, tutto sta nella comunicazione. Se tu potessi dircelo, noi capiremmo. Se tu potessi condividere i tuoi sentimenti con tua moglie, i vostri sentimenti sarebbero condivisi.

Amleto   Cosa ha fatto? Cosa ha fatto? Non riesco nemmeno a parlarne. Guarda, al pensiero sto ancora tremando. Non riesco a credere che l'abbia fatto. Non posso credere che mi abbia fatto questo . . .

Ofelia & L'analista   Ma che è successo?

Amleto   Volete saperlo? Volete saperlo? Bene, ve lo dirò. Ieri mattina, a colazione . . . (*Sussurra qualcosa all'orecchio dell'* **analista**.)

L'analista   Odddiiiioooo!

Amleto   Sì, questo è quel che ha fatto.

L'analista   Di certo è una situazione difficile. Però sono sicuro che, se noi la risolveremo, sarà risolta. I divorzi sono la causa principale del divorzio. Ma tutto il resto va bene?

Ofelia   Oh, sì. Tutto il resto va bene. Abbiamo un ottimo matrimonio.

Amleto   Oh, sì. Il lavoro va bene, i soldi ci sono, i bambini sono morti.

L'analista   Solo allora si può dire di aver raggiunto una condizione di vera saggezza, quando non si permette alle emozioni di interferire con l'imparzialità oggettiva nel giudizio intellettuale. La conclusione che si raggiunge deve sempre essere data a priori, o dedotta dall'esperienza empirica che si è accumulata. Non ci si deve mai fidare nel fare dichiarazioni che sono prive di una profonda imparzialità intellettuale. Solo allora si può dire qualcosa di veramente e profondamente imparziale, di veramente e imparzialmente profondo. (*È sorpreso per la sua stessa ingegnosità, sorride e annuisce con la testa valutando ciò che ha appena detto, ma se lo scorda subito e comincia a pulirsi il naso.*)

Ofelia (*alla scrivania, intenta a dattilografare*)   Com'è singolare quella cosa chiamata piacere, e quanto è curiosamente collegata al dolore, al punto che si potrebbe pensare come il suo opposto; non arrivano mai a un uomo insieme, eppure chi insegue l'uno, generalmente è costretto a prendere l'altro.

TV (*lezione*)   La donna, il cui piacere sessuale è originariamente auto-rappresentativo in modo diverso da quello dell'uomo, potrebbe anche non avere un clitoride: l'imene che resta per sempre (*in*)violato, su cui il seme è sparso nella disseminazione, non serve all'utero. È questa la scena di violenza che si chiama amore in trasformazione contenuta nella nostra unica perfetta triade? Se le donne sono sempre state usate come strumento di auto-decostruzione maschile, questa è l'ultima svolta della filosofia?

Ofelia (*da analista*)   Mi piace credere che tu sai quel che stai facendo, e non sei solo intrappolato negli imbrogli autolesionisti della virilità americana, che alla fine ti lasceranno emotivamente svuotato, intellettualmente affamato e sessualmente incompetente.

Amleto (*con aria indifferente, mentre gioca con un videogame*)   Vuoi che ti ammazzi in una drammatica scenata di gelosia, così schiacciante da farmi perdere i sensi? Vuoi che ti ammazzi mentre stai venendo, così potrai fonderti con l'universo nell'orgasmo eterno, e potrai pensare di vivere per sempre catturata in questo attimo? Vuoi che ti ammazzi mentre ti sussurro all'orecchio dolci scemenze sulla mia disperazione? Vuoi che ti ammazzi e poi ti segua suicidandomi, in un dramma della morte diretto con attenta regia?

Ofelia *fluttua nello spazio. Prova ad afferrare qualche pagliuzza, ma il mondo scompare all'orizzonte. Prova a camminare, ma non c'è nessuna superficie su cui farlo. Trova il telecomando e lo manovra disperatamente per un po'. Resti umani e carcasse di animali galleggiano sul fiume Gange.* **Ofelia** *si lava i capelli e lascia le orme sulla sabbia del deserto. Il suo cuore sanguina. Le sue vene sono fatte di fili metallici.* **Ofelia** *trasporta il suo stesso cadavere oltre il confine del deserto.*

Amleto   Se dovessi camminare in una valle oscura,
    non temerei alcun male, perché sei con me;
    il tuo bastone e il tuo vincastro mi danno sicurezza.
    Davanti a me tu prepari una mensa, sotto gli occhi dei miei nemici.

Ofelia (*è seduta alla sua scrivania, in mimetica militare verde. Con calma stoica, continua a dattilografare come se niente fosse*)   Per favore, tesoro, l'auto-deprezzamento non è un agente necessario nel valore di mercato individuale; la nostra purezza è del tutto formale, così come le nostre perversioni tanto care a tua madre e pubblicizzate in ogni spot commerciale. Tesoro, devi sapere che lei si è automaticamente preservata per la prima notte di nozze con candele e desideri plasmati con cura in TV, perciò è una novità per la nostra generazione. Il terrore, tesoro, il terrore. Credo fermamente in

Dio e nella dignità umana, tranne quando ci si trova in trincea con la testa abbattuta dalla virtù di qualcun altro e ciò si commette in nome della passione per la vita, così come credo che tu sia l'unico in grado di raggiungere le profondità interiori con un'intensità sconosciuta alle mie membra indebolite. Sì, sì, tesoro, mi puoi scrivere una poesia o mi puoi scopare con una certa foga, ma sono sicura che in ogni caso rimarremo fedeli a una nostra convinzione di lunga data: l'immortalità è portata a compimento dalla bontà del cuore, mentre l'unione delle anime è tormentata dall'odio reciproco e dall'amore verso gli altri, che passano le loro giornate nell'armonia dei rituali igienici, del discorso postmoderno a vari livelli intellettuali, e del lavoro che ci renderà liberi dall'abbondanza materialistica o dalle carenze – a seconda che la procreazione abbia raggiunto la sua media statistica, o si esprima nell'individualismo egoistico dell'auto-adorazione. Sono certa che la mia convinzione mi lascerà fiducia in me stessa così come farebbe una qualsiasi altra cosa, per cui mi ringrazierai quando ti verserò un bicchiere di vino e ti massaggerò le spalle. La punta del tuo pene ha un potenziale ontologico, sicché ficco la tua spada nella tua uretra per esaminare se lo spazio è ingannevole a sufficienza per assorbire il mio terrore e tutti gli altri accidentalmente lasciati dai futuri padri d'America e dei cinque continenti, considerando la globalizzazione delle nostre abitudini sessuali. Il padre di mia nonna è misteriosamente morto da qualche parte tra Praga e Vienna, esattamente come faremo noi.

Entra **Orazio**, *portando dei gamberetti su un vassoio d'argento.*

Orazio (*rivolgendosi ad* **Amleto**, *che è ancora seduto sul divano*)   Gamberetti?

Amleto   Grazie, ma sono a dieta.

Di colpo **Orazio** *ricorda qualcosa e alza il pugno urlando: «Libertà!» È investito da un carro armato, e il suo corpo scompare nell'asfalto nero. Un gruppo di allegri bambini è investito sul selciato, ridono e si tengono per mano. I corvi neri beccano la carne di* **Orazio**. *Il suono della stazione degli autobus.* Ding dong.

L'annunciatore   L'autobus da Parigi a New York, passando per Londra e Tokyo, è in partenza dalla pensilina 5. L'autobus da

Parigi a New York, passando per Londra e Tokyo, è in partenza dalla pensilina 5.

L'annunciatore *ripete più volte, come se ci fosse il meccanismo inceppato. Non appena parte il messaggio, entra* **Ofelia**. *Indossa un abito da sposa macchiato di sangue e un foulard da testa. Sta cercando di trovare la pensilina giusta. La segue* **Orazio**, *che porta un vassoio d'argento con sopra una testa umana guarnita da gamberetti.*

Ofelia (*impazzita*)   L'unico, l'unico. Io sono l'unico. Io sono quello che stavo aspettando. Io sono l'unico. Uno, l'unico, quello. L'unico, il Santo, l'intrinsecamente **uno, il benedetto**.

Orazio (*senza prestarle attenzione*)   Quelli di Christie's sono più freschi. Dai, ordiniamoli da Christie's.

Ofelia *si toglie gli stivali dell'esercito e batte* **Orazio** *a morte; il suo corpo scompare nell'asfalto nero.* **Ofelia** *si mette con le braccia spalancate.* **Amleto** *comincia a giocare con il cellulare. Accovacciata sul pavimento della stazione degli autobus,* **Ofelia** / **Medea** *canta per il suo bambino morto.*

Ofelia / Medea   Che il Suo grande nome sia benedetto nei secoli dei secoli.
Benedetto, lodato, glorificato, esaltato, magnificato, potente, possente e acclamato sia il Nome del Santo.
Benedetto è Lui.

Amleto   Hai letto il dolore nei miei occhi e pensi di sapere tutto. Pensi di poter capire un uomo dal suo dolore. Lo pensi perché puoi capire il dolore di un uomo che ti appartiene, sempre e per sempre.

TV (*National Geographic Channel*)   La cimice maschio ha un pene strutturato per iniettare e distribuire lo sperma nella femmina. Questa tecnica è molto violenta, dal momento che la femmina viene immobilizzata e infilzata nel corpo diverse volte per assicurare l'inseminazione. Tale metodo si è sviluppato per dribblare il passaggio genitale della femmina, limitando ed eliminando qualsiasi controllo sui tempi che di solito lei ha sul suo concepimento.

Ofelia   Quando il corpo sarà il mio padrone, non ne avrò altri.
(*Urlando.*) Quando il corpo sarà il mio padrone, non ne avrò altri.

Amleto *cambia canale.*

Ofelia (*sorseggia vino e continua a scrivere*)   Gli atti
raccapriccianti di auto-rivelazione hanno il loro punto di partenza
nella benevolenza della propria mente verso le classi inferiori di
stirpe volgare. Sono sicura, tesoro, che il terrore che ti ho descritto
con tanta cura non ha un significato etico per il tuo benessere. Sono
anche certa che tu troverai un ricambio al mio squilibrio emotivo
tanto facilmente quanto lo farò io, in ogni creatura che le nostre
menti desidereranno. La scelta, segnata in modo così evidente dal
mio auto-appassimento, dipende esclusivamente dal tuo livello di
serotonina e dal desiderio prodotto da questa notte particolare. La
mia offerta è valida per il tempo della tua erezione, e scade al
momento dell'eiaculazione delle tue pietose paranoie sul mio volto
in attesa. Il desiderio costruito come una funzione matematica ha il
vantaggio della variabilità e della permanenza delle sue aspettative
che, replicate in frazioni proporzionali, acquisiscono la qualità
immateriale di una struttura solida fondamentalmente
indistinguibile da qualsiasi altra soluzione acida per i problemi
interiorizzati durante l'infanzia e rimandati per il consumo con un
calice di Chardonnay o di Sauvignon de Blanco, e pesce
delicatamente preparato in salsa di limone e caviale.

Passa **Gertrude***, parlando al telefono. Ora si è trasformata in una
macchina.*

Gertrude   Il catalogo non dice che la soddisfazione è garantita?
Ti mandano una ragazza difettosa e pensano che tu ne sia
innamorato cotto . . . Rimandala indietro e digli di mandartene una
come quella della foto, senza lentiggini . . . Di questi tempi, tesoro,
il denaro non va sciupato. Ieri ho comprato delle calze 'made in
China'. Erano difettate – te lo sto dicendo, aha-aha – e così ho fatto
un reso. Di questi tempi, non ci si può permettere di buttare via
tutti questi soldi per merce difettosa. – aha-aha – Tu hai pagato per
avere una cosa, loro ti hanno mandato la cosa sbagliata, tu la
rimandi indietro e ti riprendi il valore dei soldi . . . Yeah, yeah,
questo è quel che ti sto dicendo.

Gertrude *scompare. Comincia a nevicare.*

Amleto (*alla chetichella, come se stesse rivelando un segreto*)
A volte, quando camminiamo
uno negli occhi dell'altra come attraverso cancelli . . .
A volte, io sono come lei.
A volte, lei è quello
che sono io.

Ofelia (*continuando a dattilografare freneticamente*)   La mano destra tiene l'amore eterno con tutti i suoi fantasmi, predicamenti di una nauseante salvezza e di una squadrata routine di metafore riciclate dai cadaveri degli ex amanti e da insetti caduti in libri aperti a metà. Prometto di aver cura di me stessa: trovo così toccante il fatto di trovarmi nei tuoi occhi, proprio in quelle pupille che ti supplico così ardentemente di non chiudere quando sto venendo, e in cui le mie smorfie sono ingrandite per intelligibile invenzione della nostra immaginazione. Prometto anche di includere la tua stabilità, così a lungo desiderata e confusamente intessuta da attacchi occasionali del mio ego, per mantenerti stabile nella domanda e nell'offerta. Prometto di soddisfare le nostre fantasie edipiche e di affittare il mio utero disinteressatamente, per un'oasi e un WC in cui ci potremo alleggerire delle nostre preziose feci di sforzi intellettuali. Sono certa che l'accordo soddisferà il 40% della massa, lasciando il rimanente 60% con una bruciante insaziabilità di sospetti e di perpetuità fisica di leggerezza e gravità. La mia mano sinistra offre un amore non corrisposto: che sia il mio o il tuo, lo stabiliremo dopo. Sono sicura che, in entrambi i casi, ci adatteremo ai nostri ruoli con la naturale grazia di servo e padrone. Il desiderio è proporzionale al tempo di attesa. Tesoro, lei ha fatto pratica con le migliori puttane d'Europa, Nord America e Asia. Quelle che sei andato a trovare nelle notti solitarie o di sbornia, e nelle quali hai ficcato il tuo pene mezzo moscio nella speranza di un temporaneo sollievo dall'incubo del desiderio o dalla sua mancanza.

Ofelia *si ferma. Si ricompone. Tira fuori una pistola dal cassetto e se la punta alla testa. Echeggia uno sparo, c'è sangue dappertutto. Continua a dattilografare come se niente fosse.*

Ofelia   La malattia della morte ci sovrasta. Non vogliamo morire e non viviamo. Il terrore tra possessore e posseduto si stabilisce con la velocità di un ladro che ha rubato troppo per provare piacere e troppo poco per sentire altro, e se ne va con un insensibile sorriso di disprezzo, gridando nascosto dietro agli angoli raggelati dell'auto-perpetuazione. I miei pensieri non scorrono con la facilità del tuo corpo promesso, né ribollono con grata insaziabilità . . .

TV (*National Geographic Channel*)   Lo scorpione maschio e lo scorpione femmina si avvinghiano in un intenso abbraccio, sferzandosi a vicenda con i loro pungiglioni. Tenendo le bocche chiuse, il maschio infilza ripetutamente la femmina con la sua coda. Per ritorsione, spesso la femmina annienta il suo compagno.

Entra **Ofelia**. *Il suo abito da sposa è a brandelli. Ha alcuni dispositivi di detonazione legati con una cinghia al petto.*

Ofelia   la fame che sento non è in me
      scorre fuori e dentro
      nelle mie braccia rapaci
      perdi te stesso
      non si può essere salvati e restare condannati
      la fame che sento non è in me

Si mette sulla sedia a rotelle e si spinge fuori, ridendo istericamente.

TV News   Oggi, in California, una madre ha decapitato il proprio bambino e ne ha mangiato il cervello. (*Per un attimo la telecronista sembra triste, poi torna velocemente a un sorriso smagliante.*) E ora un'altra notizia, stavolta dal nostro 'lifestyle guru', che risponderà alla domanda più importante della stagione . . .

Comincia a suonare 'Jingle Bells'.

Sul fondale la faccia di **Amleto** *si mescola al videogame con cui sta giocando.* **Amleto** *è sul divano, e nel videogame si alza per togliersi il cappello e la giacca. Va dietro le quinte, e porta una tanica di benzina che comincia a versare dappertutto.*

Ofelia (*continua a dattilografare, mentre* **Amleto** *sparge la benzina*)   Lontano, lontano, tesoro . . . Siamo definitivamente riusciti a convincerci della nostra stessa esistenza. Messa alle strette, non ho altra scelta, se non quella di perpetuare questa convinzione. Ti prego di non negarmi ciò che appartiene di diritto a qualcun altro. Conosco il tuo impegno nelle verità e nelle falsità. Al servizio di drammi di fedi perdute, e di quelle acquistate in aste silenziose al museo degli organi di cera e delle anime. Voglio che tu capisca davvero che le promesse uscite dalle mie labbra non sono traducibili. Lego i tuoi pensieri e i miei con una peculiare attenzione ai dettagli. Volevi provare l'amore o qualsiasi cosa in materia. Il teatro dei desideri è aperto per la pubblica esibizione agli spettatori curiosi e ignari gli uni degli altri. Li ho visti ieri: passavano in città, quando noi piangevamo nascosti sotto il letto che si rifiutava di essere domato. Sono uscita con la tua testa sotto il braccio. Inciampo, inciampo nelle parole attaccate al loro potere. Non piangere, caro, la notte sta arrivando.

Accende un fiammifero. Blackout.

La Máquina de Ofelia

Translation by Camila Ymay González

Una tienda de autos, un cuarto de almacenaje o la sala de juego de un niño, llena de objetos reunidos por un viajero perdido: el David *sin brazos de Miguel Ángel lleva puesto un casco de motociclista, una pila de máscaras africanas rotas, el esqueleto de un poeta muerto riéndose histéricamente de su propia sombra, una muñeca sin sus extremidades chupando un lollipop rosado, el paraguas roto de Magritte, el teléfono viejo de Andy Warhol para contactar a Dios, un velo de matrimonio blanco y sucio colgando en alguna parte junto a más ropa, pilas de zapatos viejos y pelucas.*

Es una tierra baldía moderna, con consolas de videojuegos rotas, pantallas de televisión, y pantallas de computadores mostrando al azar escenas mudas de nuestras vidas virtuales: escenas de guerra, matanzas, genocidios, cuerpos de Auschwitz, porno, propaganda política, mujeres de Wall Street, mujeres gordas, mujeres anoréxicas, colegialas japonesas, mujeres vestidas con burkas, safaris salvajes, explosiones de libros de comic. **Hamlet** *y* **Ofelia** *beben esta sopa diaria de noticias e imágenes: una mezcolanza de contraste humano entre belleza y horror, inocencia y violencia.*

Todo está cubierto de ceniza radioactiva.

Hamlet, *vestido con jeans, una chaqueta del siglo XVI, y un sombrero de cowboy, se sienta en el sofá enfrentando a la audiencia. Mira televisión, cambiando mecánicamente las estaciones con el control remoto. Al fondo del escenario, se proyecta la mezcolanza de imágenes.* **Hamlet** *quiere entender el mundo, pero lo único que puede hacer es mirarlo.*

Atrás de él a su izquierda, **Ofelia**, *vestida de verde camuflaje militar, se sienta detrás de un escritorio flotante tipeando algo en una máquina de escribir antigua. Al lado, una copa de vino tinto rojo sangre. Ella fuma un cigarrillo y está totalmente enfocada en tipear.*

Hamlet *y* **Ofelia** *son los dos extremos del mundo. Entre ellos, el océano Atlántico lleno de cadáveres pudriéndose, pájaros muertos y orina.*

Ofelia (*tipeando*)　**Hamlet**, querido, no deseo identificarme contigo o con ella, tus soldados de juguete invadieron mi lado de la cama. Los océanos y continentes intercambian fácilmente por nostalgia política y resiliencia. Deja que los muertos entierren a los muertos, la plaga de nuestros padres. (*Hace una pausa y toma un sorbo de su vino.*)

Hamlet (*sin prestar atención, recordando tiempos mejores*)   En los dados desdichados

– seis camas por siete noches –
larvas recién nacidas se acoplan
en las orillas de su propio aserrín.

Ofelia (*continúa, inalterada*)   . . . escribir es una forma de masturbación intelectual. Desparramo mi pobre y patético yo sobre el ojo blanco de mi computador, orgullosa de dominar este difícil arte de la auto indulgencia, y así entrar a la nueva era de placeres solipsísticos. Mi auto suficiencia me deslumbra. Oh, esos puntos erotogénicos en mi cerebro, examinados pensativamente en ataques megalomaníacos de auto adoración. Si, si, ahora mismo, la guardaré automáticamente para más tarde. (*Hace una pausa y fuma de su cigarrillo.*)

TV (*señal de la National Geographic*)   Durante su ritual de apareamiento, el águila blanca hembra traba sus talones con el macho, demandando su total sumisión mientras caen en picada inertemente hacia el suelo. Sí él trata de liberarse antes de que ella esté lista, ella nunca lo dejará montarla. Sí ella espera tan solo unos segundos de más, ambos se estrellarán mortalmente en el suelo.

El sonido de un tren pasando a máxima velocidad, silbando como si tratara de advertirle a alguien parado en las vías del tren. El tren pasa. Medianoche en la estación Port Authority. Ding dong, el sonido del anunciador, balbuceando algo. **Hamlet** *continúa viendo televisión.*

Ofelia (*dándolo por hecho*)   La mayoría de las chicas en la estación Port Authority son del Bronx o Harlem. Se visten con pañuelos imitación Chanel en sus cabezas y con bolsos imitación Louis Vuitton bajo sus hombros. Tratan de verse a la moda y bien mantenidas, como si tuviesen un hombre para el que valen el par de cientos de dólares en lujos aparentemente inútiles. Algunas de

ellas tienen bebés o niños pequeños, sujetándolos con una tranquila
desesperación. Nunca se quién necesita más a quién: si ellas a sus
bebés, o sus bebés a ellas. Se sientan en el suelo o en sus maletas,
esperando pacientemente por sus autobuses. A veces, ellas andan
con un hombre, y sus ojos brillan con una suave satisfacción. Se
ven frágiles y fuertes, como si en cualquier minuto pudiesen
comenzar a llorar o a maldecir.

Ofelia *vuelve a tipear. Suena el teléfono. El sonido de un tranvía
pasando. Un niño llora en el departamento de al lado. Entra*
Gertrudis. *Cruza el escenario, lleva puesta una bata y unos tubos
onduladores en la cabeza. Se limpia los dientes con los dedos y
habla por teléfono. Sus ojos brillan.*

Gertrudis   ¡Ay no, Dios mío! ¿Tenía pecas? Ósea, hello, tú
SABES lo que YO PIENSO sobre eso. A ver . . . mira lo único que
estoy diciendo es muy simple. Tú miras a cualquier muñeca de
porcelana china ¿Tiene pecas? ¿Ah? No, no tiene. ¿La que te
enviaron tiene pecas? Entonces . . . ¡Devuélvela! . . . ¡No, no
deberías hacer eso! NO DEBERÍAS tener que pagar por el envío
de la devolución. Métela de vuelta en la caja y devuélvela. ¡Ay no!
¡Ya pagaste! . . . ¡Tú viste la foto en el catálogo, usaste tu tarjeta de
crédito y ahora tienes que recibir lo que pagaste! . . . ¿Había fotos
con una niña con pecas? ¡No! Ok. Mi punto . . . ¡Ya expresé mi
punto! . . . ¡NO, porque esto se llama FALSA
REPRESENTACIÓN! . . . Te pueden meter a la cárcel por eso,
sabías . . . Si, puedes conseguir muchas niñas buenas de China . . .

*Ella desaparece por una puerta del escenario. Su bata se queda
atascada en la puerta y ella la tira enojada.* **Hamlet** *gira y le tira
un zapato, pero falla. Le crecen alas de murciélago y vuelve a
mirar la televisión.*

Ofelia (*continúa tipeando como nada hubiese pasado*)   La
angustia, querido, la angustia; quiero que la suplantes o te hagas
cargo. Es tu decisión: la prosperidad está esperando
impacientemente que nuestros genes arrepentidos sean entregados
e inmortalizados en cinco kilos de carbón e intelecto. Si, si
querido, estoy segura de que procrear puede ser una fuente
inagotable de felicidad para las masas, pero nosotros somos mucho

más refinados. Debes entender, las voces en mi cabeza no pueden ser ensordecidas por el llanto de un niño; debes saber, incluso los gritos que produzco con tanta gracia cuando tú ejercitas compasivamente tu derecho a la insensibilidad postcoital . . . insensibilidad . . . (*Pausa. Mientras ella tipea,* **Hamlet** *mira soft porn.*) hablaba de la angustia, querido, la angustia, no insensibilidad. Estoy segura de que si lo intentas un poco más, la alcanzarás. Tu pene fue medido cuidadosamente y sus cualidades existenciales fueron evaluadas con total responsabilidad por mi propio fracaso en curar tu ser herido y definir la convención de nuestro encantador encuentro el cual espero nos deje igualmente insatisfechos. El largo de tu pene es proporcional a la angustia que sentiré fumando un cigarrillo en tus brazos cansados, y contemplando la probabilidad estadística de cáncer al pulmón o un ataque al corazón provocado por insaciabilidad sexual, y miedos no bien cuidados. Hamlet, querido, no hables de política, de tus deseos, el mundo, la muerte y la sangre que derramaste llorando por los niños hambrientos.

Ofelia*, vistiendo un vestido de novia, cruza, acompañada de* **Horacio** *y* **Gertrudis**. **Gertrudis** *maneja un caballo mecedor, agitando una espada detrás de su cabeza.* **Horacio** *viste un esmoquin, calcetines de red, y tacos rojos. Su pelo está peinado hacia atrás. Lleva un plato con camarones y una libreta de notas.*

Ofelia (*subiendo y bajando las escaleras vestida de novia*)   Bendecidos ustedes . . .

Horacio   Ese camarón luce un poco deslucido. Quizás debería llamar a la compañía de catering. No vayas a querer que alguien se enferme. Deberían empezar a vender seguros de matrimonios para este tipo de cosas. ¿Qué cree tú?

Ofelia   ¿Te preguntas a veces si es que estás con la persona indicada?

Horacio (*mirando por encima de su libreta de notas*)   Por supuesto que no querida. Jamás podrías *estar* con la persona indicada. Lo que lo hace el indicado es el hecho de que tú no estás con él. Lo que lo hace incorrecto es el hecho de que tú estás con él. (*Volviendo a su libreta de notas.*) ¿De dónde provienen los camarones? ¿La Bella Tosca, o Christie's?

Ofelia   Christie's. Tú debes asegurarte de que él es el indicado. El indicado.

Gertrudis   Oh, el indicado . . .

Ofelia (*llorando desconsoladamente*)   Quiero al indicado y para siempre, juntos, hasta que la muerte . . .

Gertrudis   Vida, muerte, amor o lujuria, el universo es infinito y se está expandiendo. ¿De dónde vienes? ¿Hacia dónde vas? *Quo vadis. Panta rei.* Grandes preguntas, querida, pero, a pesar de lo que dice tu padre, ellas no van a pagar tu renta. Deberías escribirlas ahora, esconderlas en tu lugar secreto, y volver a sacarlas cuando te hayas jubilado. Serán muy útiles, entre las clases de golf, Pilates, y los bochornos. Deja de entrecerrar los ojos. Se te corre el maquillaje.

Hamlet (*entra vestido con esmoquin*)   ¿No te vas a casar realmente con *él*, o sí?

Horacio (*poniendo los ojos en blanco*)   Él es el indicado. Él no es el indicado.

Gertrudis   ¿El indicado para hacer qué?

Ofelia   Para sanar tu alma . . .

Gertrudis y **Horacio** *se miran y ríen histéricamente.*

Gertrudis   ¿Cómo el otro?

Horacio   O el otro

Gertrudis (*filosóficamente*)   U otro.

Campanas de iglesia comienzan a sonar y **Gertrudis** *y* **Horacio** *se convierten en avatares; salen, sus voces sintetizadas se disuelven en repeticiones absurdas: '¿El indicado, u otro, cuál, alguien, cualquiera, nadie, el que hemos estado esperando, o el otro, el que ellos han estado esperando, tú has estado esperando? ¿Quién ha estado esperando? ¿Cuál?'*

Hamlet (*hablando por una pantalla mientras suenan las campanas*)   Sédate a ti mismo con llantos de los hijos del lobo

nada es real sino que
pelo duro de vómito
esta noche –
tú dormirás sin soñar
mañana –
desabrocha tu piel y déjanos entrar
la clase de anatomía del Doctor Tulp puede comenzar

Ding dong – *el sonido de una parada de autobús. La voz del anunciador balbucea, inentendible.*

Ofelia *lleva una maleta y un cubre almohada lleno de cabezas de maniquís. Entra cuidadosamente, mira el horario del autobús y trata de averiguar a qué hora sale el autobús. Es detenida por* **Hamlet**. *Él lleva una cadena de oro en su cuello.*

Hamlet   Hey, adónde vas.

Ofelia   A visitar a un amigo.

Hamlet (*chequeándola*)   ¿De dónde eres?

Ofelia   Huston, Maine.

Hamlet   ¿Dónde queda?

Ofelia   Es un pueblo pequeño; nadie sabe dónde está.

Hamlet   ¿Es un pueblo universitario? ¿Vas a la universidad?

Ofelia   No.

Hamlet   ¿Qué haces aquí? (*Ella calla, sonriendo un poco, claramente incómoda.*) Jaja, ya sé, fue un tipo. Te engatusó. Jajaja. Te engatusó. Deberías venir a Nueva York.

Ofelia   Mmm

Hamlet   ¿Qué tienes ahí adentro?

Ofelia   ¿Esto?

Hamlet Aha.

Ofelia Son cabezas de maniquíes. Estoy estudiando para ser peluquera.

Ding dong. *El anunciador de Port Authority: 'El bus de las 2:30 a Cleveland sale por la puerta 5. Por favor, no olvide su equipaje.'*

Ofelia Ese es mi autobús.

Él espera a que ella diga algo, pero ella calla, por lo que él se va. A ella le pesa la funda de almohada y la arrastra lentamente, desapareciendo del escenario. Él escupe sobre su hombro y la sigue.

Comienza a sonar 'Dream a Little Dream of ME'. **Ofelia**, *sentada detrás de su escritorio, bebe un sorbo de vino.* **Hamlet** *suelta el control remoto y comienza a jugar un video juego. Hojas secas de otoño comienzan a caer sobre ellos. La música se detiene abruptamente al abrirse la puerta.*

Entra **Gertrudis**, *hablando por teléfono. Lleva la misma bata, pero la mitad de su cabeza ya no lleva tubos. Su pelo, como el de Medusa se mueve hacia las cuatro direcciones del mundo. Ella cruza el escenario, hablando por teléfono y mirando un catálogo.*

Gertrudis . . . ¿Cuál crees que debería tener? ¿La de Rusia, Rumania, o China? Las que vienen de Rusia se ven bien, lindas y rubias, pero dicen que están dañadas. Todo ese vodka ruso que sus madres bebían . . . No estoy muy segura sobre las que vienen de Rumania; se ven pálidas, rubias pero muy pálidas. Puede que estén desnutridas. Lo mismo con las de África. Pero son tan exóticas. Me vería bien con una en mi hombro junto a mi cartera Chanel. O mejor aún, Hermès . . . ¿Qué garantía tienen? . . . ¿Dos años? . . . ¿Puedes comprar una garantía extendida? . . . ¿Y si se muere? . . . ¿Te envían una nueva de reemplazo? . . . ¿Cubren los costos del funeral? . . . ¿Y el envío? No voy a pagar por el envío otra vez. Veinticinco mil por todo el papeleo – Eso es todo . . . Si, tienes razón querida, las de Sudamérica se ven muy bien, no muy oscuras, no muy pálidas . . . Aha . . .

Ella sale, muy contenta con su idea.

TV (*desde la pantalla, Es difícil diferenciar si es una telenovela o una novela clásica*)   La dualidad de su naturaleza lo asustaba. Cada vez que él creía haberla poseído, sus ojos se convertían en los de una extraña. En un instante ella era tan familiar que él podía escuchar su voz adentro de él, y tan distante que la súbita soledad que entraba en cada célula de su cuerpo lo dañaba físicamente y lo sofocaba como la conciencia de su muerte.

Hamlet *se sienta en el sofá jugando un video juego. Su cara lentamente se va transformando en la cara de* **Ofelia**. *Ella lleva un casco militar, que cubre con un pañuelo negro.*

Ofelia (*desde la pantalla, como si estuviese diciendo una rima para niños*)   Un día

mi carne nos abandonó
dejándome a mí y a mi piel en un sorpresivo estupor
no miramos mutuamente y nos causó gracia
no teníamos nada que perder

Horacio (*leyendo unos documentos legales*)   Desde hace meses que ellos se vienen preparando para este bebé. Han comprado todo junto, la cuna, el coche, la ropa. Todo era lo mejor, lo más caro, de los catálogos más exclusivos. Él le compró un auto nuevo para que ella pudiese ir y venir de la universidad sin tener que esperar por el autobús. Cuando supieron que sería una niña, él estaba decepcionado. El quería mucho tener un niño para que continuase lo que él había comenzado. Él fantaseaba sobre las cosas que le enseñaría. Avergonzado de sus sentimientos, él escondió su decepción, se acostumbró a la idea de tener una niña y la alegró durante el embarazo, lidiando pacientemente con sus ataques de mal humor y repentina melancolía. Ella llevaba a su bebé. Por primera vez, a ella se le permitía oficialmente torturarlo y ella lentamente descubrió que no había límite sobre lo que podía hacerle. El resentimiento que ella sintió hacia él por toda las veces que ella tuvo que complacer su frágil ego, solo exasperó su imaginación. Ella lo aplastaba una y otra vez con una crueldad cada vez más refinada y él lo soportó todo con una mezcla de deber, asombro y sorpresa.

El sonido de un avión o helicóptero volando por encima y la
sombra de unas alas en la escenografía. **Ofelia** *abre sus alas*
negras y comienza a flotar por encima. Se convierte en un cuervo.
Sonidos de la gran ciudad: una ambulancia, una balacera, niñas
riendo, alguien gritando y un perro ladrando en la calle. **Ofelia**
observa desde arriba. Su cuerpo se rompe en un millón de
pequeños pedazos que ella trata de juntar en una canasta de
supermercado. La mujer de la limpieza del supermercado expulsa
a **Ofelia**, *y* **Ofelia** *le saca los ojos.*

Hamlet   Luz cae

acariciando las sombras sobre sábanas blancas
oliendo a sangre, Lysol y
la orina de ayer.

¿En qué cajón has puesto todos tus insomnios
y mosaicos compuestos de las manchas de moho en el techo
donde termina tu horizonte?

Ofelia *entra en silla de ruedas, empujada por una enfermera militar.*

Ofelia   Como una chica en silla de ruedas, de pronto me encontré
dividida: ¿a quién debía declarar mi alianza? Si ese alguien fuese
una mujer, la respuesta era simple. Si ese alguien fuese un lisiado,
la respuesta era simple. Si ese alguien fuese una mujer y lisiada, la
respuesta era simple. Pero, había una imposibilidad existencial
intrínseca ahí en la figura del hombre lisiado: ¿era él un enemigo o
un hermano martirizado? ¿Unido a su sexo o a su silla de ruedas?
Ya que no pude decidir mis políticas sobre hombres lisiados, decidí
preventivamente evitarlos a todos.

Cagados fundamentalmente en su masculinidad herida, los
hombres lisiados eran algo que yo, con mi femineidad herida,
tendía naturalmente a evitar. Incapaz de lidiar con mis propias
contradicciones – entre querer ser deseada y querer ser respetada
– Yo necesitaba un hombre fácil de mantener emocionalmente, uno
infinitamente generoso, cuyo ego y mente fuesen fuertes y robustos
como su nunca vacilante pene, con el que me convenciese una y
otra vez de mi sex appeal sin límites, incluso para gustos

adquiridos, y de mi personalidad siempre fascinante que lo capturó totalmente y sin ninguna reserva.

La silla de ruedas gira alrededor y el maniquí **Ofelia** *se evapora. La enfermera desempolva la almohada y comienza a correr en círculos: ella sabe que no puede tener una silla de ruedas vacía por lo que la llena con lo que pueda.*

TV: *Un talk show o una serie en horario prime. Terapia matrimonial.* **Ofelia** *y* **Hamlet** *se sientan en el sillón.*

Terapeuta   Hola, y gracias por venir. Qué bueno que tengan un problema para compartir.

Hamlet   No hay problema.

Terapeuta (*decepcionado*)   ¿No hay problema?

Hamlet   Oh, no, si hay un problema. No hay problema de que hayamos venido a compartir el problema contigo.

Terapeuta   Ah claro, genial. Entonces ¿Cuál es el problema?

Hamlet   Es horrible, no puedo creer lo que ella hizo. Arruinó nuestras vidas.

Ofelia   Ay mi amor, qué es lo que hice, qué es lo que hice, sin tan solo me lo dijeses. . . Ay mi amor (*llorando*). Si tan solo me dijeras qué es lo que pasa estoy segura de que estaríamos bien. No pongas en peligro nuestro amor y matrimonio con tu silencio.

Terapeuta   Así es, todo se centra en la comunicación. Si pudieses contarnos, podríamos saber. Si pudieses compartir tus sentimientos con tu esposa, tus sentimientos serán compartidos.

Hamlet   ¿Lo que ella hizo? ¿Lo que ella hizo? Ni siquiera puedo hablar de eso. Mira, todavía estoy temblando de solo pensarlo. No puedo creer que haya hecho eso. No puedo creer me haya hecho esto . . .

Ofelia Y Terapeuta   ¿Qué te hizo (*hice*)?

Hamlet   ¿Quieres saber?, ¿quieres saber? Está bien, te lo diré. Ayer en la mañana, en el desayuno. . . (*Susurra en el oído del* **Terapeuta**.)

Terapeuta   ¡Aaaaay Dios mío!

Hamlet   Si, eso es lo que hizo.

Terapeuta   Definitivamente es una situación difícil, pero estoy seguro de que si lo resolvemos, estará resuelto. Los divorcios son la razón número uno de los divorcios. ¿Pero todo lo demás está bien?

Ofelia   Si, todo está bien. Tenemos un gran matrimonio.

Hamlet   Si, el trabajo está bien, el dinero está bien, los niños están muertos.

Terapeuta   Sólo entonces podrás decir que has alcanzado un estado de sabiduría verdadera, cuando no dejas que tus emociones interfieran con tu imparcial objetivo juicio intelectual. La conclusión a la que llegues siempre debe ser dada a priori o deducida de la experiencia empírica que has acumulado. Nunca debes caer en hacer declaraciones vaciadas de una imparcialidad intelectual profunda. Sólo entonces podrás decir algo verdadera y profundamente imparcial, verdadera e imparcialmente profundo. (*Él se sorprende así mismo por ser tan inteligente; él sonríe y sacude su cabeza, ponderando lo que acaba de decir, pero pronto lo olvida, y se toca la nariz.*)

Ofelia (*detrás del escritorio, tipeando*)   Que única es esta cosa llamada placer y que curiosamente relacionada está con el dolor, lo cual se tendería a pensar que es lo opuesto; ya que nunca llegan juntos a un hombre, y sin embargo él, que persigue a cualquiera de ellos se ve generalmente obligado a tomar al otro.

TV (*cátedra*)   La mujer cuyo placer sexual es originalmente auto-representativo en una forma diferente a la del hombre bien podría no tener un clítoris: el himen que permanece para siempre (in)violado, sobre el cual la semilla es para siempre derramada a lo lejos en diseminación, no tiene uso para el hysteron. ¿Es esta la escena de violencia llamada amor en transformación contenida en nuestra triada perfecta? ¿Si las mujeres siempre han sido usadas como instrumento de auto-deconstrucción masculina, es este el giro más nuevo de la filosofía?

Ofelia (*como terapeuta*)   Me gusta creer que sabes lo que estás
haciendo y que no estás atrapado en los predicamentos auto-
derrotistas de la masculinidad estadunidense, que eventualmente te
dejarán emocionalmente drenado, intelectualmente desnutrido y
sexualmente incompetente.

Hamlet (*mientras juega un video juego, casualmente*)   ¿Quieres
que te mate en un acto dramático de celos tan abrumador que
podría perder mis sentidos? ¿Quieres que te mate mientras te estás
viniendo para que puedas derretirte con el universo en un clímax
eterno, y así puedas creer que vas a vivir para siempre capturada en
este momento? ¿Quieres que te mate mientras susurro en tu oído
cositas románticas acerca de mi propia desesperación? ¿Quieres
que te mate y me mate para seguirte en el drama de la muerte
dirigido tan cuidadosamente?

Ofelia *flota en el espacio. Trata de aferrarse, pero el mundo
desaparece en el horizonte.* **Ofelia** *trata de caminar pero no hay
superficie por sobre la que caminar. Ella encuentra el control
remoto y lo presiona desesperadamente un par de veces.
Esqueletos humanos y animales flotan por el río Ganges.* **Ofelia** *se
lava el pelo y camina por la arena del desierto. Su corazón sangra.
Sus venas están hechas de cables.* **Ofelia** *lleva su propio cadáver
por la frontera del desierto.*

Hamlet   Aunque pase por el valle de la muerte,

No temeré mal alguno, porque tú estás conmigo;
tu vara y tu cayado me infunden aliento.
Tú preparas la mesa delante de mí en presencia de mis enemigos.

Ofelia (*sentada detrás de su escritorio vestida en verde militar.
Calmada y estoica, continúa tipeando como si nada hubiese
ocurrido*)   Por favor, querido, el autodesprecio no es un agente
necesario de nuestro valor de mercado; nuestra pureza es
puramente formal al igual que nuestras perversiones tan apreciadas
por tu madre y promocionadas en cada comercial de jabón.
Querido, debes saber que ella se guardó automáticamente para la
noche de bodas con velas y deseos esculpidos cuidadosamente por
la televisión, y por lo tanto nuevos para nuestra generación. La

angustia, querido, la angustia. Creo verdaderamente en Dios y la dignidad humana, excepto cuando yace en las trincheras con su cabeza reventada por la virtud de otro y su compromiso por la pasión por la vida, ya que creo que eres tú el que calará hondo adentro con una profundidad cercana a mis extremidades debilitadas. Si, si, querido, me puedes escribir un poema, o simplemente cogerme fuerte; estoy segura de que de cualquier forma, seguiremos fieles a nuestra ya larga convicción de inmortalidad lograda por la bondad del corazón, y la unión de las almas cargadas con su mutuo amor y odio hacia la otra, pasando sus días en la armonía de rituales higiénicos, discursos post-modernos de variados niveles intelectuales y mano de obra que nos liberará de la abundancia materialista o la escasez dependiendo de si la procreación alcanzó su promedio estadístico o se auto expresó en el individualismo egoístico de la auto adoración. Estoy segura de que mi convicción me dejará confiada en mí misma como lo haría cualquier otro, por lo que me agradecerás cuando te sirva una copa de vino y masajee tus hombros. La punta de tu pene tiene un potencial ontológico, por lo que introduzco tu espada en tu uretra para examinar si es que el espacio es lo suficientemente espacioso para absorber mi angustia y todos los otros dejados accidentalmente por los futuros padres de los Estados Unidos y otros cinco continentes considerando la globalización de nuestros hábitos sexuales. El padre de mi abuela pereció misteriosamente en algún lugar entre Praga y Viena, exactamente de la forma que lo haremos nosotros.

Horacio *entra con una bandeja plateada con camarones.*

Horacio (*a* **Hamlet**, *que sigue sentado en el sofá*)   ¿Camarones?

Hamlet   Gracias, estoy a dieta.

De pronto **Horacio** *recuerda algo y alza su puño, gritando: " ¡libertad! " Es arrollado por el tanque y su cuerpo desaparece en el asfalto negro. Un grupo de niños sonrientes pasan por el pavimento, riéndose y tomados de las manos. Los cuervos negros pican la carne de* **Horacio**. *El sonido de la estación de buses. Ding dong.*

El Anunciador　El bus de París a Nueva York, vía Londres y Tokio, saliendo por la Puerta 5. El bus de París a Nueva York, vía Londres y Tokio, saliendo por la Puerta 5.

El anuncio se repite un par de veces como si el mecanismo se hubiese quedado pegado. En cuanto comienza el anuncio, entra **Ofelia** *vistiendo un vestido de novia manchado con sangre y un pañuelo en la cabeza. Está tratando de encontrar la puerta correcta. Es seguida por* **Horacio**, *quién lleva una bandeja de plata con una cabeza humana encima, rodeada de camarones.*

Entra **Ofelia**.

Ofelia (*intensamente*)　La elegida, la elegida. Soy la elegida. Soy la elegida que he estado esperando. Soy la elegida. Una, solo una, cuál. La elegida, la santa, la inherentemente **elegida, la bendecida**.

Horacio (*no prestándole atención*)　Los de Christie's son más frescos. Pidamos los de Christie's.

Ofelia *se quita su bota militar y golpea a* **Horacio** *hasta matarlo. Su cuerpo desaparece en el asfalto negro.* **Ofelia** *sale con sus brazos abiertos.* **Hamlet** *comienza a jugar con su celular.* **Ofelia/Medea** *en el suelo de la estación de buses le canta a su bebé muerto.*

Ofelia/Medea　Bendito sea Su gran Nombre para siempre, por toda la eternidad.

Sea bendito, elogiado, glorificado, exaltado, ensalzado, magnificado, enaltecido y alabado Su Santísimo Nombre. Bendito sea.

Hamlet　Tú lees el dolor en mis ojos y crees saberlo todo. Tú crees que puedes leer a un hombre a partir de su dolor. Tú crees eso porque puedes leer el dolor de un hombre que te pertenece, por siempre y para siempre.

TV (*Señal National Geographic*)　El chinche macho tiene un pene diseñado para inyectar y llevar la esperma hacia la hembra. Esta técnica es muy violenta, ya que la hembra es acorralada y apuñalada muchas veces en su cuerpo para asegurar la inseminación. Este método ha evolucionado para evitar el conducto genital de la hembra, restringiendo y removiendo cualquier control que la hembra usualmente tendría sobre su concepción.

Ofelia   Cuando mi cuerpo sea mi amo, no tendré otro. (*Gritando.*) Cuando mi cuerpo sea mi amo, no tendré otro.

Hamlet *cambia de señal.*

Ofelia (*toma un poco de vino y continúa tipeando*)   Los espantosos actos de auto revelación tienen su punto de partida en la benevolencia de nuestra propia mente hacia las clases más bajas de decendencia vulgar. Estoy segura, querido, que la angustia que te he descrito tan cuidadosamente no tiene significancia ética para tu bienestar. También estoy segura de que encontrarás el remplazo de mi inestabilidad emocional tan fácilmente como yo lo haré en cada criatura que nuestras mentes desearán. La decisión marcada tan claramente por mi ser marchito depende puramente de tus niveles de serotonina y el deseo producido por esta noche específica. Mi oferta es válida durante el tiempo de tu erección y expira en el momento en que eyacules tus paranoias despreciables en mi cara expectante. El deseo construido como una función matemática tiene sus ventajas en la volatilidad y permanencia de sus expectaciones, las cuales, replicadas en proporciones fractales, adquieren la cualidad efímera de una estructura sólida fundamentalmente indistinguible de cualquier otra solución acídica a los problemas internalizados durante la niñez y pospuesta para consumo con una copa de Chardonnay o Sauvignon Blanc, y pescado, cocido a medio punto con salsa de limón y caviar.

Pasa **Gertrudis**, *hablando por teléfono. Ahora ella se ha convertido en una máquina.*

Gertrudis   ¿No decía en el catálogo satisfacción garantizada? Te mandan una niña defectuosa y piensan que vas a tener que quedarte con ella. . .Devuélvela y diles que te manden una como en la fotografía, sin pecas. . .En estos días, querido, una tiene que cuidar su dinero. Ayer, compré unos calcetines hechos en China. Estaban defectuosos – te estoy diciendo que – aha – aha – así que los devolví. Una no puede en estos días darse el lujo de malgastar

tanto dinero en cosas defectuosas. – Aha – aha – Pagas por algo, te
mandan algo incorrecto, lo devuelves y recuperas tu dinero. . .
Exacto, exacto, a eso me refiero.

Gertrudis *desaparece. Comienza a caer nieve.*

Hamlet (*a escondidas, como diciendo un secreto*)   A veces,
cuando caminamos a través

de los ojos del otro como a través de puertas
A veces, soy como ella
A veces, ella es quién
soy.

Ofelia (*tipeando, frenéticamente*)   La mano derecha sostiene el
amor eterno con todos sus dilemas fantasmales de salvación
nauseabunda y rutina rectangular de metáforas recicladas de los
cadáveres de amantes pasados e insectos caídos sobre libros
abiertos en la mitad. Te prometo atesorar mi ser que encontré tan
conmovedoramente en tus ojos justo adentro de las pupilas las
cuales te rogué tan apasionadamente que no cerraras cuando me
estoy viniendo y en las cuales mis muecas se magnifican en
fantasías audibles de nuestra imaginación. También te prometo
incluir la estabilidad que tanto deseabas y confusión entretejidas
por el puño ocasional de mi propio ego para mantenerte estable en
la oferta y demanda. Te prometo satisfacer nuestras fantasías
Edípicas y arrendar mi útero desinteresadamente por un oasis y un
baño en donde podamos aliviar nuestras preciadas heces de
esfuerzo intelectual. Estoy segura de que el acuerdo satisfará el
cuarenta por ciento de nuestra masa dejando el sesenta restante en
una ardiente insaciabilidad de sospechas y perpetuidad física de
gravedad y ligereza. Mi mano izquierda ofrece amor no
correspondido, mío o tuyo, lo estableceremos después. Estoy
segura de que de cualquier forma nos adaptaremos a nuestros roles
con la gracia natural de esclavo y maestro. El deseo es
proporcional al tiempo de espera. Querido, ella ha recibido el
entrenamiento de las mejores prostitutas de Europa, Norte América
y Asia. Las cuales visitaste en noches solitarias o de borrachera y
en las cuales insertaste tu pene semi fláccido con la esperanza de
un alivio temporal de la pesadilla del deseo o la falta de este.

Ofelia *se detiene. Se recupera.* **Ofelia** *toma un pistola de su cajón y se vuela la cabeza. El sonido del disparo y sangre por todos partes. Ella continua tipeando como si nada hubiese pasado.*

El mal de la muerte nos vence. Deseamos no haber muerto y no haber vivido. La angustia entre poseído y poseer se establece asi misma con la velocidad de un ladrón que robó demasiado para sentir placer y demasiado poco para sentir algo más y alejándose con una entumecida sonrisa de desprecio, llora escondido detrás de esquinas congeladas de autoperpetuación. Mis pensamientos no fluyen con la facilidad que tu cuerpo prometió ni hierven con agradecida insaciabilidad . . .

TV (*Señal de la National Geographic*)   El escorpión macho y la hembra se entrelazan en un abrazo intenso, azotándose el uno al otro con sus aguijones. Con sus bocas trabadas, el macho apuñala repetidamente a la hembra con su cola. En represalia, la hembra a menudo consume a su pareja.

Entra **Ofelia**. *Su vestido de novia está en harapos. Ella lleva dispositivos de detonación atados a su pecho.*

Ofelia   El hambre que siento no está en mi

fluye afuera y adentro
en mis brazos rapaces
te pierdes a ti mismo
uno no puede ser salvado y permanecer condenado
el hambre que siento no está en mi

Ella se sienta en la silla de ruedas y da vueltas, riendo histéricamente.

Señal de Noticias   Hoy en California, una madre decapitó a su bebé y se comió su cerebro. (*La presentadora se ve triste por un momento, luego cambia rápidamente a una gran sonrisa.*) Y en otras noticias, nuestra gurú de estilo de vida responderá la pregunta más importante de esta temporada . . .

Comienza a sonar 'Jingle Bells'.

El rostro de **Hamlet** *en el fondo se funde con el videojuego que él está jugando. El* **Hamlet** *en el sofá y en el videojuego se para y se* *saca su sobrero y su chaqueta. Va tras bastidores y trae un galón de gasolina, que comienza a verte por todas partes.*

Ofelia (*tipeando mientras* **Hamlet** *vierte gasolina*) Muy lejos, muy lejos, querido. . . logramos definitivamente convencernos a nosotros mismos de nuestra propia existencia. Llevado a tal extremo, no tengo más remedio que perpetuar esta convicción. Te ruego que no me niegues lo que por derecho pertenece a otro. Conozco tu compromiso con verdaderos y falsos. Servidos con pedazos de creencias perdidas y comprados en subastas silenciosas en museos de órganos y almas de cera. Quiero que de verdad entiendas que las promesas de mis labios no son traducibles. Amarro tus pensamientos y los míos con tan especial atención a los detalles. Querías sentir amor o cualquier cosa para tal caso. El teatro de los deseos está abierto al público para espectadores curiosos y ajenos unos a otros. Los vi ayer paseando por la ciudad cuando lloramos escondidos debajo de la cama que se negaba a ser domada. Salí con tu cabeza bajo mi brazo. Me trabo, me trabo en las palabras atadas a su poder. No llores querido, se acerca la noche.

Ella prende un fósforo. Apagón.

オフィーリアマシーン

エグリントンみか訳

（車屋、倉庫、もしくは子供の遊び場のような舞台に、行方不明となった旅行者が集めたオブジェが溢れている。バイク・ヘルメットを被った腕のないミケランジェロ作のダビデ像、壊れたアフリカの仮面の数々、自分の影を見てヒステリックに笑う死んだ詩人の骸骨、ピンク色のロリポップをくわえた手足のない赤ちゃん人形、ルネ・マグリットの壊れた傘、アンディ・ウォーホルが描いた神に繋がる電話、他の衣類に混じって汚れた白いウェディングベール、古臭い靴やウィッグの山々。

　戦争シーン、大量殺人、大量虐殺、アウシュビッツの死体、ポルノ、政治的広告、ウォール街の女性、太った女性、拒食症の女性、日本の女子学生、ブルカに覆われた女性、ワイルドサファリ、散乱する多量のコミック本などがランダムに映し出される壊れたゲーム機、テレビ、コンピューターのスクリーンは、仮想生活の無言のシーンをランダムに映し出す。現代の荒地である。

　ハムレットとオフィーリアは、美と恐怖、無垢と暴力という人間のコントラストを混ぜ合わせたニュースやイメージのスープを、日々飲み干している。

　全てが、放射能の灰に覆われている。

　ジーンズに16世紀のジャケットを着込み、カウボーイハットを被ったハムレットが、観客席に向かってソファに座っている。彼はテレビを見ながら、無心にリモコンでチャンネルをめくっている。舞台の背景には、様々な映像の寄せ集めが投影されている。ハムレットは世界を理解しようとするものの、世界を見つめることしかできない。

　ハムレットの後方、舞台上手には迷彩服を着たオフィーリアが机の後ろに座り、古風なタイプライターで何かを打ち込んでいる。傍らには血のように赤いワインの入ったグラスが置かれている。オフィーリアはタバコを吸いながら、タイプに没頭している。

　ハムレットとオフィーリアは、世界の両極端にいる。その間には腐乱死体や死んだ鳥が累々と浮かぶ小便で出来た大西洋が広がっている。）

オフィーリア：（タイプを打ちながら）

　ハムレット、私の愛しい人、私は、あなたにも彼女にもなりたくはない。あなたのおもちゃの兵隊が、私のベッドに侵入してきた。大海も大陸も、政治的郷愁と忍耐にいとも容易く変換されてしまう。死者に死者を埋葬させよ。疫病たる我々の父祖を。（オフィーリアは手を止め、ワインを一口飲む。）

ハムレット：（古い良き時代を思い、ぼんやりしながら）

　祝福されないサイコロで

――六つのベッドと七つの夜――

　孵化したばかりの幼虫は
　　おがくずで出来た岸辺に自ら身を潜ませる

オフィーリア：（平静を保ったまま）
　・・・　書くこととは、知的自慰行為の一形態である。難解な自己陶酔の技術を習得し、それ故に孤独な快楽の新時代に入ったことを誇りに思いながら、哀れな自分をコンピューターの白目に溢す。自分でもこの自己満足感には驚いてしまう。ああ、この脳内性感帯は、自己崇拝の誇大妄想的な発作において、思慮深く吟味されたもの。はい、はい、今すぐ、自動的に自分自身を後世のために保存する。（手を止め、タバコを一服する。）

テレビ（ナショナル・ジオグラフィック・チャンネル）
　交尾の儀式において、メスの白鷺はオスの体にその爪を食い込ませ、オスに完全なる服従を求めながら、地面へと急降下する。メスの準備が整う前にオスが飛び立とうとするならば、メスは決してオスに交尾を許さない。数秒でも長過ぎると、二羽とも地面に激突して死んでしまう。

（通過列車が全速力で走り過ぎる。線路上に立っている人に警告しようとするかのように、口笛が響き渡る。列車が通過する。真夜中のポート・オーソリティ。キンコンとチャイム音、アナウンス、つぶやき声が響く。ハムレットはテレビを見つめている。）

オフィーリア：（当たり前といった風に）

ポート・オーソリティーにいる女の子は、ブロンクスかハーレム出身が多い。頭に偽物のシャネルのスカーフを巻き、肩に偽物のルイ・ヴィトンのバッグを下げている。一見無駄な贅沢品を数百ドルも払って買ってくれる男がいるかのように、おしゃれをして大切にしてもらっているかのように振る舞う。小さな赤ん坊や幼児を、静かな絶望感を持って抱いている女たちもいる。女たちが赤ん坊を必要としているのか、赤ん坊が女たちを必要としているのか、どちらなのか私には判別できない。彼女たちは地面やスーツケースの上に座り、辛抱強くバスを待っている。時には男が一緒にいることもあり、その時は彼女らの目は、ささやかな満足感で輝いている。今にも泣き出しそうで、今にも罵り合いそうで、儚げで、たくましい。

(オフィーリアは再びタイプを打ち出す。電話の呼び出し音。路面電車の通過音。隣のアパートで子供が泣く。ガートルードが入場する。ローブを着て、頭に炎のようなローラーをつけ、舞台を横切る。歯を磨きながら、電話で話している。その日はギラギラしている。)

ガートルード:
  なんてこと! そばかすがあったのね! 私がどう思っているか、分かるでしょ? つまり... 私が言いたいのは、とても簡単なこと。普通の陶磁器人形にそばかすがある? え? ないでしょ。送られてきた人形にそばかすがあるから、送り返すのよ! ダメ、そんなことする必要はないの。返送料を払う必要はないはずよ。その箱に戻して、送り返して。あ、ダメ、代金を支払ったのだから。カタログの写真を見て、クレジットカードで支払ったものが送られてくるべきでしょ。 そばかすのある女の子の写真もあったって? いいえ、そう、私の言いたいことは... 私の言いたいこと、分かる? いいえ、これは「不当表示」、「詐称」よ! それで刑務所送りになることもあるのに。... ええ、中国にはたくさん素敵な娘がいるかもしれないけれど...。

(ガートルードがステージ・ドアから出て行く。ローブがドアに引っかかり、怒りを込めてそれを引っ張る。ハムレット

が振り返り、ガートルードの背後に靴を投げるが、外れる。ハムレットはコウモリの羽を生やし、テレビを見つめる。）

オフィーリア：（何事もなかったかのようにタイプし続ける）
　恐怖、ダーリン、恐怖。恐怖に浸るか、恐怖を背負うか、どちらかを選んで欲しい。あなたが選択するの。繁栄は、我々の残念な遺伝子が、12ポンドの炭素と知性で不滅になるのを、待ち焦がれている。そう、そうよ、ダーリン、確かに子孫繁栄は、大衆にとっては限りない喜びの源となり得るけれど、我々はもっとずっと洗練されているのだから。私の頭の中の声は、子供の泣き声に掻き消されない ・・・ 。（一時手を止める。オフィーリアがタイプしている間、ハムレットはソフトポルノを見ている。）その恐怖は、ダーリン、私が話していた恐怖は、麻痺ではない。もう少し辛抱すれば、きっと届くはず。あなたのペニスは慎重に測定され、その実存的資質が評価された。傷ついたあなたの自我を癒すことができず、私たちの素敵な出会いの慣習を定義することができなかった全責任は、私たちが満たされないままになることを望んでいる。あなたのペニスの長さは、あなたの疲れた腕の中でタバコを吸いながら、性的欲求が満たされないことによって引き起こされる肺がんや心臓発作の統計的確率を熟考したときに私が感じるであろう苦痛、適切に対処されなかった恐怖に比例する。ハムレット、ダーリン、政治や欲望や世界や死や、飢えた子供たちのために泣きながら流した血のことは話さないで。

（花嫁衣裳を着たオフィーリアが、ホレイショとガートルードを伴って舞台を横切っていく。ガートルードはロカビリー馬を駆り、頭の後ろで剣を振っている。ホレイショはタキシード姿で、網タイツと赤いヒールを履いている。髪は後ろでまとめている。エビの大皿と手帳を手にしている。）

オフィーリア：（ウエディングドレス姿で階段を上り下りしながら）
　祝福されし、あなた。

ホレイショ：
　あのエビ、ちょっとヤバかったわ。ケータリング会社に電話しようか。誰も病気にならないようにね。こういう事態に備えて、結婚式保険とか、あるべきだと思わない？

オフィーリア：
　彼が運命の人なのかどうか、不安になることってない？

ホレイショ：（ノートから顔を上げて）
　もちろん、そんな事ないの、ダーリン。運命の人と結ばれる事自体、ないから。彼が運命の人なのは、あなたとは結ばれないから。彼と結ばれたら、それは運命の人じゃないって事よ。（手帳を見ながら）このエビ、どこの？　ラ・ベラ・トスカ？　それともクリスティーズ？

オフィーリア：
　クリスティーズよ。彼が運命の人かどうか、確かめないと。

ガートルード：
　ああ、あの人 . . .

オフィーリア：（心の中の声を叫びながら）
　ずっと、ずっと、死ぬまで一緒にいたい . . .

ガートルード：
　生も死も、愛も欲も、宇宙は無限大に広がっている。あなたはどこから来たのか、どこへ行くのか？　どこへ行くのか、万物は流転する。ダーリン、いい質問だけど、あなたのお父さんが何と言おうと、家賃は払ってもらえないの。この事を今すぐ書き留めて、秘密の隠れ家にしまい込んで、引退したら取り出してみて。ゴルフのレッスンやピラティス、ホットフラッシュなどの合間なんかに、重宝するはずよ。目を細めてはダメ。化粧がヨレるでしょ。

ハムレット：（タキシード姿で入場）
　本当に結婚するつもりなのか？　あんな奴と。

ホレイショ：（目玉をぐるぐる回しながら）
　彼が運命の人か、否か。

ガートルード：
　どういう人？

オフィーリア：
　あなたの魂を癒す人 . . .
（ガートルードとホレイショは顔を見合わせ、ヒステリックに大笑いし始める。）

ガートルード：
　伴侶みたいな？

ホレイショ：
　伴侶。

ガートルード：（哲学的に）
　あるいは別の何か？

（教会の鐘が鳴り始め、ガートルードとホレイショはアバターに変わり、合成された音声が不可解な繰り返しとして響く中、退場していく。「これか、あれか、どれか、だれか、だれでも、だれでもない。私たちが待ち続けていた人、別の人、彼らが待ち続けていた人、それともあなたが待ち続けていた人？　誰を待っていた？　どの人？」

ハムレット：（鐘が鳴り響く中、スクリーンから話しかける）
　オオカミの子の叫びで心を落ち着かせ
　真実など存在せず
　嘔吐物で髪が硬くなった
　今夜
　あなたは夢を見ずに眠るだろう
　明日
　皮膚ジッパーを開けて我々を中に入れてくれ

　テュルプ博士の解剖学講義でも始めようか

（「キンコン」というバス停の音。音声案内は途切れがちで、ほぼ意味不明である。）

オフィーリア：
（オフィーリアはスーツケースとマネキンの頭を詰めた枕カバーを持っている。慎重な素ぶりでバスの時刻表を眺め、何時にバスが出発するかを確認している。ハムレットに呼び止められる。首から重い金の鎖を下げている。）

ハムレット：
　ねえ、どこに行くの？

オフィーリア：
友達を訪ねるの。

ハムレット：（オフィーリアを眺めながら）

　　どこから来たの？

オフィーリア：
　メイン州のハストン。

ハムレット：
　それってどこ？

オフィーリア：
　小さな町。誰も知らないような。

ハムレット：
　大学都市？　学生なの？

オフィーリア：
　いいえ。

ハムレット：
　そこで何するの？（オフィーリアは黙って、かすかに微笑んでいる。明らかに不快そうである。）へへ、分かった、男だね。そこでヤリまくるってか。へへ。そこでヤリまくるってか。ニューヨークに住んでみたら。

オフィーリア：
　んー。

ハムレット：
　何が入っているの？

オフィーリア：
　これ？

ハムレット：
　そう。

オフィーリア：
マネキンの頭。美容師になるための訓練中なの。

（「キンコン」ポート・オーソリティーの音声案内「午前2時30分発のクリーブランド行きバスは、5番ゲートから出発します。お荷物をお忘れにならないように」）

オフィーリア：
　私の乗るバスよ。

（ハムレットはオフィーリアが何か言うのを待ったが、黙ったままなので、その場を離れる。オフィーリアは枕カバーを引きずりながら、舞台から消えていく。ハムレットは肩越しに唾を吐き、その後を追う。

'Dream a Little Dream' が流れ始める。オフィーリアが背後の机に座り、ワインを一口飲む。ハムレットはリモコンを捨て、テレビゲームを始める。二人の上に乾いた秋の葉が落ち始める。ドアが開き、音楽が突然止まる。

ガートルードが電話で話しながら入ってくる。以前と同じローブを着ているが、頭の半分のローラーが外れている。その髪は、メデューサのように世界の四方八方に流れている。彼女は電話中でカタログをめくりながら、舞台を横切っていく。）

ガートルード：
　．．．どれにすればいいかしら？ロシア産、ルーマニア産、それとも中国産？ロシア産は金髪が似合うけど、傷ついている見たい。母親が飲んだロシア産ウォッカのせいで．．．ルーマニアの子たちは青白い。金髪だけど青白すぎる。栄養失調かもしれない。アフリカの子も同じ。でも、とてもエキゾチック。シャネル・バッグと一緒に、肩がけが似合いそう。エルメスでもいいわね。．．．保証はどうなっているの？ 2年？ 延長保証はできるの？　．．．死んだらどうするのよ？．．．新しいものを送ってくれるの？ 交換してくれるの？　葬儀費用は負担してくれるのかしら？ 送料は？ また送料を払うつもりはないわよ。書類作成に2万5千ドルもかかるの。そうね、あなたの言う通り、南米産のものはとても素敵ね、黒すぎず、青白すぎず、　ウフフ

（ガートルードは買い物に満足しつつ、舞台から退出する）。

（テレビ・スクリーンから投影される。
ソープオペラなのか、古典小説なのか、判別しがたい。）

　彼女のこの二面性が彼を恐がらせた。自分が彼女を所有していると確信するたびに、彼女の目は見知らぬ人のそれになった。彼女は自分の中で彼女の声が聞こえる程に身近な存在でありながら、あまりにも遠い存在であったため、突然の孤独感が彼の全身の細胞に入り込み、まるで自分の死を意識しているかのように体を痛め、息苦しくなった。

（ハムレットはソファに座ってビデオゲームをしている。ハムレットの顔はゆっくりとオフィーリアの顔に変容していく。オフィーリアは軍隊ヘルメットを被り、それを黒いスカーフで覆っている。）

オフィーリア：（スクリーンに向かって、子供の童謡を言うように）
　ある日
　私の肉は私たちを見捨てた
　驚きのあまり茫然自失となる

　私たちは互いに顔を見合わせ
　もはや何も失うものなどない

ホレイショ：（法律文書を読みながら）
　もう何ヶ月も前から、彼らは赤ちゃんのために準備をしてきた。ベビーベッド、ベビーカー、洋服などを一緒に購入してきた。ベッドもベビーカーも洋服も、すべてが高級なカタログに載っているような高価なものばかり。大学までバスを待たずに往復できるようにと、新品の車も買ってやった。女の子が生まれると知ったとき、彼はがっかりした。自分が始めたことを受け継いでくれる男の子が欲しいと心から思っていたから。どんなことを教えてくれるのだろうと、空想に耽った。自分の気持ちを恥じながら、その落胆を隠し、女の子という概念に慣れ、妊娠中は彼女を応援し、ユーモアや時々陥る鬱状態にも辛抱強く対応した。彼女は彼の子供を身ごもっていた。初めて公式に彼を拷問することが許され、彼女は徐々に自分ができることに限界がないことを知った。そして、彼の自尊心を傷つけたことへの憤りが、彼女の想像力を刺激した。彼女は、ますます洗練された残酷さで彼を何度も何度も潰し、彼は義務感と畏怖と驚きの入り混じった感覚でそれに耐えていた。

（頭上を飛行機かヘリコプターが飛ぶ音、セットに翼の影が映し出される。オフィーリアは黒い腕を広げ、上空を浮遊し始め、カラスに変身する。大都会の喧騒。救急車のサイレン、銃声、少女たちの嬌声、誰かの叫び声、路上で吠える犬。オフィーリアは上空から見ている。その体は100万個の小さな破片になり、それを買い物かごに集めようとする。スーパー

の掃除婦に追い出され、オフィーリアは自分の目をくり抜く。)

ハムレット：
　光がこぼれ落ち
　白いシーツの上の影を愛撫する
　血とリゾールと
　昨日の尿の匂いがする

　あなたの不眠症は、どの引き出しに入っているのか？
　天井のカビのシミでできたモザイク画
　あなたの地平線はどこで果てるのか？

(従軍看護婦に押された車椅子のオフィーリアが登場する)

オフィーリア：
　車いすの少女だった私は、突然、引き裂かれた。誰と同盟を結べばいいのか。もし女性なら、答えは簡単。もし障害者なら、答えは簡単。女性で、かつ障害者なら、答えは簡単。でも、男性の障害者には、本質的な存在不可能性があった。敵なのか、殉教者なのか、性に縛られているのか、車椅子に縛られているのか。私自身が障害者をめぐる政治的見解を決めかねていたので、先手を打って、障害者を完全に避けることにした。傷ついた男らしさに根ざした男性障害者たちは、傷ついた女らしさに根ざした私にとって、自然と避ける存在となっていた。欲望されたいという気持ちと尊敬されたいという気持ちの矛盾に対処できない私は、精神的に自立し、限りなく寛大で、自分のエゴと心が決して萎える事のないペニスのように強靭で、たとえ後天的な好みであっても、私の尽きる事のない性的魅力と、彼を余す事なく魅了する私の魅力について、幾度となく私に確認させてくれる男性が必要だった。

(車椅子が回転し、オフィーリア・マネキンが蒸発する。看護婦は枕の埃を払い、円を描くように走り始める。空の車椅子は許されないので、そこにある物を使って座席を埋めようとする。)

(テレビのゴールデンタイムに流れるトークショーが、結婚相談を行い。オフィーリアとハムレットがソファに座っている。)

セラピスト：
　こんにちは、お越しいただきありがとうございます。問題を共有してくださり、感謝いたします。

ハムレット：
　問題ないよ。

セラピスト：（がっくりして）
　問題がない？

ハムレット：
　いやあ、問題はある。問題をあなたと共有する事には問題がないって事。

セラピスト：
　そうですか、それは素晴らしい。では、何が問題なのですか？

ハムレット：
　最悪だよ、妻がした事が理解できないんだ。俺たちの人生を台無しにした。

オフィーリア：
　ああ、ハニー、私が何をしたというの。もしあなたが私に言ってくれれば．．．ああ、ハニー（泣きながら）。教えてくれれば、きっとうまくいくわ。あなたの沈黙で、愛と結婚を危険にさらさないで。

セラピスト：
　そう、すべてはコミュニケーションなのです。話してもらえれば、わかる。奥様に気持ちを伝えていただけたら、気持ちは伝わります。

ハムレット：
　妻が何をしたって？　妻が何をしたって？　話すことすらできない。思い出すだけで震える。妻がやったとは信じられない。俺にこんな事をしたなんて．．．

オフィーリア＆セラピスト：
　何をしたというの？

ハムレット：

　知りたいか？知りたいのか？　よし、教えてやる。昨日の朝、朝食時に...

　（セラピストの耳元で囁く）。

セラピスト：
　えええええええ、そんな！

ハムレット：
　それが、彼女がしたことだ。

セラピスト：
　確かに難しい状況ですが、解決すればきっと解決します。離婚の1番の原因は離婚です。

でも、それ以外は問題ないのですか？

オフィーリア：
　ええ、すべて順調よ。素敵な結婚生活なの。

ハムレット：
　そう、仕事もいい、金もいい、子供もいない。

セラピスト：
　感情によって公平で客観的な知的判断が妨げられない時にこそ、真の知恵へと到達できるのです。あなたが導き出す結論は、常にアプリオリに与えられたものでなければならないし、あなたが蓄積してきた経験則から演繹されたものでなければなりません。深い知的公平性を欠いた発言に安住してはなりません。そうしてこそ、真に深遠な公平さ、真に公平な深遠さを語ることができるのです。　（自分自身の堅実な発言に驚き、微笑みながら頭を振りながら、その発言について思いをめぐらせようとするが、すぐに忘れて鼻をほじり始める。）

オフィーリア：　（机に座ってタイプしている）
　快楽と呼ばれるものがいかに特異であるか、また、その反対と見なされる苦痛といかに不可解な関係にあるか。この二つは決して一緒に人間の前に現れることはないのに、どちらかを追求する者は、もう一方をも選ばざるを得ない。

テレビ（講義）：

　性的快感が男性とは元来異なり、自己表現的である女性は、クリトリスを持たないほうがよいかもしれない。永遠に侵（入）され続け、種が永遠に散布され続ける処女膜は、ヒステロンには無用である。これは、唯一にして完璧なるかの三位一体の中に含有される変容する愛と呼ばれる暴力の光景なのだろうか。女性が常に男性の自己解体の道具として利用されてきたとしたら、これが哲学の最新の展開なのだろうか?

オフィーリア：（療法士）
　私は、あなたが自分のしていることを理解していて、自堕落なアメリカの男らしさの苦境に陥っているのではないと信じたいのです。もしそうであれば、あなたは感情的に消耗し、知的に飢え、性的に不能になってしまうでしょう。

ハムレット：（ゲームをしながら、さりげなく）
　嫉妬に負けて正気を失うほど劇的な行為で殺して欲しいのか? 永遠のクライマックスで宇宙と溶り合い、この瞬間に捕らわれて永遠に生き続けることを実感できるように、絶頂に達している間に殺して欲しいのか?自分の絶望を耳元で甘く囁きながら殺してほしいのか?おまえの死と、その後を追って、入念に演出された死のドラマの中で、俺に殺されたいのか?

（オフィーリアは宇宙に浮かんでいる。藁にもすがる思いだが，世界は地平線の彼方に消えていく。オフィーリアは歩こうとするが、歩けるような表面はない。リモコンを見つけ、必死で何度も押す。ガンジス川には人や動物の死骸が流れている。オフィーリアは髪を洗い、砂漠の砂を踏みしめる。心臓から血が出る。血管は針金でできている。オフィーリアは自分の死体を担いで砂漠の国境を越えていく）。

ハムレット：
　たとえ死の陰の谷を歩むとも

　私は災いを恐れない。
　あなたは私と共におられ
　あなたの鞭と杖が私を慰める。
　私を苦しめる者の前で
　あなたは私に食卓を整えられる。

オフィーリア　：（アーミーグリーンの服を着て、デスクに座っている。何事もなかったかのように、冷静かつストイックにタイプし続ける。）

　お願い、ダーリン、自己卑下は自分の市場価値を高めるために必要な要素ではないと理解して。私たちの純粋さは、あなたのお母さんが大事にし、あらゆる石鹸のコマーシャルで宣伝している私たちの倒錯と同様に、純粋に形式的なものなの。ダーリン、知っているでしょう、お母さんはテレビによって丁寧に彫刻された蝋燭と欲望で結婚式の夜に自動的に身を救ったことを。故に私たちの世代にとっては新規に映る。恐怖、ダーリン、恐怖。私は神と人間の尊厳を心から信じている。ただし、それが誰かの美徳と人生への情熱に頭を吹き飛ばされて塹壕に横たわっている時は別だけど。私の弱った手足に近づき、私の奥深くに到達できるのは、あなただけと信じているから。そう、ダーリン、詩を書いてくれてもいいし、ただ激しくファックしてくれてもいい。いずれにせよ、私たちは善意と互いへの憎しみを取り除いた愛と魂の結合によって到達する不滅を信仰し、衛生的な儀式、様々な知的レベルのポストモダンの言説、出産が統計的平均に達したか、自己崇拝の利己的な個人主義で表現したかに応じ、物質的な豊かさをもたらし、窮乏から解放してくれる労働を日々続けている。この確信を抱く事によって、他の人たちと同じように、私も自分に自信を持てるとも確信している。あなたにワインを注ぎ、肩を揉んであげたら、あなたは私に感謝するでしょう。あなたのペニスの先端には存在論的可能性があり、私はあなたの剣を尿道に刺して、私の恐怖とアメリカと他の5つの大陸の未来の父たちが偶然残したその他のすべてを吸収するのに十分な広さがあるかを、我々の性的習慣のグローバル化を考慮して検討する。私の祖母の父親は、プラハとウィーンの間のどこかで、我々と全く同じように、謎の死を遂げた。

（エビが盛られた銀の皿をホレイショが持って入ってくる）

ホレイショ：（まだソファに座っているハムレットに）
　エビはいかが？

ハムレット：
　ありがとう、でもダイエット。

（ホレイショは突然何かを思い出し、叫びながら第一声を上げる。「自由だ！」彼は戦車に轢かれ、その体は黒いアスファルトの中に消えていく。その上を子供たちが笑いながら手をつないで走っていく。黒いカラスがホレイショの肉をつんでいる。バスターミナルの音、キンコン。）

音声案内：
　パリ発、ロンドン・東京経由、ニューヨーク行きのバスは、5番ゲートから発車します。

パリ発、ロンドン・東京経由、ニューヨーク行きのバスは、5番ゲートから発車します。

　（アナウンスが、壊れた機械のように、何度か繰り返される。アナウンスが始まると同時に、血まみれのウエディングドレスとスカーフを身につけたオフィーリアが登場し、出発ゲートを探す。その後には、エビとその中央に男性の頭が盛られた銀の大皿を運ぶホレイショが続く。）

（オフィーリー登場）

オフィーリア；（狂ったように）
　かの人、かの人。私が、私が待ち望んでいたかの人は、この私。私がかの人なのです。私が、かの人、唯一のかの者、聖なる者、本来あるべき者、祝福されし者。

ホレイショ：（オフィーリアには目もくれず）
　クリスティーの方が新鮮よ。クリスティーに注文しましょう。

　（オフィーリアが軍靴を脱ぎ、ホレイショを殴り殺す。彼の体は黒いアスファルトの中に消えていく。オフィーリアは両腕を大きく広げて存在する。ハムレットは携帯電話をいじり始める。バスターミナルの床でオフィーリア/メディアは死んだ我が子に歌いかける。）

オフィーリア/メディア：
　主の御名が永遠に永久に褒め称えられますように
　祝福と賛美、栄光と賞賛
　崇拝と称賛が聖なる方の御名にありますように
　神はほむべきかな

ハムレット：

　あなたは私の目から痛みを読み取り、すべてを知っていると考える。痛みから人を読み取れると思っている。人の痛みが分かるから、その人は自分のものだと思っているのだ、いつまでも、永遠に。

テレビ：（ナショナル・ジオグラフィック・チャンネル）

　オスのナンキンムシのペニスは、メスの体内に挿入され、精子を送り込むように設計されている。この方法は非常に暴力的で、メスを押さえつけ、何度も体を刺すことで確実に受精させる。この方法は、メスの性器を迂回するように進化してきたため、メスが妊娠のタイミングをコントロールすることが難しくなっている。

オフィーリア：

　私の体が私の主人である時、私は他の主人を持たないでしょう。（悲鳴）私の体が私の主人である時、私は他の主人を持たないでしょう。

（ハムレットはチャンネルを切り替える）

オフィーリア：（ワインを飲みながらタイプする）

　身の毛もよだつような自己顕示は、低俗な下層階級に対する博愛心から生起する。ダーリン、私が注意深く説明した恐怖は、あなたの幸福にはいかなる倫理的意義を持たない事は分かっている。私の感情の不均衡の代用品を、あらゆる生き物に求めるのと同じように、あなたも簡単に見つけられる事も十分わかっている。枯れていく私に提示された選択肢は、純粋にあなたのセロトニン・レベルと、この特別な夜が生み出す欲望にかかっている。私の申し出は、あなたが勃起している間のみ有効であり、あなたの哀れなパラノイアを期待で膨らんだ私の顔に射精する瞬間に時間切れとなる。数学的関数として構築された欲望は、その期待の変動性と永続性に利点があり、フラクタル比率で複製されると、幼少期に内面化され、シャルドネやソーヴィニョン・デ・ブランコで満たされたグラスと、レモンソースとキャビアでマイルドに仕上げた魚料理と一緒に消費されるために延期された諸問題に対する他の酸性の解決策と基本的に区別できない固体構造の風通しの良い品質を獲得する。

（ガートルードが電話で話しながら舞台を横切る。彼女は今、機械と化している）

ガートルード：

　カタログに満足保証って記載されているでしょ？　欠陥商品を送りつけて、それで泣き寝入りしろと奴らは思っているのでしょう。人形を送り返して、写真の通り、そばかすのないものを送るように伝えて。．．．最近では、自分で自分のお金の管理をしないとダメなのよ。昨日、中国製の靴下を買ったんだけど、欠陥品だったので、言っておくけど、ああ、ああ、返品したのよ。最近では、欠陥品を買ってお金をドブに捨てる訳にはいかないの。ああ、ああ、代金を支払ったのに、相手が間違ったものを送ってきたら、送り返してそのお金の価値を取り戻すこせるのよ。．．．はい、はい、それ、それが私が言っている事よ。

（ガートルードが退場し、雪が降り始める。）

ハムレット：（こっそり、秘密を漏らすかのように）
　時々、門をくぐるよう、
　互いに目を配りつつ歩いていると
　時々、私も彼女のようになる

　時々、彼女は
　私になる

（ガートルードが退場し、雪が降り出す）

オフィーリア：（必死にタイプしている）

　私の右手は、吐き気を催す救済という幻想的な苦境と、昔の恋人の死体の中心に開いた本に落ちた虫から再利用された長方形の比喩を伴う永遠の愛を掲げている。私は、あなたの瞳孔のすぐ内側に映る私自身を大切にする事を誓う。私が絶頂に達する瞬間にその瞳を絶対に閉じないように乞い、私の苦渋の表情が想像の産物にまで拡大されるように願う。私は、あなたが長い間望んでいた安定した生活に、需要と供給の安定を保つために時折爆発する私のエゴの発作を織り交ぜた混乱を混ぜ合わせる事も誓う。私は、エディプス幻想を実現し、私の子宮を、私たちの知的努力の結果の貴重なクソを排出するためのオアシスとトイレとして、無私に貸与する事も誓う。その結果、私たちの40％が満足し、残りの60％は猜疑

心と重力と軽さの物理的な永続性の中で燃え続けると確信する。私の左手は報われない愛を捧げる。私のものであれ、あなたのものであれ、後々決めるが、いずれにせよ、私たちは奴隷と主人の自然な恵みで自分たちの役割に適応すると確信している。欲望は待ち時間に比例する。ダーリン、彼女はヨーロッパ、北アメリカ、アジアの最高の売春婦の訓練を受けてきた。孤独な夜や酔った夜に訪れ、欲望や欲望の欠如の悪夢から一時的に解放されることを期待して、半分ぐったりしたペニスを挿入してきた。

（オフィーリアの動きが止まる。心を落ち着かせてから、引き出しから銃を取り出し、オフィーリアの頭を吹っ飛ばす。銃声が響き渡り、あたりは血の海になる。オフィーリアは何事もなかったかのようにタイプし続ける。）

　死の弊害が私たちに打ち勝つ。私たちは死なないように、生きないようにと願う。所有する事と所有される事の間の恐怖は、喜びを感じるために多くを盗み、他の何かを感じるには少なすぎる泥棒の速さで確立され、軽蔑が麻痺した笑顔で立ち去り、叫びは自己増殖の凍った隅に隠される。私の思考は、あなたの体が約束したようには容易く流れないし、飽くなき不安定性さで沸き立つこともない．．．

テレビ　：（ナショナル・ジオグラフィック・チャンネル）
　オスとメスのサソリは激しい抱擁を交わし、針で互いを刺す。口を閉ざしたしたまま、オスは尻尾でメスを何度も刺す。その報復として、しばしメスはオスを捕食する。

　（オフィーリアが入ってくる。ウエディングドレスはボロボロ。胸には起爆装置が括り付けられている。）

オフィーリア：
　私の感じる飢えは、私の中にはない
　外から内へと流れていく
　私の強引な腕の中で
　あなたは己を見失う
　救われず、断罪され続ける
　私の感じる飢えは、私の中にはない

　（オフィーリアは車椅子に座ってまま回転し、ヒステリックに笑う）

テレビのニュース：

今日、カリフォルニアで母親が赤ん坊の首を切り、その脳を食べました。（若い女性キャスターは一瞬悲しそうな表情をするが、すぐに満面の笑みを見せる。）　新しいニュースです。今回はライフスタイル・グルがこの季節の最も重要な質問にお答えします。

（「ジングル・ベル」が流れ始める。

背景のスクリーンに投影されるハムレットの顔は、彼が遊んでいるビデオゲームに溶け混んで行く。ハムレットはソファーの上に立ち上がり、帽子とジャケットを脱ぐ。　舞台裏に行き、ガソリンの入った缶を持ってきて、舞台にまき始める。）

オフィーリア：（ハムレットがガソリンをまく中、タイプし続ける）

遠く、遠く、ダーリン．．．私たちは自分自身の存在を確認するに至った。ここまで来たら、私にはこの信念を貫く以外の道はない。お願いだから、他の誰かの信念を否定しないで。真実と虚偽にあなたが拘泥する事は承知の上よ。失われた信仰の断片と、蝋人形と魂の博物館での無言のオークションで買った物を一緒に捧げるから。私の唇が発した約束は、翻訳不可能である事を、理解して欲しい。私は、あなたの思考と私の思考を、細部まで異様なこだわりを持って結びつけている。あなたが愛や何かを感じたいと思ったから。欲望の劇場は、好奇心旺盛ながら互いに無関心な観衆にも公開されている。昨日、街を通り過ぎる奴らを見かけた。私たちが飼い慣らされることを拒んでベッドの下に隠れて泣いている時に。私はあなたの頭を脇に抱えて歩き去った。奴らの力に付随する言葉に、何度も、何度もつまずく。泣かないで、ダーリン、夜がまた来る。

（オフィーリアがマッチを点ける。暗転）

오필리어기계 (Opheliamachine)

번역. 남기윤 (Kee-Yoon Nahm)

역자주: 번역본 리딩에 참여해 주신 신지이, 김성민, 오은지, 한태경, 유용석 님께 감사드립니다.

Translator's note: I would like to thank Shin Ji-i, Kim Seong Min, Oh Eun-ji, Han Taekyoung, and Yoo Yong Suk for participating in a reading of this translation.

(자동차 성비소 혹은 창고 혹은 아이의 놀이방. 길 잃은 여행자가 수집한 가지각색 물건들로 가득하다. 오토바이 헬멧을 쓴 미켈란젤로의 〈다비드〉상, 망가진 아프리카 가면 더미, 자기 그림자를 향해 미친듯이 웃는 죽은 시인의 해골, 분홍색 막대사탕을 입에 문 팔 없는 아기 인형, 마그리트의 부러진 우산, 신과 통화할 수 있는 앤디 워홀의 전화기, 옷 더미 사이에 걸린 얼룩진 흰색 면사포, 낡은 신발과 가발 더미 등.

황폐한 현대적 풍경에는 망가진 게임기, TV 스크린, 컴퓨터 스크린 등이 가득하다. 이 화면들에는 우리의 가상 생활을 담은 장면들이 수리 없이 지나간다: 전쟁, 대량 살인 사건, 대량 학살, 이유슈비츠에 늘어진 시체들, 포르노, 성지 션선, 월가의 여성들, 뚱뚱한 여성들, 거식증 여성들, 일본 여학생들, 부르카를 두른 여성들, 야생 사파리, 만화책의 폭발 장면, **햄릿**과 **오필리어**는 인간적 아름다움과 공포, 순수와 폭력이 대비되는 이 뉴스와 이미지의 소용돌이를 매일 들이킨다.

이 모든 것은 방사능 오염에 뒤덮여 있다.

햄릿은 청바지와 16세기 영국풍 재킷을 입고 카우보이 모자를 쓰고 있으며 관객을 향해 소파에 앉아 있다. 그는 생각 없이 리모컨으로 채널을 돌리며 TV를 본다. 무대 뒤편에는 화면에 나오는 이미지의 소용돌이가 프로젝션된다. **햄릿**은 세상을 알고 싶지만 그저 쳐다보기만 할 수 있다.

그의 뒤, 상수에는 **오필리어**가 국방색 군복을 입고 벽에 설치된 테이블에 앉아 옛날식 타자기로 무언가를 쓰고 있다. 그녀 옆에는 핏빛 와인 한 잔이 있다. 그녀는 담배를 피우며 타자에 열중한다.

햄릿과 **오필리어**는 세계의 양 극단에 있다. 둘 사이에는 부패한 시체, 죽은 새, 오줌으로 가득한 대서양이 있다.)

오필리어
(타자를 치며)
나의 햄릿, 난 당신이나 그 여자와 동일시되고 싶지 않아. 당신의
장난감 병정들이 침대 내 쪽으로 침범했어. 바다와 대륙은
정치적 향수와 인내랑 쉽게 맞바꿀 수 있어. 이제 우리 죽은
자들을 묻고 아버지들의 역병을 뒤로 하자. (그녀는 멈추고
와인을 한 모금 마신다.)

햄릿
(더 좋았던 시절을 회상하며 멍하게)
축복을 받지 못한 주사위로
– 일곱 밤 동안 침대 여섯 개 –
새로 알에서 깨고 나온 애벌레들이
자신들의 톱밥으로 이루어진 해변에 도달한다.

오필리어
(아랑곳하지 않고 계속한다)
. . . .글쓰기는 일종의 지적 자위 행위라고 할 수 있지. 나는
컴퓨터의 하얀 눈동자 위에 나의 불쌍하고 초라한 자아를
쏟아내고 있어. 어렵고도 어려운 방종의 기술에 통달한 것이
자랑스러워서, 곧 유아론적인 쾌락의 신세계에 진입하기 위해서
말이야. 나는 놀라우리만치 자급자족이 가능해. 아, 과대망상적
자기애가 치솟을 때마다 깊게 고찰하는 나의 뇌 곳곳에 포진한
성감대 있잖아. 그래, 그래, 바로 지금. 나중을 위해 자동으로
저장해 둬야지. (그녀는 멈추고 담배를 한 모금 피운다.)

TV (내셔널 지오그래픽 채널)
암컷 흰꼬리독수리는 짝짓기를 할 때 수컷과 발톱을 깍지
낍니다. 이 상태로 수컷이 완전히 항복할 때까지 지면으로
곤두박칠 치죠. 암컷이 준비되기 전에 수컷이 깍지를 풀려 하면
암컷은 짝짓기를 결코 허락하지 않습니다. 반면, 암컷이 몇
초라도 지체하면 둘 다 추락해 죽고 말죠.

(전속력으로 질주하며 지나가는 기차 소리. 마치 철로에 서 있는
사람에게 경고라도 하듯 경적 소리를 낸다. 기차가 지나간다.
포트 오소리티 터미널[1], 자정이다. 딩동, 웅성거리는 안내방송
소리가 들린다. **햄릿**은 TV를 계속 본다.)

---

[1] 포트 오소리티(Port Authority)는 뉴욕 맨하탄에 있는 대규모 버스 터미널이다.
뉴욕과 뉴저지를 연결하는 대중교통 허브다.

오필리어

(태연히)

포트 오소리티에 있는 여자들은 대부분 브롱스나 할렘에서 왔어.
머리는 가짜 샤넬 목도리로 싸고 옆구리에는 가짜 루이비통
가방을 끼고 있지. 다들 나 패션 감각 있다, 의지할 사람 있다,
이렇게 보이려고 애를 써. 마치 자기한테 아무 짝에도 쓸모 없는
몇 백 달러짜리 사치품을 기꺼이 사줄 남자 쯤은 있다는 듯이.
어떤 여자들은 절박한 마음을 조용히 감춘 채 갓난아기나 유아를
데리고 다녀. 누가 누구를 더 필요로 하는지 난 지금도 헷갈려:
여자가 아기를 필요로 하는지, 아니면 아기가 여자를 필요로
하는지. 그들은 맨 바닥이나 여행가방에 앉아서 버스를 기다려.
가끔은 남자랑 같이 있는데 그럴 때면 눈에서 부드러운 만족감이
번뜩이는 것 같아. 그 여자들은 유약하면서도 강단이 있지.
언제라도 울기 시작하거나 욕을 쏟아낼 것처럼.

(**오필리어**는 다시 타자를 친다. 전화가 울린다. 전화가 끊기는
소리. 아파트 옆집에서 아기가 우는 소리가 들린다. **거투르드**
입장. 목욕 가운을 걸치고 머리에는 펌 롤러를 요란하게 단 채
무대를 가로지른다. 이를 쑤시며 전화통화를 한다. **거투르드**
눈에서 광채가 뿜어져 나온다.)

거투르드

어머 세상에 뭐라고? 주근깨가 있었다고? 야, 야, 내 생각이
어떤지 너도 잘 알잖아. 정말... 아니, 한 마디만 하면 돼.
도자기 인형 아무거나 찾아서 한 번 봐봐라, 주근깨 있나. 있어?
없지. 근데 너한테 보낸 거엔 있다고? 반송해! 아니, 그걸 왜
니가 내! 운송비는 당연히 그쪽에서 내야지. 다시 상자에 넣어서
돌려보내버려. 야, 말도 안돼. 돈 냈잖아. 제품 소개 봤고 카드로
결제 했으니까 당연히 제대로 된 제품을 받아야지! 사진에
주근깨 있는 여자애가 있었어? 아니잖아. 무슨 말이냐고? 내가
무슨 말을 하려는지 아직도 모르겠어? 아니, 그러니까 이건
허위광고잖아! 그거 감옥 갈 수 있는 거야, 몰라? 그러니까.
괜찮은 중국산 여자애 엄청 많아 . . . .

(**거투르드**는 문 너머로 사라진다. 문틈에 목욕 가운이 끼자
짜증을 내며 잡아당긴다. **햄릿**은 뒤를 돌아 그녀를 향해 신발을
던지지만 맞추지 못한다. 그의 팔에서 박쥐 날개가 돋아난다.
그는 다시 TV를 시청한다.)

오필리어
(아무 일 없었다는 듯 타자를 계속 친다.)
불안 말이야, 불안. 당신이 가득 채우거나 책임을 졌으면 해.
선택은 당신 거야. 번영은 우리의 초라한 유전자를 건네뛸
준비를 하며 조급하게 기다리지. 탄소와 지성 5 킬로그램 어치
안에 영원히 보존될 수 있게 말이야. 그래, 그래, 번식은 대중에게
끝없는 희열을 안겨줄 지도 모르지. 하지만 우린 그보다 더
고상하잖아. 당신이 알아야 할 게, 내 머릿속에서 메아리치는
목소리들은 아이 우는 소리에 묻힐 수 없어. 내가 말하는데, 내
입에서 우아하게 흘러나오는 신음 소리는, 그러니까 당신이
고맙게도 섹스 후 당당히 선보이는 그 무감각... 그 무감각은...
(사이. **오필리어**가 타자를 치는 동안 **햄릿**은 에로 영화를 본다.)
아니, 난 불안에 대해 말하고 있었지. 무감각이 아니라. 당신도
노력을 조금만 더 하면 느낄 수 있을 거야. 당신의 성기는
정밀하게 측정됐고 그 존재론적 속성들이 완벽하게 분석됐지.
당신의 상처받은 자아를 치료하지 못하는 것에 대해 내가
전적인 책임을 지고 우리의 매력적인 만남의 관습들을 정의할 수
있도록 말이야. 그 덕에 우리 둘 다 똑같이 만족을 느끼지 못하게
됐기를 바래. 당신 성기의 길이는 내가 당신의 지친 팔을 베고
누워 담배를 피울 때 느끼는 비탄에 비례하지. 난 누운 채 성적
불만족 때문에 폐암이나 심장마비가 발병할 수 있는 통계적
확률, 그리고 제대로 돌보지 않은 불안들에 대해 사색해. 햄릿,
부디 정치 얘기, 욕망 얘기, 세계 얘기, 죽음 얘기, 굶주림에
허덕이는 아이들을 생각하며 흘린 피눈물 얘기는 꺼내지 말아줘.

(웨딩 가운을 입은 **오필리어**가 **호레이쇼**와 **거투르드**를 대동하며
무대를 가로지른다. **거투르드**는 흔들목마를 타고 머리 위로
칼을 휘두른다. **호레이쇼**는 턱시도를 입고 그물스타킹과 빨간
하이힐을 신고 있다. 그녀는 머리를 뒤로 묶고 있다. 손에는 새우
한 접시와 공책을 들고 있다.)

오필리어
(웨딩 드레스를 입고 계단을 오르내리며)
. . . 너희에게 복이 있나니 . . .

호레이쇼
이 새우 맛이 좀 갔는데? 케이터링 업체에 전화해봐야 하나?
누가 먹고 아프면 안 되잖아. 웨딩 보험 같은 거 팔기 시작해야
하는 거 아니야? 어떻게 생각해?

오필리어

혹시 지금 내가 사랑하는 사람이 나한테 맞는 사람인가 의심이
들 때 없어?

호레이쇼

(공책을 보다가 고개를 들며)

안 맞는 게 당연하지. 진짜 나랑 맞는 사람하고 같이 존재한디는
건 불가능해. 어떤 사람이 너하고 맞을 수 있는 이유는 같이
있지 않기 때문이야. 같이 있다는 사실만으로 맞는 사람이 될 수
없는 거고. (다시 공책을 본다.) 이 새우 어디서 보낸 거지? 라
벨라 토스카였나? 크리스티스였나?

오필리어

크리스티스. 적어도 그 사람에게 확신이 들어야 해. 확신이.

거투르드

확신이라. . .

오필리어

(펑펑 울며)

난 확신이 느는 사람을 위해. 영원히, 죽는 날까지 함께 할 수
있는 . . .

거투르드

삶, 죽음, 사랑이냐 정욕이냐, 우주는 무한하고 끊임없이
팽창한다. 그대는 어디에서 왔는가? 어디로 가는가? 쿠오
바디스.[2] 판타 레이.[3] 좋은 질문이야, 근데 얘, 너희 아버지가
뭐라고 했던 간에 그 사람들이 네 월세를 내줄 것 같아? 천만에.
지금은 그 이름들을 적어놓고 너만의 비밀 공간에 고이
모셔뒀다가 은퇴하고 나서나 꺼내보는 게 좋을 거야. 그땐
쓸모있을 거야. 골프 레슨이나 필라테스 사이, 또 몸에 열이 오를
때 말이야. 자꾸 그렇게 눈을 찌푸리지 마. 화장 번지잖아.

햄릿

(턱시도를 입고 입장)

설마 그 사람이랑 진짜로 결혼하려는 건 아니지?

---

[2]Quo vadis: 라틴어로 '어디로 가는가?'
[3]Panta rei: 라틴어로 '모든 것을 흐른다.'

호레이쇼
(어이없다는 듯)
확신이 든다잖아. 확신.

거투르드
뭐에 대한 확신?

오필리아
내 영혼을 치유할...

(**거투르드**와 **호레이쇼**가 눈빛을 교환하고 미친 듯이 웃기
시작한다.)

거투르드
지난 번 그 놈 처럼 말이야?

호레이쇼
아님 걔 말고 딴 남자?

거투르드
(심오하게)
아니면 또 하나의 남자?

(교회 종소리가 울리기 시작하더니 종들이 인터넷 아바타들로
변한다. 종들의 합창이 부조리한 반복구들로 탈바꿈한다: '그
남자, 딴 남자, 어느 남자, 어떤 남자, 아무 남자, 없는 남자,
우리가 기다려온 남자, 또 다른 남자, 그들이 기다려온 남자,
당신이 기다려온 남자. 누가 기다려 왔나? 어느 남자일까?')

햄릿
(종들이 울리는 동안 모습이 화면에 나타난다)
새끼 늑대들의 울음소리에 잠들어라
모든 게 가짜지만
머리카락은 마른 토사물에 빳빳하게 굳었다
오늘밤 –
당신은 꿈 없는 잠에 빠질 것이다
내일 –
피부를 벗어제끼고 우리를 안에 들이라
툴프 선생의 해부학 수업이 시작된다

(딩동 – 버스 정류장 소리. 알아들을 수 없는 소리의 안내방송이
웅성거린다.)

오필리어
(여행가방과 마네킹 머리로 가득한 베갯잇을 들고 있다.
조심스럽게 입장해 버스 시간표를 올려보며 언제 버스가
출발하는지 알아내려 한다. **햄릿**이 그녀를 방해한다. 그는 목에
무거운 금목걸이를 걸고 있다.)

햄릿
저기, 어디 가요?

오필리어
친구 만나러요.

햄릿
(위아래로 훑어보며)
어디서 왔어요?

오필리어
허스턴이요. 메인 주 히스턴이요.

햄릿
그게 어디에요?

오필리어
작은 도시에요. 아무도 어디에 있는지 몰라요.

햄릿
대학 도시에요? 대학생이에요?

오필리어
아니요.

햄릿
어기서 뭐 해요? (**오필리어**는 말없이 희미하게 웃을 뿐이다.
이 자리게 불편하다.) 호호, 알겠다. 남자죠? 거기서
남자한테 당했죠? 흐흐. 맞네, 남자한테 당했네. 뉴욕으로 이사
와요.

오필리어
흠.

햄릿
그 안에 뭐 들었어요?

오필리어
이거요?

햄릿
네.

오필리어
마네킹 머리요. 미용 배우고 있거든요.

(딩동. 포트 오소리티 아나운서 목소리: '클리블랜드행 오전 2시 30분 버스가 5번 게이트에서 출발합니다. 짐을 다 챙기셨는지 다시 한 번 확인하시기 바랍니다.')

오필리어
제 버스에요.

(**햄릿**은 **오필리어**가 무슨 말을 더 하기를 기다리지만 그녀가 말이 없자 떠난다. 그녀는 힘겹게 베갯잇을 질질 끌며 무대 뒤편으로 퇴장한다. **햄릿**은 고개를 돌려 침을 퉤 뱉고 그 뒤를 따라간다.

'Dream a Little Dream of Me'가 흘러나온다. 책상에 앉은 **오필리어**가 와인을 한 모금 마신다. **햄릿**은 리모컨을 버리고 비디오 게임을 하기 시작한다. 그들 위로 낙엽이 떨어지기 시작한다. 문이 열리면 음악이 갑자기 꺼진다.

거투르드가 전화를 들고 입장한다. 그녀는 전과 똑같은 목욕 가운을 입고 있지만 펌 롤러 절반은 뺀 상태다. 그녀의 머리카락은 메두사의 뱀들처럼 사방으로 뻗친다. 전화통화를 하며 카탈로그를 넘긴다.)

거투르드
. . .어느 걸로 사면 좋을까? 러시아산? 루마니아산? 아니면 중국산? 러시아산은 다 괜찮아 보여. 예쁘고 금발이고. 근데 다 부분 파손이래. 엄마들이 보드카를 너무 마셔서. . . 루마니아산은, 글쎄 난 잘 모르겠다. 금발인 건 좋은데, 너무 창백하지 않아? 영양실조에 걸렸을 수도 있어. 아프리카산도 마찬가진데, 너무 이국적이지 않니? 어깨에 하나 걸치고 있으면 멋져 보일 것 같지 않아? 샤넬 백 바로 옆에 말이야. 아니, 에르메스가 낫겠다. . . 보증기간이 어떻게 되지? 고작 2년? 장기 보증 옵션 없나? . . .혹시나 죽으면 어떡하지? . . .새로 보내주나? 장례비도 지원해주나? . . .운송비는? 운송비 두 번

다시는 안 낼 거야. 그 서류 다 정리하는데 2만5천이나
들었다니까. 그래 맞아, 맞아 맞아, 네 말이 맞아. 남미산이
괜찮아 보이네, 정말. 너무 검지도 않고 너무 창백하지도
않고. . .그래. . ..

(자기 결정에 만족해 하며 퇴장한다.)

TV 화면
(연속극인지 고전소설인지 분간하기가 어렵다.)
그녀는 자신의 이중적인 본성을 두려워했다. 그가 그녀를
사로잡았다고 확신할 때마다 그녀의 눈은 낯선 사람의 것으로
변했다. 어느 순간에는 그녀가 너무나도 가깝게 느껴져 자기
머릿속에 그녀의 목소리가 들리기까지 했다가, 또 갑자기 너무
멀어져 그의 세포 하나하나에 스며든 외로움이 쓰라렸고 자신의
죽음을 인지한 것처럼 그를 숨막히게 했다.

(햄릿은 소파에 앉아 비디오 게임을 한다. 그의 얼굴은 점차
오필리아의 것으로 변한다. 그녀는 검은 두건으로 싼 군용
선두보를 쓰고 있다.)

오필리어
(얼굴이 화면에 나타난다. 마치 동시를 읊조리듯 말한다.)
어느날
나의 살점들이 우리를 버리고 떠났네
나와 내 피부는 놀라서 멍하니 있었네
우린 재미있어 서로를 바라봤지
왜냐하면 더 잃을 게 없었거든

호레이쇼
(법률 문서를 읽는다)
그들은 몇 달 째 아기를 맞이할 준비를 하고 있었다. 아기침대,
유모차, 아기 옷 등 모든 쇼핑을 함께 했다. 모든 것을 최고급,
최상가, 최고로 유명한 브랜드 카탈로그에서 골랐다. 그는
그녀가 버스를 기다리지 않고도 대학 캠퍼스를 오갈 수 있도록
새 차를 사줬다. 아기가 딸이라는 것을 알게 되자 그는 실망했다.
그는 자신의 업적을 물려받을 아들을 정말 원했다. 그는
아들에게 가르쳐줄 수 많은 것들을 상상하곤 했다. 그는 실망한
것이 부끄러워 자기 마음을 숨겼다. 딸을 가지게 될 것이라는
사실을 받아들였고 임신 기간 내내 그녀에게 힘이 돼주려 했다.
그녀가 날카로워지거나 갑자기 우울해질 때마다 조용히

보듬어줬다. 그녀는 그의 아기를 품고 있었다. 그녀는 처음으로
대놓고 그를 괴롭힐 수 있게 됐으며, 뭘 해도 다 받아준다는
것을 점차 알게 됐다. 그의 소심함을 포용해야 했던 그 많은
순간들 때문에 쌓인 불만은 그녀의 상상력을 더욱 자극했다.
그녀는 점차 치밀하게 잔혹한 방식으로 그를 짓밟고 또
짓밟았다. 그는 책임감, 충격, 경이로움을 동시에 느끼며 이 모든
것을 감당했다.

(머리 위로 비행기나 헬기가 지나가는 소리. 무대에 날개
그림자가 드리워진다. **오필리어**는 검은 팔을 벌리고 점차
공중으로 떠오르기 시작한다. 그녀는 까마귀로 변신한다.
대도시의 소음들: 앰뷸런스, 무차별 총격, 웃는 여자 아이들,
비명을 지르는 사람, 길에서 개 짖는 소리 등. **오필리어**는
하늘에서 이 모든 것을 내려다본다. 그녀의 몸은 수 백 만
조각으로 부숴진다. 그녀는 몸의 파편들을 장바구니에 모아
담으려 한다. 마트 청소부 아줌마가 그녀를 쫓아내자 **오필리어**는
자기 눈알을 뽑아낸다.)

햄릿
빛이 들렀다 간다,
흰 시트에 떨어진 그림자를 어루만지며,
거기에서 피, 락스,
어제 싼 오줌 냄새가 난다.

지평의 끝에 있던 그 많던 불면증과
천장에 난 곰팡이 얼룩들로 만든 모자이크들,
다 어느 서랍에 넣어뒀는가?

(**오필리어**는 군 간호사가 미는 휠체어에 앉아 입장한다.)

오필리어
어렸을 때부터 휠체어를 탄 나는 갑자기 딜레마에 빠졌어.
누구한테 충성을 맹세해야 하지? 그 대상이 여성이라면 답은
쉽지. 그 대상이 병신이라면 답은 쉽지. 그 대상이 여성인 동시에
병신이라면 답은 쉽지. 하지만 장애를 가진 남성의 모습에는
실존적 불가능성이 내재해 있었어. 그는 적인가, 아니면
순교당한 동지인가? 그는 젠더에 종속돼 있는가 휠체어에
종속돼 있는가? 난 남성 장애인에 대한 정치적 입장을 정리하지
못했기 때문에 아예 피해버리기로 결정했어. 장애를 가진
남자들은 상처받은 남성성 때문에 본질적으로 망가져 있었기

때문에 여성성이 상처받은 나는 자연스럽게 그들을 피하게 된
거야. 내 안에 담긴 모순들, 그러니까 욕망의 대상이 되고 싶은
동시에 존중의 대상이 되고 싶은 마음을 해결하지 못했기
때문에 감정적으로 많은 걸 요구하지 않는 남자가 필요했던
거야. 무한히 관대하고, 지칠 줄 모르는 성기처럼 자아와 정신이
강인하고 듬직한 남자. 내가 어마어마한, 그치만 호불호가 갈릴
수노 있는, 섹스 어필과 늘 매력적인 성격을 가지고 있다는 것,
그가 완전히 또 조금의 주저함도 없이 나에게 사로잡혔다는
것을 그 성기가 확인시켜주지.

(휠체어가 빙글빙글 돌면서 **오필리어** 마네킹이 증발한다.
간호사는 베개에서 먼지를 털어내고 원을 따라 달리기
시작한다. 간호사는 휠체어를 비워둘 수 없다는 것을 알기
때문에 뭐든지 그 위에 쌓아올린다.)

(TV: 토크쇼나 인기 드라마 소리. 부부 심리상담 시간.
오필리어와 **햄릿**은 소파에 앉는다.)

심리상담사
안녕하세요, 와주셔서 감사합니다. 문제를 이렇게 함께
나눈다는 게 쉬운 일이 아닐 텐데.

햄릿
아 뭐, 문제 없죠.

심리상담사
(실망하며)
문제가 없어요?

햄릿
아, 아니요. 문제가 있어요. 문제를 나누는 게 문제 없다고요.

심리상담사
아, 그렇군요. 좋습니다. 그래서 문제가 뭔가요?

햄릿
너무 끔찍해요. 이 사람이 한 짓이 믿기지가 않아요. 우리 삶을
망가뜨렸어요.

오필리어
자기야, 자기야, 내가 뭘 어떻게 했는데, 내가 뭘 어떻게 했냐고.
제발 말 좀 해줘, 자기야. (운다.) 그게 뭔지 얘기만 해주면 다

괜찮아질 거야. 그렇게 입을 닫아버리면 우리 사랑, 우리 결혼이 위험에 빠지잖아.

심리상담사
맞아요, 커뮤니케이션이 중요해요. 얘기를 해주셔야 저희가 알죠. 아내에게 감정표현을 하시면 그 감정을 나눌 수 있을 거예요.

햄릿
뭘 했냐고? 뭘 했냐고요? 말 꺼내기도 힘들어요. 이것 봐요, 생각만 해도 몸이 덜덜 떨린다니까요. 아직도 믿기지 않아요. 나한테 어떻게 그럴 수 있었는지 . . . .

오필리어 & 심리상담사
뭘 어떻게 했는데(요)?

햄릿
알고 싶어요? 정말로 알고 싶어요? 알았어요, 얘기할 게요. 어제 아침에 말이죠, 밥을 먹는데. . . (**심리상담사의 귀에 속삭인다.**)

심리상담사
이런 맙소사!!!

햄릿
진짜로 그랬다니까요.

심리상담사
아, 이건 확실히 어려운 상황이네요. 그런데 말이죠, 우리가 이 문제를 해결하면, 문제가 해결될 거라고 굳게 믿습니다. 이혼 사유 1위가 뭔지 아세요? 바로 이혼입니다. 근데 그것 말고 생활은 어떤가요?

오필리어
다 괜찮아요. 결혼 생활이 좋아요.

햄릿
네, 일하는 것도 괜찮고, 벌이도 괜찮고, 애들은 죽었어요.

심리상담사
감정이 균형 잡히고 객관적인 지성적 판단을 방해하지 않을 때, 바로 그 때 진정으로 현명해졌다고 말할 수 있죠. 두 분께서는 항상 선험적 결론을 제시하시든지, 아니면 축적된 경험적

증거를 가지고 귀납적으로 결론을 도출하셔야 합니다. 심오한
정신적 객관성이 결여된 명제들을 쉬지 않고 계속 제기해야만
해요. 오직 그래야만 객관적으로 진정한 것을 진정으로
객관적으로 말할 수 있게 됩니다. **(심리상담사**는 자기가
얼마나 천재적인지 놀란다. 그는 자기가 방금 한 말을 곱씹으며
웃고 고개를 흔든다. 그러나 곧 잊어버리고 코를 후비기
시작한다.)

오필리어
(책상에 앉아 타자를 친다)
쾌락이라는 것은 어찌 이리도 특별할까. 또 어찌나 신기하게도
고통과 결부돼 있을까. 반대일 줄 알았는데. 왜냐하면 남자는
그걸 동시에 느낄 수는 없지만 어느 쪽이건 하나를 좇으면 다른
하나도 따라올 수 밖에 없거든.

TV
(강연)
성적 쾌락을 표현하는 방식은 근본적으로 자기반영적이라서
남성과 다른 여성은 차라리 클리토리스가 없는 게 나을 수도
있습니다. 왜냐하면 영원히 찢어지지 않는 처녀막은 히스테론을
필요로 하지 않기 때문이죠. 그 위로 쓰기 영원히 신공될
뿐입니다. 이것이 바로 이른바 사랑이라는 폭력의 현장일까요?
우리에게 유일하게 주어진 완벽한 삼위일체 안에 담긴 변화하는
사랑 말입니다. 여성이 늘 남성의 자기해체에 동원되는 도구에
불과했다면 이거야말로 철학의 새로운 반전 아닐까요?

오필리어
(심리치료사가 되어)
전 당신이 합리적으로 행동하고 있다고 믿고 싶어요.
자기패배에 젖은 미국식 남성성의 함정들에서 자유롭다고요.
그걸 방치하면 결국 감정적 소진, 지적 결핍, 성적 무능에 빠지게
될 거예요.

햄릿
(비디오 게임을 하며 태연하게)
내가 정신을 잃을 정도로 압도적인 질투심에 휩싸여 너를
극적으로 살해해 주기를 원해? 당신이 오르가즘을 느낄 때 죽여
무한한 절정을 느끼며 우주와 하나가 될 수 있게 해주기를 원해?
당신이 영원히 그 순간을 살 수 있다고 믿을 수 있게 말이야.
내가 당신의 귀에 내 절망에 관한 달콤한 헛소리를 속삭이며

죽여주기를 원해? 정교하게 연출한 죽음의 연극이 완성되도록
당신을 살해하고 나서 나도 같이 죽기를 원해?

(**오필리어**가 공중에 떠오른다. 지푸라기 잡는 심정으로 손을
뻗지만 세계는 지평선 너머로 사라진다. **오필리어**는 걸으려
하지만 딛을 땅이 없다. 리모컨을 찾아 다급하게 몇 번 버튼을
누른다. 갠지스 강 하류로 사람과 동물 시체가 떠내려간다.
오필리어는 물에 머리를 감고 사막 모래를 밟는다. 심장에서
피가 난다. 그녀의 핏줄은 철사로 돼 있다. **오필리어**는 자신의
시체를 짊어지고 사막 국경을 건넌다.)

햄릿
내가 사망의 음침한 골짜기로 다닐지라도
해를 두려워하지 않을 것은 주께서 나와 함께 하심이라
주의 지팡이와 막대기가 나를 안위하시나이다
주께서 내 원수의 목전에서 내게 상을 차려 주시고

오필리어
(위장무늬 군복을 입고 책상에 앉아 있다. 아무 일도 없었다는
듯 침착하고 감정 없이 타자를 계속 친다.)
나의 햄릿, 당신 시장가치를 올리려고 꼭 자기비하에 의지할
필요는 없어. 우리의 순수함은 온전히 형식적인 것이야. 당신
어머니가 그토록 애지중지했고, 보이는 비누 광고에서마다
부각된 우리의 변태 기질도 마찬가지고. 당신이 알아야 할 게
있는데, 그녀는 양초와 텔레비전으로 정교하게 조형된, 그렇기
때문에 우리 세대에게 새로운, 욕망을 품고 자동적으로
첫날밤까지 자신의 처녀성을 지켰어. 불안 말이야, 불안. 타인의
미덕과 삶에 대한 확고한 열정이 있기에 나는 신과 인간의
존엄성을 진정으로 믿어. 대가리가 날아간 채 참호에 누워 있을
때만 아니면 말이야. 내가 나약한 팔로 감싸안은 그 깊고 심오한
곳 안에까지 닿을 수 있는 사람이 바로 당신이 될 거라고 생각해.
그래, 맞아 햄릿. 나에게 시를 써주든지 날 세게 박아주든지 해.
어느 쪽이건 간에 우리는 오랫동안 간직한 불멸에 대한 의지를
계속 이어나가게 될 거야. 그 의지는 우리의 선량한 마음, 서로에
대한 사랑, 또 증오를 청산한 영적 화합을 통해 실현되겠지.
개인위생의 의식들, 다양한 지적 수준에서 벌어지는
포스트모던한 대화, 그리고 번식이 통계적 평균에 도달했는지
혹은 자기애의 이기적 개인주의에 불과한지에 따라 물질적 풍요

혹은 결핍을 해결해줄 수 있는 노동의 조화 속에서 하루하루를
보내며 말이야. 나의 신념은 타인과 마찬가지로 나에게
자신감을 안겨줄 거라 생각해. 그 덕에 내가 당신에게 와인을 한
잔 따라 주고 안마를 해줄 때 당신이 고맙다고 하겠지. 당신의
성기 끄트머리에는 존재론적 가능성이 있어. 그러므로 나는
당신의 요도에 당신의 칼을 찔러 넣고 그 안의 공간이 나의
불안을, 그리고 잎으로 태어날 미국의 아버지들, 아니 우리의
성생활을 감안하면 다른 다섯 대륙도 포함시켜야겠구나, 아무튼
그들이 실수로 두고 간 불안들을 모두 수용할 만큼 넓은지
확인하겠어. 우리 할머니의 아버지는 프라하와 비엔나 사이
길가 어딘가에서 의문의 죽음을 당하셨어. 우리도 정확히
그렇게 죽게 될 거야.

(호레이쇼가 새우를 담은 은쟁반을 들고 입장한다.)

호레이쇼
(아직도 소파에 앉아있는 **햄릿**에게)
새우 먹을래?

햄릿
아니. 다이어트 중이야.

(**호레이쇼**는 갑자기 무언가가 기억났는지 주먹을 불쩍 들고
"자유!"라고 외친다. 탱크가 그를 짓밟고 지나가고 그의 시체는
검은 아스팔트 속으로 사라진다. 웃는 아이들이 손을 잡고
아스팔트 위로 뛰어간다. 까마귀들이 **호레이쇼** 시체의 살을
파먹는다. 버스 터미널 소리. 딩동.)

터미널 안내원
파리발, 런던 도쿄 경유, 뉴욕행 버스가 5번 터미널에서 곧
출발합니다. 파리발, 런던 도쿄 경유, 뉴욕행 버스가 5번
터미널에서 곧 출발합니다.

(기계가 고장난 것처럼 인내방송이 몇 번 반복된다. 안내방송이
시작되면 **오필리어**가 피에 젖은 웨딩드레스를 입고 머리에
스카프를 두른 채 입장한다. 그녀는 승차장을 찾고 있다. 그녀의
뒤로 **호레이쇼**가 어떤 남자의 잘린 머리와 새우가 올려진
은쟁반을 들고 따라온다.)

(**오필리어** 입장.)

오필리어
(미친 듯이)

확신, 확신이 드는, 나에게 확신이 들어. 내가 기다려온 사람은 바로 나야. 바로 나야. 바로 그 자, 유일한 자, 어느 자. 그 자, 신성한 자, 당연한 자, 축복받은 자.

호레이쇼
(그녀에게 신경을 쓰지 않는다.)
크리스티스 게 더 신선하네. 크리스티스에서 주문하자.

(오필리어는 군화를 벗어 그것으로 **호레이쇼**를 때려 죽인다. 그의 시체가 검은 아스팔트 속으로 사라진다. **오필리어**는 양 팔을 벌리고 퇴장한다. **햄릿**은 핸드폰을 가지고 놀기 시작한다. **오필리어/메데아**는 버스 터미널 바닥에 앉아 죽은 아이에게 노래를 불러준다.)

오필리아/메데아
그의 이름이 영원토록 축복받을지어다,
주님의 이름은 축복받고, 찬양받고, 영광받고, 고귀하고, 극찬받고,
강인하고, 광활하고, 찬미받을 지어다.
그는 축복받을 지어다.[4]

햄릿
당신은 내 눈 안에 담긴 고통을 보고 다 안다고 생각하지. 한 남자의 고통을 보면 모든 걸 알 수 있다고 생각하지. 한 남자의 고통을 알아볼 수 있으면 그 남자는 언제나 영원히 내 것이 된다고 생각하지.

TV
(내셔널 지오그래픽 채널)
수컷 빈대는 암컷에게 정액을 주입하도록 설계된 생식기를 가지고 있습니다. 빈대의 짝짓기는 매우 폭력적입니다. 왜냐하면 암컷을 못 움직이게 누른 채 생식기로 여러 번 찔러야만 수정이 안정적으로 되기 때문입니다. 이 방법은

---

[4] 유대교 장례식에서 암송하는 카디시(kaddish)의 일부.

암컷의 생식 통로를 우회하도록 진화가 됐는데, 그 결과로
암컷이 임신 시기를 조절할 수 있는 능력은 제한되고
제거됩니다.

오필리어
내가 내 몸의 주인이 되면 다른 주인은 받아들이지 않겠어.
(소리를 지르며) 내가 내 몸의 주인이 되면 다른 주인은
받아들이지 않겠어.

(햄릿은 채널을 바꾼다.)

오필리어
(와인을 한 모금 마시고 계속 타자를 친다.)
자기계시의 참혹한 행동들은 천박한 혈통의 하층민들을 향한
자비로운 마음에서 시작되는 법이지. 내가 당신에게 섬세하게
묘사하는 불안은 당신이 잘 사는 데에 아무런 윤리적 영향을
미치지 않을 거야, 분명히. 그리고 나의 불안정한 감정을 대체할
무언가를 쉽게 찾을 수 있을 거야, 분명히. 나 또한 우리가
욕망하는 모든 생명체에서 대체물을 찾듯이. 수그리드는 나의
사아가 정확하게 가리키는 선택은 오직 당신의 세라토닌 수치와
오늘 이 밤이 생성하는 욕망에 달려 있어. 너의 제안은 낚시이
발기돼 있는 동안 유효하고 너의 기내에 찬 얼굴에 당신이 그
애지로운 편집증을 사정하는 순간 만료돼. 수학 공식으로
구성된 욕망에도 나름의 장점이 있어. 기대감이 요동치는
동시에 영구불변할 수 있기 때문이지. 그걸 프랙털 비율로
복제하면 고체 조직의 가벼운 성질을 띠게 돼. 어렸을 때
학습돼서 먼 훗날 샤르도네나 소비뇽 블랑 한 잔, 레몬 소스와
캐비어로 맛을 낸 생선 요리를 먹을 때 회사할 수 있게 미뤄둔
개인적인 문제들 있잖아. 그런 문제에 대한 시름한 해결책과
근본적인 차이가 없겠지.

(거투르드가 전화를 하며 지나간다. 그녀는 이제 기계로 변신해
있다.)

거투르드
카탈로그에 써 있었잖아. 고객 만족 보장. 불량품 애를
보내놓기만 하면 그냥 가만히 있을 줄 아나 본데, 당장 반품하고
사진과 똑같이 생긴 걸로 다시 보내라고 해. 주근깨 없는... 얘,
요즘 같은 세상에 돈 관리를 얼마나 철저하게 해야 하는데. 내가
어제 중국산 양말을 샀는데, 글쎄 불량품인 거 있지?

그렇다니까, 어, 어. 그래서 반품했어. 불량품에 허비할 돈이
남아도는 줄 알아? 어, 어. 돈을 냈는데 제품을 잘못 보냈으면
반품하고 제대로 된 걸 받아야 한다니까. 그래, 그래, 내 말이
바로 그거야.

(거투르드 퇴장. 눈이 내리기 시작한다.)

햄릿
(마치 비밀을 알려주듯 은밀하게)
어떨 때, 우리가 대문을 지나듯
서로의 눈 속을 통과할 때
어떨 때, 나는 그녀와 같다
어떨 때, 그녀는
내가 된다

오필리어
(분주하게 타자를 치며)
오른손에는 영원한 사랑이 들려 있어. 하지만 그 안에는 지난
연인의 시체와 펼쳐진 책 위로 떨어진 곤충을 재활용해 만든
구역질 나는 구원, 또 비유의 각진 습관들이 남긴 곤란한 감정의
흔적들이 도사리고 있지. 당신의 눈동자 안에 사랑스럽게 담긴 나
자신을 아끼겠다고 약속할 게. 그러니까 내가 오르가즘을 느낄
때, 그리고 찌푸린 나의 인상이 소리를 낼 것 만 같은 상상으로
확대될 그 때 제발 눈을 감지 말아줘. 또 당신이 그토록 오랫동안
바라던 안정을 갖추도록 노력하겠다고 약속할 게. 당신의 수요와
공급이 원활할 수 있게 때때로 내가 자존심을 내세우는 것과
뒤섞인 혼란도 갖출 게. 우리의 오이디푸스적 환상을 충족하기로
약속하고 나의 자궁이 오아시스이자 우리의 지적 노력의
배설물을 담을 수 있는 변기가 될 수 있도록 헌신하도록 노력할
게. 나는 이 합의가 우리 질량의 40 퍼센트는 만족할 거라고 믿어.
나머지 60 퍼센트는 의혹, 무거움과 가벼움에 대한 물리적
영속성의 불만족으로 타오르겠지. 나의 왼손은 되돌려 받지 못한
사랑을 내세우고 있어. 그게 내 것인지 당신 것인지는 나중에
결정하자고. 어느 쪽이건 간에 우리는 노예와 주인 본연의
우아함을 가지고 우리에게 주어진 역할들에 적응할 거라고 믿어.
기다리는 시간에 비례해서 욕망은 커지지. 나의 햄릿, 그녀는
유럽, 북미, 그리고 아시아 최고의 창녀들로부터 교육을 받았어.
당신이 외로움에 몸부림 치거나 술에 취하는 밤이면 찾아가 반쯤

단단해진 성기를 삽입한 그 창녀들 말이야. 욕망의 악몽이나 그 부재로부터 잠시만이라도 벗어날 수 있기를 염원하며.

(**오필리어**는 멈춘다. 자신을 추스른다. 그 후 서랍에서 총을 꺼내 자기 머리를 쏜다. 발사 소리가 크게 울리고 사방에 피가 튄다. 그녀는 아무 일 없었다는 듯 계속 타자를 친다.)

죽음의 병이 우리를 압도해. 우리는 죽지 않기를 희망하고 살지 않기를 희망하지. 소유당하는 것과 소유하는 것 사이의 불안감은 쾌감을 느끼기에는 너무 많이 훔쳤지만 다른 감정을 느끼기에는 너무 조금 훔친 도둑의 속도로 자리를 잡아. 멸시의 굳은 미소를 지으며 떠나지. 자기 존속의 얼어붙은 구석들 뒤에 숨은 울음들이 들려. 당신의 육체가 약속한 만큼 내 생각은 유연하게 흐르지 못해. 그렇다고 해서 당신에게 고마워하는 불만족으로 끓어오르지도 않아 . . ..

TV
(내셔널 시오그래픽 채널)
암컷괴 수컷 전갈은 깅렬하게 서로를 붙들고 독침으로 서로를 찌르려 합니다. 입으로 서로를 문 채 수컷은 꼬리로 암컷을 수 차례 찌를 것입니다. 암컷은 보통 수컷을 잡아먹는 것으로 응수합니다.

(**오필리어** 입장, 그녀의 웨딩드레스는 너덜너덜해져 있다. 가슴에는 폭탄 기폭 장치가 장착돼 있다.)

오필리어
내가 느끼는 굶주림은 내 안에 있는 게 아니야
내 안으로 흘러들어왔다가 나가지
당신은 나의 탐욕스러운 팔 안에서
자기 자신을 잃어버려
구원을 받는 동시에 선고받을 수는 없지
내가 느끼는 굶주림은 내 안에 있는 게 아니야

(그녀는 휠체어에 앉아 미친 듯이 웃으며 휠체어를 굴려서 퇴장한다.)

TV 뉴스
오늘 캘리포니아에서 한 어머니가 자기 아기의 목을 베고 뇌를 파먹는 사건이 있었습니다. (젊은 앵커우먼은 잠깐 동안 슬퍼 보이다가 재빠르게 환한 웃음을 짓는다.) 다음 소식으로 넘어가죠. 저희 라이프스타일 전문가를 만날 시간인데요, 이번 시즌 가장 핫한 질문에 답을 해주신다고 합니다 . . . .

('징글벨'이 들린다.

배경에 투사된 **햄릿**의 얼굴은 그가 하고 있는 비디오 게임 안으로 녹아든다. 소파에 앉은 **햄릿**과 비디오 게임 속의 **햄릿**이 동시에 일어나 모자와 자켓을 벗는다. 그는 무대 뒤로 들어가 휘발유 한 통을 들고 나와 사방에 뿌리기 시작한다.)

오필리어
(**햄릿**이 휘발유를 뿌리는 동안)
저 멀리, 저 멀리, 나의 햄릿. . . 우리는 우리 존재에 대한 확신을 스스로 찾은 게 분명해. 부디 다른 사람이 가져야 마땅한 것을 내가 못 뺏도록 막지는 말아 주기를 바래. 밀랍 장기, 영혼 등이 즐비한 박물관에서 열리는 무언의 경매장에서 구매한 물건들과 잃어버린 신념의 조각을 곁들여 밥상에 올린 진실과 거짓에 당신이 목숨을 건다는 걸 난 알아. 내 입에서 나오는 약속들은 번역이 불가능하다는 걸 당신이 진짜로 이해해 주기를 바래. 난 세심한 곳 하나하나까지 신경을 쓰며 당신과 나의 생각들을 연결해. 당신은 사랑을 느끼기를 원했지. 아니, 뭐라도 느끼기를. 욕망의 연극은 만인 앞에 공개돼 있어. 호기심 가득하고 서로의 존재를 인식하지 못하는 관람객에게 말이야. 나는 어제 우리가 길들여지기를 거부하는 침대 밑으로 기어들어가 울고 있었을 때 그 관람객들이 도시를 거니는 것을 봤어. 나는 옆구리에 당신 머리를 끼고 외출을 했어. 나는 말들 때문에 발을 헛디뎌. 그 말들의 힘에 연결된 채. 나의 햄릿, 울지 마. 밤이 다가오고 있어.

(그녀는 성냥불을 켠다. 암전.)

Opheliamachine

Traducere Una Toma

Un service auto, un depozit sau camera de joacă a unui copil, plin de obiecte adunate acolo, de un călător rătăcit: Statuia lui David fără brațe purtând o cască de motocicletă, o grămadă de măşti africane sparte, scheletul unui poet mort râzând isteric de propria lui umbră, un bebeluş de jucărie, cu membrele lipsă, sugând o acadea roz, umbrela stricată a lui Magritte, vechiul telefon către Dumnezeu al lui Andy Warhol, un voal de mireasă alb şi murdar atârnând undeva cu alte haine, grămezi de pantofi vechi şi peruci.

E o groapă de gunoi modernă, cu console de jocuri stricate, ecrane TV şi ecrane de computer care difuzează la întâmplare scene mute din viețile noastre virtuale: scene de război, crime în masă, genocide, cadavre de la Auschwitz, filme porno, campanii politice, femei de pe Wall Street, femei grase, femei anorexice, eleve din Japonia, femei acoperite în burka, safari sălbatic, explozii din benzi desenate. **Hamlet** *şi* **Ophelia** *beau supa asta zilnică de ştiri şi imagini: un mish-mash de contraste umane, de frumusețe şi groază, inocență şi violență.*

Totul e acoperit de cenuşă radioactivă.

Hamlet, *îmbrăcat în blugi, o jachetă de secol XVI şi pălărie de cowboy, stă aşezat pe canapea cu fața la spectatori. Se uită la televizor, schimbând neatent canalele cu telecomanda. Pe fundalul scenei este proiectat mish-mash-ul.* **Hamlet** *vrea să înțeleagă lumea, dar tot ce poate face e să se holbeze la ea.*

În stânga scenei, în spatele lui, **Ophelia**, *îmbrăcată în costum militar de camuflaj verde, stă în spatele unui birou plutitor scriind ceva la o maşină de scris demodată. Un pahar de vin roşu sângeriu e aşezat lângă. Fumează o țigară şi este concentrată la ce scrie.*

Hamlet *şi* **Ophelia** *sunt la cele două capete ale lumii. Între ei, oceanul Atlantic plin de cadavre în putrefacție, păsări moarte şi urină.*

Ophelia (*scrie*)   Hamlet, dragul meu, nu-mi doresc să mă identific cu tine sau cu ea, soldații tăi de jucărie au invadat partea mea de pat. Oceanele şi continentele se dau la schimb uşor pentru nostalgie politică şi anduranța. Lasă morții să-şi îngroape morții, ciuma taților noştri. (*Face o pauză şi ia o gură din paharul de vin.*)

Hamlet (*absent, amintindu-şi de vremuri mai bune*)   În zarurile
nesfinţite
Şase paturi pentru şapte nopţi
larve nou născute au acostat
pe malurile din propriul lor rumeguş.

Ophelia (*continuând, netulburată*)   . . . scrisul e o formă de
masturbare intelectuală. Îmi vărs fiinţa săracă, patetică peste ochiul
alb al computerului meu, mândră că stăpânesc arta asta dificilă a
auto-indulgenţei, şi, prin urmare, mândră să intru în noua eră a
plăcerilor solipsiste. Autosuficienţa mea mă uimeşte. O, acele
puncte erogene din creierul meu, examinate cu atenţie în crize
megalomanice de auto-adorare. Da, da, chiar acum. O s-o salvez
automat pentru mai târziu. (Face o pauză şi trage un fum din ţigară.)

TV (*National Geographic Channel*)   În timpul ritualului de
împerechere, vulturul alb femelă îşi împreunează ghearele cu
masculul, cerând supunerea lui totală în timp ce perechea se aruncă
inertă spre pământ. Dacă el încearcă să se elibereze înainte ca ea să
fie pregătită, nu o să-l lase să o penetreze. Dacă ea aşteaptă doar
câteva secunde prea mult, se vor prăbuşi amândoi de moarte pe
pământ.

*Sunetul unui tren care merge la viteză maximă, fluierând de parcă
încearcă să atenţioneze pe cineva care stă pe şine. Trenul trece.
Miezul nopţii la Autoritatea portuară. Ding, dong, sunetul unui
anunţ la difuzor, murmurând ceva.* **Hamlet** *se uită la TV în
continuu.*

Ophelia (*lipsită de emoţie, raţională*)   Majoritatea fetelor de la
Autoritatea portuară sunt fie din Bronx, fie din Harlem. Poartă
eşarfe Channel fake pe cap şi genţi Louis Vuitton fake pe braţ.
Încearcă să arate la modă şi îngrijite, de parcă au un bărbat pentru
care merită să cheltui câteva sute de dolari pe luxuri evident
inutile. Unele dintre ele au bebeluşi mici sau copii cu ele, ţinându-i
în braţe cu o disperare tăcută. Niciodată nu sunt sigură cine are mai
multă nevoie de cine: ele de copiii lor sau copiii lor de ele. Stau pe
jos sau pe valizele lor, aşteptându-şi răbdător autobuzele. Par atât
fragile, cât şi dure, de parcă ar putea începe să plângă sau să înjure
în orice moment.

Ophelia *se întoarce la scris. Sună telefonul. Sunetul tramvaiului trecând. Plânsete de copil în apartamentul vecin. Intră* **Gertrude.** *Traversează scena, purtând un halat și bigudiuri de culoare aprinsă în cap. Se scobește între dinți și vorbește la telefon. Ochii îi strălucesc.*

Gertrude   O, Doamne, nu! Avea pistrui?! Păi, alo, ȘTII ce CRED EU despre asta. Adică . . . uite tot ce vreau să zic e atât de simplu. Te uiți la o păpușă de porțelan obișnuită, are pistrui? Hm? Nu, nu are. Cea pe care ți-o trimit ei are pistrui? Deci . . . trimite-o înapoi! . . . Nu, nu ar trebui să faci asta! NU ar trebui să plătești TU pentru livrarea returului. Pune-o imediat înapoi în cutia aia și trimite-o înapoi. O, nu! Ai plătit pentru ea! Ai văzut poza în catalog, ți-ai introdus cardul de credit și acum ar trebui să primești ce doreai! . . . Era o fată cu pistrui în poze? Nu! ok. Ce vreau să zic . . . m-am făcut înțeleasă?! . . . NU, pentru că asta se numește REPREZENTARE GREȘITĂ! . . . Pot fi băgați la pușcărie pentru asta, știai? . . . . Mda, poți să iei multe fete drăguțe din China . . .

Dispare în spatele ușii din scenă. I se prinde halatul în ușă și ea trage de el nervoasă. **Hamlet** *se întoarce și aruncă cu un pantof după ea, dar ratează. Îi cresc aripi de liliac și revine la a se uita televizor.*

Ophelia (*continuă să scrie de parcă nimic nu s-ar fi întâmplat*)   Teama, dragule, teama; Vreau să o umpli sau să o iei asupra ta. E alegerea ta: prosperitatea așteaptă nerăbdătoare ca genele noastre sărace să treacă, și să se imortalizeze în cinci kilograme de carbon și intelect. Da, da, dragule, sunt sigură că procreația poate fi o sursă de bucurie nesfârșită pentru mase, dar noi suntem cu mult mai rafinați. Trebuie să înțelegi, vocile din capul meu nu pot fi asurzite de plânsetul unui copil; trebuie să știi, chiar și țipetele pe care le produc cu atâta grație când îți exerciți milostiv dreptul la amorțeală post-coitală . . . amorțeală . . . (*Pauză. Pe măsură ce scrie,* **Hamlet** *se uită la soft porn.*) teama, dragule, teama despre care vorbeam, nu amorțeală. Sunt sigură că dacă încerci puțin mai tare, vei ajunge la ea. Penisul tău a fost măsurat cu atenție și calitățile sale existențiale au fost evaluate cu deplină

responsabilitate pentru propriul meu eşec de a-ţi vindeca fiinţa
rănită şi de a defini convenţia întâlnirii noastre fermecătoare care
sper că ne va lăsa la fel de nesatisfăcuţi. Lungimea penisului tău
este proporţională cu angoasa pe care o s-o simt fumând o ţigară în
braţele tale obosite, şi contemplând probabilitatea statistică a
cancerului pulmonar sau a unui atac de cord provocat de
insaţiabilitate sexuală şi temeri de care nu s-a îngrijit nimeni.
Hamlet, dragă, nu vorbi despre politică, despre dorinţele tale, lume,
moarte şi sângele pe care îl verşi plângând pentru copiii înfometaţi.

Ophelia, *purtând o rochie de mireasă, traversează scena,
acompaniată de* **Horatio** *şi* **Gertrude**. **Gertrude** *conduce un cal
de jucărie fluturând o sabie deasupra capului.* **Horatio** *poartă un
frac, ciorapi de plasă şi tocuri roşii. Părul ei este prins la spate.
Ţine un platou cu creveţi şi un caiet.*

Ophelia (*urcând şi coborând scările în rochia de
mireasă*)   Binecuvântat eşti Tu . . .

Horatio   Crevetele ăla arată puţin stricat. Poate ar trebui să sun
compania de catering. Nu vrei să se îmbolnăvească nimeni. Chiar
ar trebui să înceapă să vândă asigurare de nuntă pentru situaţii de
genul ăsta. Tu ce crezi?

Ophelia   Te întrebi vreodată dacă eşti cu persoana potrivită?

Horatio (*ridicându-şi ochii din caiet*)   Evident că nu eşti, dragă.
Nu poţi niciodată chiar SĂ FII cu persoana potrivită. Ce îl face
potrivit e faptul că nu eşti cu el. (*întorcându-se la caiet*) De unde
sunt creveţii? La Bella Tosca sau Christie's?

Ophelia   Christie's. Ar trebui să te asiguri că el e acela. Acela.

Gertrude   O, acela . . .

Ophelia (*plângându-şi inima*)   Îl vreau pe cel ales pentru
totdeauna, împreună, până la moarte . . .

Gertrude   Viaţă, moarte, iubire sau dorinţă, universul e infinit şi
se extinde. De unde ai venit? Unde te duci? *Quo vadis. Panta rei.*
Bune întrebări, dragă, dar, în ciuda a ce spune tatăl tău, nu o să-ţi
plătească chiria. Ar trebui să le scrii acum, să le pui deoparte în

ascunzătoarea ta secretă, şi să le scoţi când ieşi la pensie. O să-ţi
fie de folos atunci, între lecţii de golf, Pilates şi bufeuri. Chiar
ar trebui să încetezi să te mai încrunţi aşa. Ţi se întinde tot
machiajul.

Hamlet (*intrând, în frac*)   Chiar o să te căsătoreşti cu EL?

Horatio (*dându-şi ochii peste cap*)   El e acela. Nu el e acela.

Gertrude   Acela pentru ce?

Ophelia   Să-ţi vindece sufletul . . .

Gertrude *şi* **Horatio** *se uită unul la celălalt şi încep să râdă
isteric.*

Gertrude   Ca celălalt?

Horatio   Sau celălalt.

Gertrude (*filosofic*)   Sau altul.

*Încep să sune clopote de biserică şi ei se transformă în avataruri;
pleacă, vocile lor sintetizate se dizolvă în repetiţii absurde; 'acela,
sau celălalt, care, cineva, oricine, nimeni, cel pe care l-am
aşteptat, sau celălalt, cel pe care l-au aşteptat, l-aţi aşteptat? cine
a aşteptat? care?'*

Hamlet (*vorbind din ecran în timp ce bat clopotele*)   Sedează-te
cu plânsetele copiilor lupului
nimic nu e real dar
părul întărit de vomă
în noaptea asta –
o să dormi fără să visezi.
mâine –
dezbracă-ţi pielea şi lasă-ne înăuntru
lecţia de anatomie a doctorului Tulp poate începe.

*Ding dong – sunetul staţiei de autobuz. Vocea anunţului murmură
neinteligibil.*

Ophelia *cară o valiză şi o faţă de pernă plină cu capete de
manechine. Întră cu atenţie, căutând orarul autobuzelor şi
încercând să-şi da seama la ce oră pleacă autobuzul. Este*

oprită de **Hamlet**. *El poartă un lanţ de aur masiv în jurul gâtului.*

Hamlet   Hei, unde mergi?

Ophelia   Să vizitez un prieten.

Hamlet (*scanând-o din cap până în picioare*)   De unde eşti?

Ophelia   Huston, Maine.

Hamlet   Unde e asta?

Ophelia   E un oraş mic; nimeni nu ştie unde e.

Hamlet   E un oraş studenţesc? Eşti studentă?

Ophelia   Nu.

Hamlet   Ce faci acolo? (*Ea tace, zâmbeşte chinuit, clar inconfortabil.*) Haha, ştiu, e o chestie de băieţi. El te-a prins în poveste acolo. Haha. Te-a prins cu totul în poveste acolo. Ar trebui să vii aici la New York.

Ophelia   Hmm.

Hamlet   Ce ai acolo?

Ophelia   Asta?

Hamlet   Aha.

Ophelia   Sunt capete de manechin. Învăţ să devin coafeză.

Ding dong. Anunţul Autorităţii portuare spune: 'Autobuzul către Cleveland de la ora 2:30 AM pleacă de la poarta 5. Vă rugăm nu vă uitaţi bagajele.'

Ophelia   Ăla e autobuzul meu.

El aşteptă ca ea să zică ceva, dar ea tace aşa că el pleacă. Se chinuie cu faţa de pernă şi o tărăşte încet după ea, dispărând în culise. El scuipă peste umăr şi o urmăreşte.

Se aude melodia 'Dream a Little Dream'. **Ophelia**, *stând în spatele biroului ei, ia o gură de vin.* **Hamlet** *abandonează telecomanda şi începe să se joace un joc video. Frunze de toamnă* *uscate încep să cadă peste ei. Muzica se opreşte abrupt când se deschide uşa.*

Intră **Gertrude**, *vorbind la telefon. Poartă acelaşi halat, dar nu mai are bigudiuri în jumătate din cap. Părul ei, ca al Medusei curge în toate cele patru direcţii ale lumii. Traversează scena, vorbind la telefon şi căutând prin catalog.*

Gertrude   . . . pe care crezi că ar trebui să mi-o iau? Pe cea din Rusia, România sau China? Cele din Rusia arată bine, drăguţe şi blonde, dar cred că sunt defecte. Toată vodca aia rusească pe care au băut-o mamele lor . . . Nu sunt aşa sigură în legătură cu cele din România; arată palide, blonde, dar prea palide. E posibil să fie subnutrite. La fel şi cu alea africane. Dar sunt aşa exotice. Mi-ar sta bine cu una pe umăr lângă geanta Channel. Sau şi mai bine, Hermes . . . Cât au garanţia? . . . Doi ani? Se poate cumpăra garanţie extinsă? . . . şi dacă moare? . . . îţi trimit una nouă ca s-o înlocuiască? Acoperă costurile de înmormântare?   Dar livrarea? Nu o să mai plătesc livrarea o dată. Douăzeci şi cinci de mii pentru toate actele – asta e tot . . . Da, ai dreptate dragă, cele din America de sud arată drăguţ, nici prea închise, nici prea palide . . . Ah-aha . . . .

Pleacă, destul de mulţumită de ideea ei.

TV (*de pe ecran, E greu de zis dacă e o telenovelă sau ecranizarea unui roman clasic*)   Această dualitate a naturii ei îl speria. De fiecare dată când era sigur că îi aparţine, ochii ei deveneau aceia ai unui străin. Într-un moment era atât de familiară încât îi putea auzi vocea înăuntrul lui, şi atât de distantă încât singurătatea îi intra brusc în fiecare celulă a corpului, îl durea fizic şi îl sufoca precum conştientizarea propriei morţi.

Hamlet *stă pe canapea jucându-se un joc video. Faţa lui se transformă încet în faţa* **Ophelia**. *Ea poartă o cască militară, pe care o acoperă cu un şal negru.*

Ophelia (*din ecran, de parcă recită o poezie pentru copii*)
într-o zi
carnea mea ne-a părăsit
lăsându-ne pe mine şi pielea mea stupefiate

ne-am uitat una la cealaltă amuzate
nu mai aveam nimic de pierdut

Horatio (*citind din nişte documente legale*)   De luni bune se
pregătesc pentru acest bebeluş. Au cumpărat totul împreună,
pătuţul, căruciorul, hainele. Totul era de cea mai bună calitate, cel
mai scump, din cele mai exclusive cataloage. El i-a cumpărat o
maşină nou-nouţă ca ea să poată ajunge de la Universitate înapoi
fără să aştepte autobuzul. Când au aflat că va fi fată, el a fost
dezamăgit. El chiar vroia să aibă un băiat care să continue ce a
început. Avea fantezii cu lucrurile pe care urma să-l înveţe. Ruşinat
de propriile sentimente, şi-a ascuns dezamăgirea, s-a obişnuit cu
ideea că i se va naşte o fată şi a încurajat-o pe parcursul sarcinii. Ea
îi purta copilul. Pentru prima oară, îi era permis oficial să îl
tortureze şi încet-încet şi-a dat seama că nu era nicio limită la ceea
ce putea să facă. Resentimentul pe care îl simţea faţă de el pentru
toate dăţile în care fusese nevoită să-i gâdile ego-ul fragil îi
exaspera imaginaţia. L-a zdrobit din nou şi din nou cu cruzime din
ce în ce mai rafinată şi el a suportat totul cu un simţ amestecat de
datorie, veneraţie şi uimire.

Sunetul unui avion sau elicopter zburând deasupra şi umbra
aripilor pe decor. **Ophelia** *îşi întinde braţele negre şi începe să*
plutească deasupra. Se transformă într-un corb. Sunetele unui oraş
mare: o ambulanţă, împuşcături, fete care râd, cineva care ţipă şi
un câine lătrând în stradă. **Ophelia** *se uită de deasupra. Corpul ei*
se sparge într-un milion de bucăţele pe care încearcă să le adune
într-un coş de cumpărături. Femeia de serviciu din supermarket o
dă afară şi îi smulge ochii.

Hamlet
Lumina trece
mângâind umbrele pe aşternuturi albe
mirosind a sânge, dezinfectant şi
urina de ieri.

În ce sertar ţi-ai pus toate insomniile
şi mozaicurile compuse din petele de mucegai de pe tavan
unde se termină orizontul tău?

Ophelia *în scaun cu rotile intră, împinsă de o soră medicală a armatei.*

Ophelia   Ca fată într-un scaun cu rotile, am fost brusc nehotărâtă: cui să mă declar credincioasă? Dacă cineva era o femeie, răspunsul era simplu. Dacă cineva era infirm, răspunsul era simplu. Dacă cineva era și femeie și infirmă, răspunsul era simplu. Dar, era o imposibilitate existențială intrinsecă în figura unui bărbat infirm: era un dușman sau un frate martirizat? Țintuit de sexul lui sau de scaunul lui cu rotile? Cum nu m-am putut decide asupra politicilor mele în privința bărbaților infirmi, am decis preventiv să-i evit cu totul. Fundamental futuți în masculinitatea lor rănită, bărbații infirmi erau ceva ce eu, cu feminitatea mea rănită, eram natural predispusă să evit. Incapabilă să fac față propriilor mele contradicții – între a vrea să fiu dorită și a vrea să fiu respectată – aveam nevoie de un bărbat care nu necesita mult efort emoțional, unul infinit generos, ale cărui propriu ego și minte erau puternice și rezistente ca pula lui niciodată șovăitoare, cu care m-ar fi convins din nou și din nou de sex-appeal-ul meu nemărginit, chiar dacă e ceva care cere obișnuință, și de personalitatea mea veșnic fascinantă care l-a captivat cu totul și fără rezervă.

Scaunul rulant se învârte și manechinul **Ophelia** *se evaporă. Asistenta scutură perna de praf și începe să alerge în cercuri: știe că nu poate avea un scaun rulant gol așa că îndeasă în el tot ce prinde.*

TV: *Talk show sau serial de oră de vârf. Consiliere de cuplu.* **Ophelia** *și* **Hamlet** *stau pe canapea.*

Terapeut   Bună, mulțumesc că ați venit. E așa drăguț din partea voastră să aveți o problemă de împărtășit.

Hamlet   Nicio problemă.

Terapeut (*dezamăgit*)   Nici o problemă?

Hamlet   Ah, nu, este o problemă. Nicio problemă că am venit să împărtășim problema cu dumneavoastră.

Terapeut   Ah, am înțeles, ce minunat. Deci care e problema?

Hamlet   E oribil, nu pot să cred ce a făcut. Ne-a distrus viețile.

Ophelia   O, iubire, ce am făcut, dacă mi-ai zice odată . . . o, iubire (*plângând*). Dacă doar mi-ai putea spune ce este sunt sigură că o să fim bine. Nu pune în pericol dragostea și căsătoria noastră cu tăcerea ta.

Terapeut   Da, totul este despre comunicare. Dacă ne-ai putea spune, vom știi. Dacă ai putea să-ți împărtășești sentimentele cu soția ta, sentimentele tale vor fi împărtășite.

Hamlet   Ce a făcut? Ce a făcut? Nici nu pot să vorbesc despre asta. Uite, încă tremur doar gândindu-mă. Nu pot să cred că a făcut asta. Nu pot să cred că mi-a făcut mie asta . . . .

Ophelia Și Teraput   Ce a (*am*) făcut?

Hamlet   Vreți să știți? Vreți să știți? Bine, vă spun. Ieri dimineață, la micul dejun . . . (*Îi șoptește la ureche* **Terapeutului**.)

Terapeut   O, doaaaaamneeee!

Hamlet   Da, asta a făcut.

Terapeut   Este cu siguranță o situație dificilă, dar sunt sigur că dacă o rezolvăm, va fi rezolvată. Divorțurile sunt motivul numărul unu pentru divorțuri. Dar, în rest e totul bine?

Ophelia   O, da, totul e bine. Avem o căsătorie grozavă.

Hamlet   O, da, munca merge bine, stăm bine cu banii, copiii sunt morți.

Terapeut   Doar atunci poți spune că ai atins o stare de înțelepciune adevărată, când nu dai voie emoțiilor să intervină în judecata intelectuală imparțială obiectivă. Concluzia pe care o tragi necesită un *a priori* sau să fie dedusă din experiența empirică pe care ai acumulat-o. Nu trebuie niciodată să te limitezi la afirmații care sunt lipsite de imparțialitate intelectuală profundă. Doar atunci poți spune ceva cu adevărat profund imparțial, cu adevărat imparțial profund. (*E surprins de propria istețime; zâmbește și își scutură capul, cântărind ce tocmai a spus, dar uită repede, începând să se scobească în nas.*)

Ophelia (*în spatele biroului ei, scriind*) Cât de singular e lucrul numit plăcere și cât de curios înrudit cu durerea, care ar putea fi considerată opusul acestuia; fiindcă niciodată nu vin la om împreună, și totuși cel care o urmărește pe oricare din ele este în general obligat să o ia și pe cealaltă.

TV (*conferință*) Femeia a cărei plăcere sexuală este la origine auto-reprezentativă într-un mod diferit de a unui bărbat ar putea la fel de bine să nu aibă clitoris: himenul care rămâne veșnic (*in*)violat, asupra căruia sămânța este veșnic vărsată în timpul diseminării, nu are nevoie de el. E asta scena de violență numită iubire în transformare conținută în singura noastră triadă perfectă? Dacă femeile au fost dintotdeauna folosite ca instrument al deconstrucției masculine, e ăsta cel mai nou val filosofic?

Ophelia (*o terapeută*) Îmi place să cred că știi ce faci și că nu ești doar blocat în situațiile dificile ale masculinității americane auto-distructive, care în cele din urmă te va lăsa stors emoțional, înfometat intelectual și incompetent sexual.

Hamlet (*în timp ce joacă un joc video, relaxat*) Vrei să te ucid într-un act dramatic de gelozie atât de copleșitoare încât să mă facă să-mi pierd simțurile? Vrei să te ucid în timp ce termini ca să te poți topi cu universul în climaxul etern, ca să poți crede că vei trăi veșnic capturată în acest moment? Vrei să te ucid în timp ce îți șoptesc în urechi nimicuri dulci despre propria mea disperare? Vrei să te ucid și să mă ucid și pe mine ca să te urmăresc în drama morții atât de atent regizată?

Ophelia *plutește în spațiu. Încearcă să apuce paie, dar lumea dispare la orizont.* **Ophelia** *încearcă să meargă dar nu e nici o suprafață pe care să mergi. Găsește telecomanda și apasă disperată de câteva ori. Cranii umane și animale plutesc în jos pe râul Gange.* **Ophelia** *își spală părul și calcă pe nisipul deșertic. Inima ei sângerează. Venele ei sunt făcute din sârme.* **Ophelia** *își cară propriul cadavru peste granița deșertului.*

Hamlet Chiar dacă ar fi să umblu prin valea umbrei morții, Nu mă tem de niciun rău: căci Tu ești cu mine;

Toiagul și nuiaua ta mângâie.
Tu îmi întinzi masa în fața potrivnicilor mei.

Ophelia (*stând în spatele biroului ei în verde militar. Calm și stoic, continuând să scrie, de parcă nimic nu s-ar fi întâmplat*)   Te rog, dragule, auto-deprecierea nu e în mod necesar un indicator al valorii de piață a cuiva: puritatea noastră e pur formală așa cum sunt și perversitățile noastre atât de prețuite de mama ta și promovate în fiecare reclamă la săpun. Dragule, trebuie să știi că ea s-a păstrat automat pentru noaptea nunții cu lumânări și dorințe atent sculptate de televizor, prin urmare cu totul noi pentru generația noastră. Teama, dragule, teama. Cred cu adevărat în Dumnezeu și în demnitatea umană, mai puțin când zace în tranșee cu capul explodat de virtutea și angajamentul altcuiva față de pasiunea pentru viață, așa cum cred că tu ești acela care să ajungă adânc înăuntru cu o profunzime inaccesibilă membrelor mele slăbite. Da, da, dragule, poți să-mi scrii o poezie, sau să mă futi îndeajuns de tare; Sunt sigură că oricum ne vom aminti cu credința de vechea noastră convingere a imortalității construită din bunătatea inimii, și uniunea sufletelor conduse de ura reciprocă și iubirea unul față de celălalt, trecându-și zilele în armonia ritualurilor igienice, discurs post-modern de diferite niveluri intelectuale și muncă ce ne va elibera de abundența materialistă sau de lipsuri, depinzând dacă procreația și-a atins media statistică sau s-a exprimat prin individualismul egoist al auto-adorării. Sunt sigură că convingerea mea mă va lăsa încrezătoare în mine cum ar face-o cu oricare alta, lucru pentru care îmi vei mulțumi când o să-ți torn un pahar de vin și o să-ți masez umerii. Vârful penisului tău are un potențial ontologic, așa că îți înfig sabia în uretră ca să examinez dacă spațiul e îndeajuns de amăgitor ca să-mi absoarbă teama și toate celelalte lăsate accidental de viitorii tați din America și din cinci alte continente ce iau în considerare globalizarea obiceiurilor noastre sexuale.

Horatio *intră cu un platou de argint cu creveți*

Horatio (*către **Hamlet**, care încă stă pe canapea*)   Creveți?

Hamlet   Mersi, sunt la dietă.

Horatio *îşi aminteşte ceva brusc şi îşi ridică pumnul, ţipând:* '*Libertate!' Este călcat de tanc şi corpul lui dispare în asfaltul negru. Un grup de copii zâmbitori fuge pe trotuar, râzând şi ţinându-se de mâini. Corbii negri ciugulesc din carnea lui* **Horatio.** *Sunetul staţiei de autobuz. Ding dong.*

AnunŢul   Autobuzul de la Paris la New York, cu opriri în Londra şi Tokyo, pleacă de la poarta 5. Autobuzul de la Paris la New York, cu opriri în Londra şi Tokyo, pleacă de la poarta 5.

Anunţul se repetă de câteva ori de parcă s-ar fi blocat mecanismul. Când începe anunţul, intră **Ophelia** *purtând o rochie de mireasă pătată de sânge şi o eşarfă pe cap. Încearcă să găsească poarta corectă. E urmărită de* **Horatio,** *care cară o tavă de argint cu un cap de mascul uman pe ea, înconjurat de creveţi.*

Ophelia *intră.*

Ophelia (*înnebunită*)   Acela, acela. Eu sunt acela. Eu sunt acela pe care l-am tot aşteptat. Eu sunt acela. Unul, singurul, care . . . Acela, cel Sfânt, cel inerent, cel binecuvântat.

Horatio (*nefiind atent la ea*)   Cei de la Christie's sunt mai proaspeţi. Hai să-i comandăm pe cei de la Christie's.

Ophelia *îşi dă jos bocancul militar şi îl bate pe* **Horatio** *până la moarte.* **Ophelia** *iese cu mâinile larg întinse.* **Hamlet** *începe să se joace pe telefon.* **Ophelia/Medea** *pe podeaua staţiei de autobuz îi cântă copilului ei mort.*

Ophelia/Medea

Fie numele Său cel mare binecuvântat în veci şi în vecii vecilor.
Binecuvântat, slăvit, fălit, înălţat,
ridicat, mărit şi lăudat fie numele celui Atotsfânt
Binecuvântat fie el.

Hamlet   Citeşti durerea în ochii mei şi crezi că ştii totul. Crezi că poţi citi un bărbat din durerea lui. Crezi că, pentru că poţi citi durerea unui bărbat, el îţi aparţine, veşnic şi întotdeauna.

TV (*National Geographic Channel*)   Ploşniţa mascul are un penis făcut să injecteze şi să livreze spermă în femelă. Această tehnică este foarte violentă, femela este ţinută la pământ şi înjunghiată de mai multe ori în corp pentru a asigura inseminarea. Această metodă a evoluat pentru a ocoli pasajul genital femeiesc, restrângând şi îndepărtând orice control pe care femela l-ar avea în mod normal asupra momentului reproducerii.

Ophelia   Când corpul este stăpânul meu, nu voi mai avea altul. (*Ţipând.*) Când corpul este stăpânul meu, nu voi mai avea altul.

Hamlet *schimbă canalele.*

Ophelia (*ia o gură de vin şi continuă să scrie*)   Actele macabre de auto-revelare au punctul de plecare în bunăvoinţa minţii cuiva faţă de clasele de jos de descendenţă vulgară. Sunt sigură, dragule, teama pe care ţi-am descris-o atât de atent nu are nicio semnificaţie etică pentru bună-starea ta. Sunt, de asemenea, sigură că vei găsi înlocuitorul pentru dezechilibrul meu emoţional la fel de uşor cum o să o fac eu în orice creatură vor dori minţile noastre. Alegerea atât de clar marcată de fiinţa mea devastatoare depinde complet de nivelul tău de serotonină şi de dorinţa produsă în mod specific de această noapte. Oferta mea e valabilă pe timpul erecţiei tale şi expiră până când îţi ejaculezi jalnicele gânduri paranoice în chipul meu doritor. Dorinţa construită ca funcţie matematică îşi are avantajele în volatilitatea şi permanenţa aşteptărilor ei, care, replicate în proporţii fractalice, dobândesc calitatea eterică a unei structuri solide ce nu poate fi distinsă de nici o altă soluţie acidă la problemele internalizate în timpul copilăriei şi amânate pentru consum cu un pahar de Chardonnay sau Sauvignon de Blanco, şi peşte, gătit blând în sos de lămâie şi caviar.

Gertrude *trece, vorbind la telefon. Acum s-a transformat într-o maşinărie.*

Gertrude   Catalogul nu menţiona satisfacţie garantată? Îţi trimit o fată defectă şi ei cred că rămâi cu ea de gât . . . Trimite-o înapoi şi spune-le să-ţi trimită una ca în imagini, fără pistrui. . . . În zilele astea, dragă, trebuie să avem grijă de banii noştri. Ieri, am cumpărat nişte şosete făcute în China. Erau defecte – Îţi zic – aha

– aha – aşa că le-am returnat. Cineva pur şi simplu nu-şi poate
permite să arunce cu banii pe articole defecte în zilele astea. –
aha – aha – Ai plătit pentru ceva, ţi-au trimis lucrul greşit, ai
dreptul să-l trimiţi înapoi şi să-ţi recuperezi banii . . . mda, mda,
asta zic.

Gertrude *dispare. Începe să cadă zăpada.*

Hamlet (*pe furiş, de parcă spune un secret*)
Uneori, când mergem prin
ochii unul altuia ca prin porţi
Uneori, sunt ca ea
Uneori, ea e cine
Sunt eu.

Ophelia (*scriind, frenetic*)   Mâna dreaptă ţine iubirea eternă cu
toate dificultăţile fantomă de salvare bolnăvicioasă şi rutină
rectangulară de metafore reciclate de la cadavre ale foştilor
îndrăgostiţi şi insecte căzute în cărţi deschise la mijloc. Voi promite
să preţuiesc fiinţa mea pe care am găsit-o cu atâta înduioşare în
ochii tăi chiar înăuntrul pupilelor pe care te implor cu înflăcărare să
nu le închizi când îmi dau drumul şi în care grimasele mele sunt
amplificate în închipuiri perceptibile ale imaginaţiei noastre. De
asemenea promit să includ stabilitatea mult dorită de tine şi
confuzia împletită cu lovituri ocazionale din partea ego-ului meu ca
să-ţi echilibreze cererea şi oferta. Promit să îndeplinesc fanteziile
noastre Oedipiene şi să-mi închiriez pântecul fără interes pentru o
oază şi o toaletă în care ne putem retrăi fecalele preţioase de eforturi
intelectuale. Sunt sigură că aranjamentul va satisface 40% din
materia noastră, lăsând restul de 60% într-o insaţiabilitate arzătoare
de suspiciuni şi perpetuitate fizică a gravităţii şi uşurinţei. Mâna
mea stângă oferă dragoste neîmpărtăşită, a mea sau a ta, vom stabili
asta mai târziu. Sunt sigură că, oricum, ne vom adapta la rolurile
noastre cu graţia naturală a sclavului şi maestrului. Dorinţa e
proporţională cu timpul de aşteptare. Dragule, ea a fost instruită de
cele mai bune curve din Europa, America de nord şi Asia. Cele pe
care le-ai vizitat în nopţi singuratice sau de beţie şi în care ţi-ai
introdus penisul pe jumătate flasc în speranţa eliberării temporare de
coşmarul dorinţei sau al lipsei ei.

Ophelia *se oprește. Se adună.* **Ophelia** *scoate o armă din sertar și se împușcă în cap. Sunetul împușcăturii și sânge peste tot. Continuă să scrie de parcă nu s-ar fi întâmplat nimic.*

Boala morții ne învinge. Ne dorim să nu fi murit și să nu fi fost în viață. Teama dintre a fi posedat și a poseda se instalează cu viteza unui hoț care a furat prea mult ca să simtă plăcere și prea puțin ca să simtă orice altceva și, plecând cu un zâmbet amorțit de mulțumire, plânge ascuns în spatele colțurilor înghețate ale auto-perpetuării. Gândurile mele nu curg cu ușurința promisă de corpul tău, nici nu fierb cu insațiabilitate recunoscătoare.

TV (*National Geographic Channel*) Scorpionul mascul și cel femelă se strâng într-o îmbrățișare intensă, biciuindu-se unul pe celălalt cu cozile. Cu gurile blocate, masculul o va înjunghia în mod repetat pe femelă cu coada. Drept revanșă, femeia adeseori își va mânca partenerul.

Ophelia *intră. Rochia ei de mireasă este zdrențuită. Are aparate de detonare legate de piept.*

Ophelia

foamea pe care o simt nu e în mine
curge afară și înăuntru
în brațele mele lacome
tu te pierzi
cineva nu poate fi salvat și rămâne condamnat
foamea pe care o simt nu e în mine

Stă în scaunul cu rotile și iese, râzând isteric.

Știri TV Astăzi în California, o mamă i-a tăiat capul bebelușului ei și apoi i-a mâncat creierul. (Prezentatoarea pare tristă pentru o secundă, apoi îi apare brusc un zâmbet larg pe față.) Acum continuăm cu alte știri, de la guru-ul nostru de lifestyle, care va răspunde la cele mai importante întrebări ale sezonului . . . .

Se aude 'Jingle Bells'

Fața lui **Hamlet** *de pe fundal se amestecă cu jocul video pe care îl joacă.* **Hamlet** *pe canapea și în jocul video se ridică în picioare și*

îşi dă jos pălăria şi jacheta. Se duce în culise şi aduce o canistră
de benzină, pe care începe să o verse peste tot.

Ophelia (*scriind, în timp ce* **Hamlet** *varsă benzina*)   Departe,
departe, dragule . . . cu siguranţă am reuşit să ne convingem de
propria noastră existenţă. Dusă la aşa o extremă, nu am de ales
decât să perpetuez această convingere. Te implor să nu-mi refuzi
ceea ce aparţine de drept altcuiva. Ştiu de angajamentul tău faţă de
adevăruri şi falsităţi. Servit cu bucăţi de credinţe pierdute şi ele
cumpărate de la licitaţii tăcute din muzee de organe de ceară şi
suflete. Vreau ca tu să înţelegi bine că promisiunile de pe buzele
mele nu pot fi traduse. Leg gândurile tale şi ale mele cu o atenţie
atât de ciudată la detalii. Ai vrut să simţi iubire sau orice altceva.
Teatrul dorinţelor este deschis pentru afişare publică spectatorilor
curioşi şi neatenţi unii la ceilalţi. I-am văzut ieri trecând prin oraş
când noi am plâns ascunşi sub patul care refuza să fie îmblânzit.
Am ieşit cu capul tău sub braţ. Mă împiedic, mă împiedic de
cuvintele ataşate de puterea lor. Nu plânge dragule, vine noaptea.

Aprinde un chibrit. Heblu.

Maszynofelia

Przekład Anna Kowalcze-Pawlik

Wursztat samochodowy, składzik albo pokój dziecięcy zagracony
rzeczami zgromadzonymi przez zagubionego podróżnika: wśród
nich bezręki Dawid *Michała Anioła w kasku motocyklowym, stos*
połamanych afrykańskich masek, szkielet zmarłego poety, który
szczerzy się histerycznie do własnego cienia, lalka bez rąk i nóg
z różowym lizakiem w buzi, zepsuty parasol Magritte'a, stary
telefon do Boga Andy'ego Warhola, brudny ślubny welon zwisający
między innymi ubraniami, zwały starych butów i peruk.

To nowoczesne pustkowie upstrzone zepsutymi konsolami,
telewizorami i ekranami komputerów, które bezdźwięcznie
wyświetlają przypadkowe sceny z naszego wirtualnego życia:
obrazy wojny, masowe mordy, ludobójstwa, ciała z Auschwitz,
pornosy, reklamy polityczne, kobiety biznesu, kobiety z nadwagą,
anorektyczki, japońskie uczennice, kobiety w burkach, dzikie
safari, komiksowe eksplozje. Hamlet *i* Ofelia *spijają tę codzienną*
zupę newsów i obrazów: kolaż ludzkich komirustów zawieszonych
między pięknem a grozą, niewinnością a przemocą.

Wszystko pokrywa radioaktywny pył.

Hamlet *ubrany w dżinsy, szesnastowieczny kubrak i kapelusz*
kowbojski siedzi na kanapie zwróconej ku publiczności. Ogląda
telewizję, bezmyślnie przerzucając kanały na pilocie. Na zascentu
projekcja kolażu. Hamlet *chce zrozumieć świat, ale jedyne,*
co może, to się mu przyglądać.

Po lewej stronie sceny, za nim, Ofelia, *ubrana w wojskowe moro,*
siedzi przy składanym biurku i pisze na staromodnej maszynie.
Z boku kieliszek czerwonego wina. Pali papierosa i jest całkowicie
pochłonięta pisaniem.

Hamlet *i* Ofelia *znajdują się na dwóch krańcach świata. Między*
nimi Atlantyk pełen gnijących trupów, martwych ptaków
i uryny.

Ofelia (*pisząc na maszynie*) Hamlecie, mój drogi, nie chcę się
ani z tobą, ani z nią; twoje żołnierzyki zajęły moją stronę łóżka.
Oceany i kontynenty z łatwością da się wymienić na polityczną
nostalgię i wytrwałość. Niech umarłych grzebią umarli, to klątwa
naszych ojców. (*Przerywa i bierze łyk wina.*)

Hamlet (*z roztargnieniem, wspominając lepsze czasy*)
W kościach wyklętych
– łóżek sześć choć siedem nocy –
cumują świeżo wyklute larwy
u brzegów własnych trocin.

Ofelia (*ciągnie z niezmąconym spokojem*) . . . pisanie jest formą
intelektualnej masturbacji. Wylewam swoje biedne, żałosne ja na
białe oko mojego komputera, dumna, że opanowałam tę trudną
sztukę dogadzania sobie, a tym samym wkroczyłam w nową erę
solipsystycznej przyjemności. Zadziwia mnie moja
samowystarczalność. Och, te erotogenne sfery w moim mózgu,
badane w zamyśleniu, w megalomańskich napadach
samouwielbienia. Tak, tak, teraz, automatycznie sejwuję,
oszczędzam siebie na później. (*Przerywa i zaciąga się
papierosem.*)

Telewizja (*kanał National Geographic*)   Podczas rytuału
godowego samica orła białego zwiera szpony na szponach samca,
żądając jego całkowitej uległości, a w międzyczasie oboje
bezwładnie opadają ku ziemi. Jeśli samiec spróbuje się uwolnić,
zanim ona będzie gotowa, samica nie pozwoli mu się dosiąść.
Jeśli orlica będzie zwlekała o kilka sekund za długo, oboje
roztrzaskają się o ziemię.

*Dźwięk pociągu jadącego na pełnej prędkości, gwizd, jakby
maszynista próbował ostrzec kogoś stojącego na torach. Pociąg
przejeżdża. Północ na nowojorskim dworcu autobusowym Port
Authority. Ding dong, sygnał systemu komunikacji dworcowej, głos
coś mamrocze.* **Hamlet** *ogląda telewizję.*

Ofelia (*rzeczowo*)   Większość dziewcząt widywanych w Port
Authority pochodzi z Bronksu lub Harlemu. Noszą podróbki
szalów Chanel na głowach i fałszywki Louisa Vuittona pod pachą.
Starają się wyglądać na modne i zadbane, jakby miały mężczyznę,
dla którego są warte te kilkaset dolarów pozornie bezużytecznego
luksusu. Niektóre z nich mają ze sobą niemowlęta lub małe dzieci
i podtrzymują je z cichą desperacją. Nigdy nie jestem pewna, kto
kogo bardziej potrzebuje: one swoich dzieci czy te dzieci ich.
Siedzą na ziemi lub na walizkach, cierpliwie czekając na autobusy.

Czasami towarzyszy im mężczyzna, a wtedy w ich oczach pojawia się błysk delikatnej satysfakcji. Wydają się kruche, a zarazem twarde, jakby zaraz miały wybuchnąć płaczem albo potokiem przekleństw.

Ofelia *wraca do pisania. Dzwoni telefon. Dźwięk przejeżdżającego tramwaju. W sąsiednim mieszkaniu płacze dziecko. Wchodzi* **Gertruda.** *Przechodzi przez scenę, ubrana w szlafrok, na głowie ma termoloki. Dłubie w zębach i rozmawia przez telefon. Jej wzrok rzuca błyskawice.*

Gertruda   O mój Boże, nie! Miała piegi?! Cóż, halo, WIESZ, co o tym MYŚLĘ. To znaczy. . . weź, jedyne, co mówię, to, że to jest naprawdę takie proste. Weź zwykłą lalkę z chińskiej porcelany, czy ona ma piegi? Co? Nie, nie ma. Czy ta, którą ci przysłali, ma piegi? No to, . . . odeślij ją!. . . Nie, naprawdę nie musisz! NIE należy płacić za przesyłkę zwrotną. Wkładasz ją z powrotem do tego pudła i odsyłasz. O nie! Już zapłaciłeś!. . . Widziałeś zdjęcie w katalogu, użyłeś karty kredytowej i teraz powinieneś dostać to, za co zapłaciłeś!. . . Czy były tam zdjęcia dziewczyny z piegami? NIE! Ok. O co mi chodzi. . . czy powiedziałam już o co mi chodzi?! . . . NIE, bo to się nazywa BŁĘDNA REPREZENTACJA!. . . Mogą za to trafić do więzienia, wiesz? . . . .Tak, można dostać mnóstwo fajnych Chinek . . .

Znika za drzwiami scenicznymi. Zatrzaskuje szlafrok w drzwiach i ciągnie go ze złością. **Hamlet** *odwraca się, rzuca za nią butem, ale nie trafia. Wyrastają mu nietoperze skrzydła, wraca do oglądania telewizji.*

Ofelia (*kontynuuje pisanie, jak gdyby nic się nie stało*)   Lęk, mój drogi, lęk; chcę, żebyś go wypełnił albo wziął na siebie. To twój wybór: dobrobyt niecierpliwie czeka, byśmy przekazali swoje geny i unieśmiertelnili je w czterech kilogramach węgla i intelektu. Tak, tak, kochanie, jestem pewna, że prokreacja może być źródłem nieskończonej radości dla mas, ale my jesteśmy o wiele bardziej wyrafinowani. Musisz zrozumieć, że głosów w mojej głowie nie można zagłuszyć płaczem dziecka; musisz wiedzieć, że nawet okrzyki, które wydaję z taką gracją, kiedy miłosiernie korzystasz

ze swojego prawa do uwiądu po stosunku. . . uwiądu. . . (*Przerwa.*
Kiedy ona pisze, **Hamlet** *ogląda miękkie porno.*) Lęk, kochanie,
lęk, o nim mówiłam, nie o uwiądzie. Jestem pewna, że jeśli
odrobinę bardziej się postarasz, dotrzesz do niego. Twojego
członka dokładnie zmierzono, a jego właściwości egzystencjalne
oceniono z pełną odpowiedzialnością za niepowodzenie, jakie to ja
poniosłam, za niewyleczenie twojego zranionego ego; za rzucenie
wyzwania konwencji towarzyszącej naszemu uroczemu spotkaniu,
które, mam nadzieję, pozostawi nas oboje w stanie równego
niespełnienia. Długość twojego penisa jest proporcjonalna do lęku,
jaki będę czuła, paląc papierosa w twoich zmęczonych objęciach
i rozważając statystyczne prawdopodobieństwo raka płuc lub
zawału serca wywołanego nienasyceniem seksualnym oraz
niewłaściwie leczonymi lękami. Hamlecie, mój drogi, nie
opowiadaj o polityce, swoich pragnieniach, świecie, śmierci i krwi,
którą przelałeś płacząc nad głodującymi dziećmi.

Ofelia, *przechodzi w sukni ślubnej, w towarzystwie* **Horacego** *i*
Gertrudy. **Gertruda** *dosiada konia na biegunach, wymachuje*
mieczem nad głową. **Horacy** *ma na sobie smoking, kabaretki*
i czerwone szpilki. Jej włosy są ściągnięte do tyłu. Trzyma półmisek
krewetek oraz notatnik.

Ofelia (*przechadza się po schodach w sukni*
ślubnej)   Błogosławionyś . . . .

Horacy   Te krewetki wyglądały na trochę przeschnięte. Może
powinnam zadzwonić do cateringu. Nie chcesz, żeby ktoś się
pochorował. Naprawdę powinni zacząć sprzedawać ubezpieczenia
ślubne na taką okoliczność. Jak uważasz?

Ofelia   Czy kiedykolwiek zastanawiałaś się czy jesteś z tą
właściwą osobą?

Horacy (*spogląda znad notatnika*)   Oczywiście, że nie, kochana.
Nigdy nie mogłabyś *być* z właściwą osobą. Właśnie to, że z nim
jesteś, sprawia, że to on jest tym niewłaściwym. (*Z powrotem*
zagląda w notatnik.) Skąd się wzięły krewetki? La Bella Tosca czy
Christie?

Ofelia   Christie. Należało by się upewnić, że on jest tym właściwym. Tym jedynym.

Gertruda   Och, ten jedyny . . .

Ofelia (*rzewny płacz*)   Chcę tego jedynego, na zawsze, póki śmierć . . .

Gertruda   Życie, śmierć, miłość czy pożądanie; wszechświat jest nieskończony i się rozszerza. Skąd pochodzisz? Dokąd zmierzasz? *Quo vadis. Panta rei.* Świetne pytania, serdeńko, ale niezależnie od tego, co powtarza twój ojciec, nie zapłacą za ciebie czynszu. Powinnaś je sobie teraz spisać, schować w tej swojej skrytce i wyjąć dopiero jak doczołgasz się do emerytury. Przydadzą ci się wtedy, akurat w przerwach między lekcjami golfa, pilatesem i uderzeniami gorąca. Naprawdę powinnaś przestać się tak mrużyć. Całkiem sobie makijaż rozmazujesz.

Hamlet (*wchodzi w smokingu*)   Nie wyjdziesz za *niego*, prawda?

Horacy (*przewraca oczami*)   Jest tym jedynym. Nie jest tym jedynym.

Gertruda   Tym jedynym, który ma zrobić co?

Ofelia   Uleczyć duszę . . .

Gertruda *i* **Horacy** *spoglądają na siebie i wybuchają histerycznym śmiechem.*

Gertruda   Niczym bratnia dusza?

Horacy   Lub ta druga dusza.

Gertruda (*filozoficznie*)   Albo dusza jakaś tam.

Zaczynają bić dzwony kościelne, a **Gertruda** *i* **Horacy** *zamieniają się w awatary; odchodzą, a ich zsyntetyzowane głosy rozpływają się wśród absurdalnych powtórzeń: 'ta druga, jakaś tam, inna, która, jakaś, żadna; ta, na którą czekałam; albo inna; ta, na którą czekali inni; ty czekałaś? Kto czekał? Na kogo?'*

Hamlet (*przemawia z ekranu, do wtóru bijących dzwonów*)   Upajaj się skowytem wilczych szczeniąt

nic nie jest prawdziwe prócz
włosów, co sztywnieją od wymiocin
dziś wieczorem –
śnić będziesz bez snów
jutro –
rozsuniesz skórę i dasz nam wstęp
Lekcję anatomii doktora Tulpa czas rozpocząć

*Ding dong – odgłosy dworca autobusowego. Głos podający
informację dworcową jest niewyraźny, niezrozumiały.*

Ofelia *niesie walizkę i poszewkę na poduszkę pełną głów
manekinów. Wchodzi ostrożnie, sprawdza rozkład jazdy i próbuje
odczytać godzinę odjazdu swojego autobusu. Zatrzymuje ją*
Hamlet. *Na szyi ma ciężki złoty łańcuch.*

Hamlet   Siema, a gdzie to koleżanka jedzie.

Ofelia   A do znajomych.

Hamlet (*wgapia się w nią*)   Skąd jesteś?

Ofelia   Huston, Maine.

Hamlet   Gdzie to?

Ofelia   To małe miasteczko, nikt nie wie, gdzie.

Hamlet   Studenckie to? Miasteczko? Na studiach jesteś?

Ofelia   Nie.

Hamlet   Co tu robisz? (*Milczy, wyraźnie zakłopotana blado się
uśmiecha.*) Hehe, wiem o co biega, to robota jakiegoś łacha.
Wydymał cie tam. Całkiem cie tam wychujał. Powinnaś przyjechać
tu, do Nowego Jorku.

Ofelia   Hm.

Hamlet   A co tam trzymiesz?

Ofelia   To?

Hamlet   No.

Ofelia   To głowy manekinów. Szkolę się na fryzjerkę.

Ding dong. System informacji dworcowej Port Authority 'Poranny autobus do Cleveland, godzina 2:30, odjeżdża ze stanowiska 5. Proszę pamiętać o zabraniu bagażu.'

Ofelia   To mój autobus.

Hamlet *czeka aż* **Ofelia** *się odezwie, ale ona milczy, dlatego* **Hamlet** *odchodzi. Ona szamocze się z poszewką i powoli ciągnie ją za sobą, znikając za kulisami. On spluwa przez ramię i rusza za nią.*

Zaczyna przygrywać 'Dream a Little Dream of Me'. **Ofelia** *siedzi przy swoim biurku, bierze łyk wina.* **Hamlet** *porzuca pilota i zaczyna grać na konsoli. Zaczynają na nich opadać suche jesienne liście. Muzyka zatrzymuje się nagle, z tą chwilą otwierają się sceniczne drzwi.*

Wchodzi **Gertruda***, z telefonem przy uchu. Ma na sobie ten sam szlafrok, ale na połowie głowy nie ma już wałków. Jej włosy, niczym węże Meduzy, unoszą się we wszystkich kierunkach świata. Przechodzi przez scenę, wciąż rozmawiając przez telefon, przegląda przy tym katalog.*

Gertruda   . . . no ale jak uważasz, którą powinnam sobie sprawić? Tę z Rosji, Rumunii, czy z Chin? Te z Rosji wyglądają dobrze, wszystkie ładne, a do tego blond, ale podobno są popsute. Cała ta rosyjska wódka, którą piły ich matki. . . Nie jestem pewna co do tych rumuńskich; wyglądają blado, są blond, ale zbyt blade. Mogą być niedożywione. To samo z tymi afrykańskimi. Ale te są takie egzotyczne. Wyglądałbym dobrze z jedną taką u boku, zaraz obok mojej Chanelki. Albo jeszcze lepiej, przy Hermèsie. . . Jaka jest na nie gwarancja?. . . Dwa lata? Czy można wykupić przedłużoną gwarancję?. . . a co jeśli umrze?. . . Czy wysyłają ci nową, aby tę pierwszą zastąpić? Czy pokrywają koszta pogrzebu?. . . A co z wysyłką? Nie zamierzam ponownie płacić za wysyłkę. Dwadzieścia pięć tysięcy za całą tę papierkową robotę – i ani centa więcej. . . Tak, masz rację kochana, te z Ameryki

Południowej wyglądają bardzo ładnie, nie za ciemne, nie za jasne. . . Aha. . . .

Wychodzi całkiem zadowolona ze swojego postanowienia.

Telewizja (*z ekranu, trudno powiedzieć czy to opera mydlana czy jakaś klasyka*)   Dwoistość jej natury przerażała go. Za każdym razem, gdy był pewien, że ją posiadł, jej spojrzenie stawało się spojrzeniem nieznajomej. Była tak mu bliska, że mógł w sobie samym wysłyszeć jej głos, a zarazem tak odległa, że nagła samotność, która dawała o sobie znać w każdej komórce jego ciała, bolała fizycznie i przytłaczała niczym świadomość własnej śmierci.

Hamlet *siedzi na kanapie i gra na konsoli. Jego twarz powoli przemienia się w twarz* **Ofelii**. **Ofelia** *ma na głowie hełm wojskowy, który chowa pod czarną chustką.*

Ofelia (*z ekranu, jak gdyby powtarzała dziecięcą rymowankę*)   Dnia pewnego, razu jednego

ciało moje nas opuściło
skórę mą i mnie zostawiło
w osłupieniu i w zaskoczeniu
się gapimy z rozbawienia
nic nie mamy do stracenia.

Horacy (*odczytuje jakieś dokumenty*)   Przygotowywali się na to dziecko od miesięcy. Wszystko kupowali razem, łóżeczko, wózek, ubranka. Wszystko było najlepsze, najdroższe, z najbardziej ekskluzywnych katalogów. Kupił jej nowiutki samochód, żeby mogła jeździć na uniwersytet bez czekania na autobus. Kiedy dowiedzieli się, że będzie dziewczynka, był rozczarowany. Bardzo pragnął syna, który kontynuowałby jego dzieło. Fantazjował o wszystkich tych rzeczach, których mógłby go nauczyć. Zawstydzony własnymi uczuciami ukrywał rozczarowanie, przyzwyczaił się do myśli o dziewczynce i kibicował jej podczas ciąży, cierpliwie znosząc napady jej złego humoru i ciągłe ataki melancholii. Nosiła jego dziecko. Po raz pierwszy miała oficjalne prawo torturować go i powoli odkrywała, że nie ma żadnych hamulców. Resentyment, jaki żywiła wobec niego za wszystkie te chwile, gdy musiała zadowalać jego kruche ego, tylko rozjątrzał jej wyobraźnię. Miażdżyła go raz po raz z coraz subtelniejszym okrucieństwem, a on znosił to wszystko z mieszaniną poczucia obowiązku, podziwu i zaskoczenia.

Dźwięk przelatującego samolotu lub helikoptera i cień skrzydeł na planie. **Ofelia** *rozkłada czarne ramiona i zaczyna unosić się w powietrzu. Zmienia się w kruka. Odgłosy wielkiego miasta: karetka pogotowia, strzelanina, śmiejące się dziewczyny, czyjś krzyk i szczekanie psa na ulicy.* **Ofelia** *przygląda się z góry. Jej ciało rozpada się na milion kawałków, które próbuje zebrać do koszyka. Sprzątaczka wyrzuca* **Ofelię** *z supermarketu, a* **Ofelia** *wydziera jej oczy.*

Hamlet   Światło wpada

pieszcząc cienie na białych prześcieradłach
które trącą krwią, lizolem
i wczorajszym moczem.

Do której szuflady schowałaś wszystkie swoje bezsenne noce
i mozaiki z plam pleśni na suficie
gdzie kończy się twój horyzont?

Pojawia się **Ofelia** *na wózku inwalidzkim popychanym przez wojskową pielęgniarkę.*

Ofelia   Jako dziewczyna na wózku nagle poczułam się rozdarta: z kim mam zawierać sojusze? Jeżeli ktosia był kobietą, odpowiedź była prosta. Jeśli ktosia był kaleką, odpowiedź była prosta. Jeśli ktosia była kobietą i kaleką, odpowiedź była prosta. W figurze okaleczonego mężczyzny kryła się jednak wewnętrzna niemożliwość egzystencjalna: czy był wrogiem, czy umęczonym bratem? Był uwikłany w swoją płeć czy w zależność od wózka? Ponieważ nie mogłam się zdecydować, jaką politykę obrać wobec kalekich mężczyzn, postanowiłam na wszelki wypadek całkowicie ich unikać. Okaleczeni mężczyźni, prawdziwie kuriozalni w swojej zranionej męskości, byli czymś, czego ja, z moją zranioną kobiecością, byłam naturalnie skłonna się wystrzegać. Nie mogąc poradzić sobie z własnymi paradoksami – między pragnieniem bycia pożądaną a pragnieniem bycia szanowaną – potrzebowałam mężczyzny, który nie wymaga dużych nakładów emocjonalnych, który przejawiałby niczym nieskrępowaną wspaniałomyślność, i którego własna jaźń i umysł były silne i wytrzymałe, jak jego niezawodny penis, którym przekonywałby mnie w kółko o moim bezgranicznym seksapilu, pomijając całe to jego upodobanie do mnie oraz moją niezmiennie fascynującą osobowość, która zawładnęła nim bez reszty i do cna.

Wózek obraca się wokół własnej osi, a manekin **Ofelii** *wyparowuje. Pielęgniarka odkurza poduszkę i zaczyna biegać w kółko: wie, że wózek inwalidzki nie może pozostać pusty, więc wypycha go, czym tylko się da.*

Telewizja: talk show lub serial w czasie największej oglądalności. Terapia par. **Ofelia** *i* **Hamlet** *siedzą na kanapie.*

Terapeuta   Dzień dobry. Dziękuję, że się pojawiliście. Naprawdę miło, że macie problem, którym możecie się podzielić.

Hamlet   Bez problemu.

Terapeuta (*rozczarowany*)   Bez problemu?

Hamlet   No nie, problem jest. Bez problemu możemy się tym problemem z tobą podzielić.

Terapeuta   No tak, rewelacja. W czym problem?

Hamlet   To straszne, nie mogę uwierzyć w to, co zrobiła. Zrujnowała nam życie.

Ofelia   Och, kochanie, co ja zrobiłam, co ja zrobiłam, gdybyś mi tylko powiedział. . . kochany (*płacze*). Gdybyś tak mógł po prostu mi powiedzieć, o co chodzi, to jestem pewna, że z nami wszystko byłoby dobrze. Nie niszcz naszej miłości i małżeństwa swoim milczeniem.

Terapeuta   Tak, wszystko zależy od komunikacji. Jeśli możesz nam powiedzieć, to się dowiemy. Jeżeli możesz podzielić się swoimi uczuciami z żoną, twoje uczucia zostaną podzielone.

Hamlet   Co zrobiła'? Co ona zrobiła? Nie mogę o tym mówić
nawet. Słuchaj, wciąż się trzęsę na samą myśl o tym. Nie mogę
uwierzyć, że to zrobiła. Nie mogę uwierzyć, że mi to zrobiła . . .

Ofelia i Terapeuta   Co ona (*ja*) zrobiła(*m*)?

Hamlet   Chcesz wiedzieć? Naprawdę chcesz wiedzieć? Dobra, to
powiem. Wczoraj rano, przy śniadaniu. . . (*Szepcze* **terapeucie** *do
ucha.*)

Terapeuta   Chryste Panie!

Hamlet   Tak, to właśnie zrobiła.

Terapeuta   To zdecydowanie trudna sytuacja, ale jestem pewien,
że jeżeli znajdziemy dla niej rozwiązanie, to ją rozwiążemy.
Rozwody są pierwszą przyczyną rozwodów. Ale poza tym
wszystko gra?

Ofelia   O tak, wszystko gra. Mamy wspaniałe małżeństwo.

Hamlet   O tak, praca jest wspaniała, pieniądze są wspaniałe,
dzieci nie żyją.

Terapeuta   Możesz powiedzieć, że osiągnąłeś stan prawdziwej
mądrości dopiero wtedy, kiedy nie pozwolisz, aby emocje
przysłaniały ci twój bezstronny, obiektywny osąd intelektualny.
Wniosek, który wyciągasz, musi być zawsze podany a priori lub
wydedukowany z empirycznego doświadczenia, które zgromadziłeś.
Nigdy nie wolno poprzestawać na składaniu oświadczeń
pozbawionych głębokiej intelektualnej bezstronności. Dopiero
wtedy można powiedzieć coś naprawdę dogłębnie bezstronnego,
naprawdę bezstronnie głębokiego. (*Jest zdziwiony, że jest taki
mądry; uśmiecha się i kręci głową, zastanawiając się nad tym, co
właśnie powiedział, ale szybko zapomina i zaczyna dłubać w nosie.*)

Ofelia (*za biurkiem, pisze*)   Jaka to dziwna rzecz, to, co ludzie
nazywają przyjemnością. Jaki dziwny jest jej stosunek do tego, co
się wydaje jej przeciwieństwem, do przykrości. Obie razem nie
chcą człowiekowi przysługiwać, ale jeśli ktoś za jedną z nich goni
i dosięgnie, bodaj że zawsze musi i drugą chwycić, jakby zrośnięte
były wierzchołkami, choć są dwie.

Telewizja (*wykład*)   Kobieta, której przyjemność seksualna jest
pierwotnie samoreprezentatywna w sposób odbiegający od
przyjemności męskiej, równie dobrze mogłaby nie posiadać
łechtaczki: błona dziewicza, która pozostaje na zawsze (nie)
naruszona, na której nieodmiennie rozpływa się nasienie, nie ma
żadnego pożytku z histerologii. Czy jest to scena przemocy, którą
nazywamy przemianą miłości zawierającej się w naszej jedynej
doskonałej triadzie? Jeśli kobiety zawsze wykorzystywano jako
narzędzie męskiej autodestrukcji, czy mamy tu do czynienia z
najnowszym zwrotem w filozofii?

Ofelia (*terapeutka*)   Lubię wierzyć, że wiesz, co robisz i że nie
trwasz tak po prostu w pułapce autodestrukcyjnej amerykańskiej
męskości, która w końcu pozostawi cię emocjonalnie
wyczerpanym, intelektualnie zagłodzonym i seksualnie
niekompetentnym.

Hamlet (*od niechcenia, nie przerywając gry*)   Chcesz, żebym cię
zabił kiedy dochodzisz, żebyś mogła zjednoczyć się z
wszechświatem w wiecznym orgazmie, żebyś mogła myśleć, że
będziesz żyć wiecznie w zachwycie tą chwilą? Chcesz, żebym cię
zabił, szepcząc ci do ucha słodkie słówka o mojej własnej rozpaczy?
Czy chcesz, żebym najpierw zabił ciebie a potem siebie, dołączając
do ciebie w starannie wyreżyserowanym dramacie śmierci?

Ofelia *unosi się w przestrzeni kosmicznej. Próbuje chwytać się
wszystkiego, ale świat znika na horyzoncie.* **Ofelia** *stara się
chodzić, ale nie ma po czym. Znajduje pilota i z desperacją naciska
go kilkukrotnie. Zwłoki ludzi i zwierząt spływają Gangesem.* **Ofelia**
*myje włosy i stąpa po pustynnym piasku. Jej serce krwawi. Jej żyły
są zrobione z drutów.* **Ofelia** *przenosi własne zwłoki przez granicę
pustyni.*

Hamlet   Choćbym nawet szedł ciemną doliną,
Zła się nie ulęknę, boś Ty ze mną,
Laska twoja i kij twój mnie pocieszają.
Zastawiasz przede mną stół wobec nieprzyjaciół moich

Ofelia (*siedzi przy biurku w wojskowej zieleni. Ze stoickim
spokojem pisze, jak gdyby nigdy nic*)   Proszę, mój drogi,

samoponiżenic nie jest czynnikiem niezbędnym, określającym czyjąś wartość rynkową; nasza czystość jest czysto formalna, podobnie jak nasze perwersje, które tak ceni twoja matka i które pojawiają się w każdej reklamie mydła. Kochany mój, musisz wiedzieć, że ona automatycznie sejwowała się, oszczędzała się na noc poślubną wśród świec i pragnień wymuskanych przez telewizję, które właśnie dlatego stanowią dla naszego pokolenia nowość. Lęk, mój drogi, lęk. Naprawdę wierzę w Boga i ludzką godność, z wyjątkiem sytuacji, gdy wykrwawia się w okopach z czaszką zmiażdżoną przez cudzą cnotę i przywiązanie do namiętności życia, ponieważ wierzę, że to ty właśnie jesteś tym, który sięga głęboko, z wnikliwością niedostępną moim omdlewającym ramionom. Tak, tak, kochanie, możesz napisać mi wiersz albo po prostu pieprzyć mnie wystarczająco mocno; jestem pewna, że tak czy inaczej pozostaniemy wierni naszemu wieloletniemu przekonaniu o nieśmiertelności osiągniętej dzięki dobroci serca i zjednoczeniu dusz uwolnionych od wzajemnej nienawiści i miłości, spędzających swoje dni w harmonii higienicznych rytuałów, postmodernistycznym dyskursie na różnych poziomach intelektualnych oraz pracy, która uwolni nas od materialistycznego nadmiaru lub braku zależnie od tego, czy prokreacja osiągnęła swoją statystyczną średnią, czy też wyraziła się w egoistycznym indywidualizmie samouwielbienia. Jestem pewna, że moje poczucie pewności siebie sprawi, że będę pewna siebie jak każdy inny, za co mi podziękujesz, kiedy naleję ci kieliszek wina i zrobię masaż barków. Czubek twojego penisa ma potencjał ontologiczny, więc wbijam twój miecz w twoją cewkę moczową, by zbadać, czy przestrzeń pomiędzy jest wystarczająco pojemna, by wchłonąć lęk mój i wszystkie inne pozostawione przypadkiem przez przyszłych ojców Ameryki i pięciu pozostałych kontynentów, co należy wziąć pod uwagę ze względu na globalizację naszych zwyczajów seksualnych. Ojciec mojej babci zginął w niewyjaśnionych okolicznościach gdzieś pomiędzy Pragą a Wiedniem, dokładnie tak jak przydarzy się to nam.

Horacy *wchodzi ze srebrną tacą pełną krewetek.*

Horacy (*do* **Hamleta**, *który wciąż siedzi na kanapie*)   Krewetkę?

Hamlet   Dzięki, jestem na diecie.

Horacy *nagle coś sobie przypomina i podnosi pięść, krzycząc:*
'Wolność!' Rozjeżdża go czołg, a jego ciało znika w czarnym
asfalcie. Grupa uśmiechniętych dzieci biegnie po chodniku,
śmiejąc się i trzymając się za ręce. Czarne kruki dziobią ciało
Horacego. *Dźwięki dworca autobusowego. Ding-dong.*

System Komunikacji Dworcowej   Autobus z Paryża do Nowego
Jorku przez Londyn i Tokio odjeżdża ze stanowiska numer 5.

Zapowiedź powtarza się kilkukrotnie, jakby mechanizm się zaciął.
Na początku zapowiedzi przechodzi **Ofelia** *w zakrwawionej sukni*
ślubnej i chustce na głowie. Próbuje znaleźć właściwe stanowisko.
Za nią podąża **Horacy,** *który niesie srebrną tacę z męską głową*
otoczoną krewetkami.

Wchodzi **Ofelia.**

Ofelia (*szaleńczo*)   Jedno, jedyne. Ja jestem jedna. Ja jestem tą,
na którą czekałam. Jedną, jedyną, która. Jedna, w jedni uświęcona,
wewnętrznie jednorodna, wybrana, błogosławiona.

Horacy (*Nie zwraca na nią uwagi*)   Te od Christie są świeższe.
Zamówmy te ze Christie.

Ofelia *zdejmuje wojskowy but i tłucze* **Horacego** *na śmierć. Jego*
ciało znika w czarnym asfalcie. **Ofelia** *istnieje, szeroko*
rozpościerając ręce. **Hamlet** *zaczyna bawić się telefonem*
komórkowym. **Ofelia/Medea** *śpiewa swojemu zmarłemu dziecku*
na podłodze dworca autobusowego.

Ofelia/Medea   Niechaj Jego wielkie Imię będzie błogosławione
na wieki i na zawsze.
Niech będzie błogosławione i pochwalone, opiewane
i wywyższone,
wyniesione i uświetnione, uwielbiane i sławione Święte Imię Jego,
który jest Błogosławiony.

Hamlet   Czytasz ból w moich oczach i myślisz, że wiesz
wszystko. Myślisz, że możesz odczytać mężczyznę w oparciu

o jego ból. Myślisz, że skoro potrafisz odczytać ból mężczyzny, to on na zawsze należy do ciebie.

Telewizja (*kanał National Geographic*)   Samiec pluskwy posiada penisa przeznaczonego do wstrzykiwania nasienia w samicę. Technika ta jest nader brutalna, ponieważ dla zapewnienia zapłodnienia samica jest przyszpilana do podłoża i kilkukrotnie dźgana w ciało. Metoda ta ewoluowała, by ominąć żeńskie narządy rodne, ograniczając i usuwając jakąkolwiek kontrolę samicy nad czasem zapłodnienia.

Ofelia   Ciało moje moim jedynym panem. (*Krzyczy.*) Ciało moje moim jedynym panem.

Hamlet *zmienia kanał.*

Ofelia (*sączy wino i nie przerywa pisania*)   Makabryczne akty samoobjawienia mają swój początek w życzliwości umysłu wobec niższych klas o wulgarnym pochodzeniu. Jestem pewną, mój drogi, że lęk, który tak dokładnie ci opisałam, nie ma żadnego etycznego znaczenia dla twojego dobrego samopoczucia. Jestem również pewna, że znajdziesz zastępnik mojej emocjonalnej nierównowagi równie łatwo jak ja, w każdym stworzeniu, jakiego zapragną nasze myśli. Wybór, który tak wyraźnie podkreśla moje obumierające ja, zależy wyłącznie od twojego poziomu serotoniny i pożądania wywołanego tej jednej konkretnej nocy. Moja oferta jest ważna jedynie na czas twojej erekcji i wygasa kiedy wytryskujesz swoje żałosne paranoje prosto w moją wyczekującą twarz. Pożądanie skonstruowane jako funkcja matematyczna ma swoje zalety: zmienność oraz trwałość jego oczekiwań, które powielone w proporcjach fraktalnych nabierają ulotnej właściwości solidnej struktury zasadniczo nie do odróżnienia od jakiegokolwiek innego cierpkiego rozwiązania konfliktów zinternalizowanych w dzieciństwie i odłożonych do spożycia z kieliszkiem Chardonnaya lub Sauvignon de Blanco i rybą, delikatnie przyrządzoną w sosie cytrynowym z kawiorem.

Przechodzi **Gertruda**, *która wciąż wisi na telefonie. Zamieniła się już w maszynę.*

Gertruda   Czy w katalogu nie było napisane, że satysfakcja
gwarantowana? Wysyłają ci wadliwą dziewczynę i myślą, że z nią
utkniesz na dobre. . . . Odeślij ją z powrotem i powiedz, żeby
przysłali ci taką jak na zdjęciu, bez piegów. . . W dzisiejszych
czasach, mój drogi, trzeba dbać o swoje pieniądze. Wczoraj
kupiłam skarpetki wyprodukowane w Chinach. Miały wadę – no
mówię ci – aha – aha – więc je zwróciłam. W dzisiejszych czasach
nie można sobie ot tak pozwolić na topienie wszystkich swoich
pieniędzy w wadliwych produktach. – aha – aha – Płacisz za coś,
wysyłają ci niewłaściwą rzecz, możesz ją odesłać i odzyskać swoje
pieniądze. . . . tak, tak, to właśnie mówię.

Gertruda *znika. Zaczyna padać śnieg.*

Hamlet (*ukradkiem, jakby zdradzał sekret*)   Czasem przenikamy
się
oczami, które są jak wrota
czasem jestem jak ona
czasem ona jest tym
kim jestem ja

Ofelia (*pisze gorączkowo*)   Prawa dłoń podtrzymuje wieczną
miłość wraz z jej właściwymi urojonymi dolegliwościami ohydnego
zbawienia i prostokątną rutyną metafor odzyskanych ze zwłok
byłych kochanków i owadów, które spadły na otwarte pośrodku
książki. Przysięgam że będę wielbić siebie, którą z taką tkliwością
odnalazłam w twoich źrenicach, w oczach, które tak gorąco błagam,
by się nie zamykały, gdy dochodzę, i w których wyraz mojej twarzy
potężnieje do rozmiaru słyszalnych wytworów naszej wyobraźni.
Obiecuję również, że dostarczę ci stałości, której tak długo
pragnąłeś oraz zagubienia przeplatanego okazjonalnymi napadami
mojego własnego ego, by zapewnić ci stabilność podaży i popytu.
Przyrzekam spełniać nasze edypalne fantazje i bezinteresownie
odnajmować moje łono jako oazę oraz toaletę, w której możemy
składować cenne resztki naszych intelektualnych wysiłków. Jestem
pewna, że ten układ zadowoli czterdzieści procent naszej masy, a
pozostałe sześćdziesiąt pozostawi w żarze nienasyconej
podejrzliwości a także fizycznej wieczystości grawitacji i
nieważkości. Moja lewa ręka ofiaruje nieodwzajemnioną miłość,

moją lub twoją, ustalimy to później. Jestem pewna, że tak czy inaczej wejdziemy w nasze role z naturalną gracją niewolnika i pana. Pożądanie jest proporcjonalne do czasu wyczekiwania. Mój drogi, ona szkoliła się u najlepszych dziwek Europy, Ameryki Północnej i Azji. Tych, które odwiedzałeś w samotne albo pijane noce i w które wpychałeś swojego na wpół sflaczałego penisa z nadzieją na chwilową ulgę od koszmaru pożądania lub jego braku.

Ofelia *przerywa. Uspokaja się.* **Ofelia** *wyjmuje pistolet z szuflady i strzela sobie w skroń. Huk wystrzału, wszędzie krew. Kontynuuje pisanie, jakby nic się nie stało.*

Ogarnia nas choroba śmierci. Chcielibyśmy nie umrzeć i nie żyć. Między zniewoleniem a posiadaniem wyrasta lęk, z szybkością złodzieja, który ukradł za dużo, by czuć przyjemność, a za mało, by czuć cokolwiek innego, i który odchodzi z drętwym uśmieszkiem pogardy, a jego wrzask cichnie wśród zamarzniętych zaułków samopowielenia. Moje myśli nie płyną z łatwością, jaką obiecywało twoje ciało, ani nie tętnią czarującym nienasyceniem . . .

Telewizja (*kanał National Geographic*)   Samiec i samica skorpiona splatają się w intensywnym uścisku i wymieniają ciosy. Podczas zwarcia szczękoczułkami samiec wielokrotnie dźga samicę żądłem. W odwecie samica często pożera swojego partnera.

Wchodzi **Ofelia***. Jej suknia ślubna jest podarta. Do tułowia ma przymocowane materiały wybuchowe.*

Ofelia   Głód, który czuję, jest poza mną
rozlewa się na zewnątrz i wtłacza
w moje nienasycone objęcia
zatracasz się
nie da się siebie ocalić skazując się na potępienie
głód, który czuję, jest poza mną

Usadawia się w wózku inwalidzkim i wyjeżdża z histerycznym śmiechem.

Dziennik Telewizyjny   Dziś w Kalifornii matka odcięła głowę swojemu dziecku i pożarła jego mózg. (*Prezenterka wygląda przez chwilę na smutną, po czym szybko przywołuje na twarz szeroki*

uśmiech.) A teraz kolejna informacja, tym razem od naszego
lifestylowego guru, który odpowie na najważniejsze pytanie
sezonu . . .

Zaczyna przygrywać 'Jingle Bells'.

*Twarz **Hamleta** wtapia się w widoczną w tle grę wideo; tę samą,
którą się wciąż zajmuje. **Hamlet** widoczny na kanapie i w grze
wideo wstaje, zdejmuje kapelusz oraz kubrak. Odchodzi za kulisy,
po czym przynosi kanister z benzyną, którą zaczyna rozlewać
wszędzie dookoła.*

Ofelia (*pisze podczas gdy **Hamlet** rozlewa benzynę*)   Daleko,
daleko stąd, kochany. . . na pewno udało się nam przekonać
samych siebie, że istniejemy. Doprowadzona do takiej skrajności
nie mam innego wyboru, jak tylko utrwalić to przekonanie.
Błagam, nie odmawiaj mi tego, co słusznie należy do kogoś
innego. Znam twoje przywiązanie do prawd i fałszów. Podawane z
odłamkami martwych przekonań i resztkami kupionymi na cichych
aukcjach w muzeach woskowych organów i dusz. Chcę, żebyś
naprawdę pojął, że obietnic, które padają z moich ust, nie da się
przetłumaczyć. Łączę Twoje i moje myśli z osobliwą dbałością o
szczegóły. Chciałeś poczuć miłość albo w ogóle cokolwiek. Teatr
pożądania jest otwarty na publiczne pokazy dla widzów
ciekawskich, nieświadomych i sobie obojętnych. Widziałam jak
wczoraj szli przez miasto, a my płakaliśmy schowani pod łóżkiem,
którego nie dało się ujarzmić. Wyszłam z twoją głową pod pachą.
Potykam się, potykam o słowa przywiązana do ich znaczeń. Nie
płacz kochanie, nadchodzi noc.

Zapala zapałkę. Światło gaśnie.

Bibliography

(2021). *Opheliamachine Trailer*. Retrieved 2023, from https://vimeo.com/562068802.

Brandes, P. (2013, 20 June). Review: '"Opheliamachine" An Uncompromising Vision at City Garage.' *Los Angeles Times*. Retrieved March 2023, from https://www.latimes.com/entertainment/arts/la-xpm-2013-jun-20-la-et-cm-theater-review-opheliamachine-at-city-garage-20130618-story.html

Byrnes, A. (2013, 25 June). Review: '"Opheliamachine." Forging Meaning: Opening the Curtain.' *KCRW*. Retrieved March 18, 2023, from https://www.kcrw.com/culture/shows/opening-the-curtain/forging-meaning

Desena, R. (2013, 25 June). Review of 'Opheliamachine.' *The Los Angeles Post*. Retrieved July 2013. https://www.thelosangelespost.org/12007/.

Douglas, E. (2022, 4 October). 'Old Classics, Remastered: October on the Berlin Stage.' *Exberliner*. Retrieved 18 March 2023, from https://www.exberliner.com/stage/old-classics-remastered-october-on-the-berlin-stage/

Leigh Morris, S.(2013, 20 June). Review of 'Opheliamachine.' *LA Weekly*. Retrieved July 2013. http://blogs.laweekly.com/arts/2013/06/hollywood_fringe_reviews.php

Meierhenrich, D. (2022, 1 October). Review: 'Playfulness Beats Text: New Discoveries in The Ambition Trap.' *Berliner Zeitung*. Retrieved 18 March 2023, from https://www.berliner-zeitung.de/kultur-vergnuegen/theater/theater-berlin-opheliamaschine-und-mein-leben-in-aspik-wenn-der-regie-nachwuchs-in-die-ehrgeizfalle-geht-li.272514

Meisel, M. (2013, 18 June). Review of 'Opheliamachine.' *The Hollywood Reporter*. Retrieved 18 March 2023, from https://www.hollywoodreporter.com/lifestyle/lifestyle-news/opheliamachine-theater-review-570065/

Miles, B. (2013, 12 July). Review of 'Opheliamachine.' *ShowMag.com*. Retrieved 2023, from http://showmag.com/index.php?option=com_content&view=article&id=250:opheliamachine&catid=1:theater&Itemid=3.

Müller, H. (2022, 16 October). Review: 'Uršulė Bartos "Opheliamaschine" am berliner ensemble.' *Zur Startseite*. Retrieved 18 March 2023, from https://www.morgenpost.de/kultur/article236682249/Ophelia-springt-aus-der-Kiste-und-ermaechtigt-sich-selbst.html

'"Opheliamaschine" (2023) by Magda Romanska in the Berliner Ensemble.' *TheaterKompas.de*. Retrieved 2023, from https://www.theaterkompass.de/beitraege/opheliamaschine-von-magda-romanska-im-berliner-ensemble-57122

'Opheliamachine' by Magda Romanska. City Garage Theatre. (n.d.). Retrieved March 2023, from https://citygarage.org/2013/06/01/opheliamachine-by-magda-romanska/

Pagani, M. P. (2014). 'Da Elsinore alla tecnosolitudine americana.' *Mimesis Journal*, 3, 1, 4–10. https://doi.org/10.4000/mimesis.467

Rakow, C. (2022, November). Review of 'Opheliamaschine.' *Theater Heute*, 53–54.

Rizzo, J. (2013, 13 June). 'Heiner Müller. "Opheliamachine" Takes on Influential 20th-Century Theatre Work.' *Cultural Daily – Independent Voices, New Perspectives*. Retrieved March 2023, from https://culturaldaily.com/opheliamachine-takes-on-influential-20th-century-theatre-work/

Romanska, M. (2014). 'Opheliamachine.' *Mimesis Journal*. https://doi.org/https://doi.org/10.4000/mimesis.479

Spitz, S. A. (2013, 20 June). Review: 'The New Age of Ophelia.' Retrieved July 2013. http://smdp.com/the-new-age-of-ophelia/123755 *Santa Monica Daily Press*.

Wikimedia Foundation. (2022, 19 April). 'Opheliamachine.' *Wikipedia*. Retrieved 18 March 2023, from https://en.wikipedia.org/wiki/Opheliamachine#The_Company